R. L. Stevenson on Fiction

✳

R. L. Stevenson on Fiction

AN ANTHOLOGY OF LITERARY AND CRITICAL ESSAYS

✳

Edited by
GLENDA NORQUAY

Edinburgh University Press

© in selection and editorial material, Glenda Norquay, 1999

Edinburgh University Press
22 George Square, Edinburgh

Typeset in Goudy
by Hewer Text Ltd, Edinburgh and
printed and bound in Great Britain by
Biddles Ltd, Guildford, Surrey

A CIP record for this book is available
from the British Library

ISBN 0 7486 0777 3 (paperback)

The right of Glenda Norquay
to be identified as author of the editorial
material has been asserted in accordance with
the Copyright, Designs and Patents Act 1988.

Contents

✳

Acknowledgements

＊

I am much indebted to the work of Roger Swearingen, author of *The Prose Writings of Robert Louis Stevenson*, and to Paul Maixner's edition of *The Critical Heritage* volume on Stevenson. Catherine Kerrigan, who has played an important role in recent Stevenson scholarship, was a great support and source of advice in the initial stages of the project; Jackie Jones of Edinburgh University Press was an encouraging and positive editor; Cairns Craig was an important early influence on my thinking about Stevenson.

I am grateful to the Beinecke Collection, Yale University Library, to Princeton University Library and to the National Library of Ireland for sending material. Staff at Liverpool John Moores University Library (Pat Williams in particular); the Sidney Jones Library, University of Liverpool; the School of Scottish Studies, University of Edinburgh, and the National Library of Scotland have also all been helpful at various times. Caroline Richardson helped the project greatly with scanning material in the initial stages, and Sam Fear resolved all kinds of technical problems.

Connie Hancock assisted with some of the fact-finding; I am also extremely grateful to Timothy Ashplant and Sheena Streather for help in tracking down information. Carol Anderson, Peter Childs, Aileen Christianson, Pat Corcoran, Jo Croft, Elspeth Graham, Alison Lumsden, Pam Morris, Jason Pierce Susan Poznar, Kathleen Peck, Kelsey Thornton, Joanna Price and Roger Webster all provided information, assistance or support in a number of ways. Annie and Duncan have also had to live with this project.

Introduction

*

In 1885 Robert Louis Stevenson wrote to his friend W. H. Low about an essay he had published in *Longman's Magazine*. 'A Humble Remonstrance' was part of the debate between Stevenson and Henry James over the nature and future of the novel as a form, and perhaps his most memorable piece of literary criticism. In the same letter he mentions a paper he has recently completed on the subject of style: both ambitiously and disparagingly, he describes this as being 'a sort of start upon my Treatise on the Art of Literature: a small, arid book that shall some day appear.'[1] At this time Stevenson was clearly giving much thought to the business of writing and to the development of fictional forms – subjects which had always interested him in a theoretical as well as practical manner and which continued to engage his attention. The 'small, arid book', however, never appeared. What he did produce was a number of essays which explore fiction-making: what makes for a good or bad book; the ways in which writers, including himself, work; the nature of literary realism; the influence of childhood reading on the adult mind; and the importance of the imagination for both writers and readers.

This collection of essays brings together some of those ideas, offering an extension of, and commentary upon, the larger writing project of Stevenson's career. Stevenson produced a large number of essays in his relatively short life, and it was a form for which he appeared to find a ready market at the time. Yet in 1951 David Daiches complained of the fact that 'our serious modern critics hang on every word which James has to utter about the art of fiction, and nobody has anything to say for Stevenson's remarks on the subject.'[2] Writing his own spirited defence of Stevenson's reputation a year later, J. C. Furnas noted that 'Lack of experience with the essay bars many modern readers from much good Stevenson outside his fiction.'[3] To an extent, we as readers now are even further removed from familiarity with that form and Stevenson's critical writing has tended to become 'background' to his own novels. Nevertheless the essays touch on a surprising number of issues which have concerned practitioners and theorists of the novel in recent years; while offering pleasures particular to their author and his time, many of the issues debated may not seem so unfamiliar to the reader acquainted with contemporary literary theory. This volume aims to focus attention on Stevenson's critical work in its own right, in terms of both its content and its textual strategies.

Although Stevenson both before and after his death was accused of a mannered style – sacrificing simplicity 'to the desire to be striking and sonorous' – the literary tactics of the pieces are both exciting and pleasurable.[4] As a theorist Stevenson tended to the personal and anecdotal, working through circumlocutory narratives to make his case: 'The Gossip', a title he adopted more than once, is an accurate description of the 'idle' talk, the ruminative tone, the enthusiasm for the subject and the intermingling of facts and fictions which characterise these pieces. The essays create little fictions within themselves, playing with the narrative 'I': in several instances Stevenson begins talking about a third-person character until finally 'admitting' that this person he knows so well is of course himself. Not only does this technique divert attention away from potential 'authority' in the speaker, but it also permits a certain collusion between writer and reader, and in some cases a blurring of roles and responsibilities; another striking feature of Stevenson's work in this collection is his dual positioning as both practising writer and enthusiastic reader, a duality which also complicates our own reading response.

Stevenson was both innovative, and immersed in the debates of his day. The Essay as a form developed extensively during the period, reaching an ever wider audience with the growth of periodicals, and Stevenson devoted much energy to participating in the world of *belles-lettres*, but opinion was sometimes divided as to his suitability in this area. An unsigned review of *Virginibus Puerisque* in the *British Quarterly Review* in 1881 praises the 'clear and graceful literary style' of the collection, as well as its 'ease, its restrained satire', but adds nevertheless 'we cannot say of it that it has the fulness, the calm air of experience of our earlier essayists'.[5] The reviewer also accuses the writer of 'affected wit' and a kind of literary 'charm' that would be unattractive to men of experience. A similarly ambivalent response can be found in William Archer's extended discussion of Stevenson's œuvre in 1885, in which Stevenson's 'lightness of touch' is both a strength and a limitation, and his theories on the importance of narrative incident linked rather disparagingly with his felicity in 'the gift of mere storytelling'.[6] For the modern reader, however, part of the attraction of these essays must lie in their lack of gravitas, in the emphasis on the personal, and in that element of play which disturbed Stevenson's contemporaries. It is in their stylistic features, as much as their proclaimed content, that these essays reveal much about his writing practices.

The intention of this volume is to bring together a number of significant essays which offer a literary map of Stevenson, drawing attention to those areas in which he makes the most significant critical interventions. The essays have appeared in separate volumes of the various collected works, but have not been brought together in a form which allows the general reader to notice the development of Stevenson's ideas, his continual exploration of the same set of issues through a variety of approaches and the frame of reference he built up from his own reading which shaped both his work and his literary value system. As with much *belle-lettriste* writing, the references are often idiosyncratic and at times obscure to the modern reader: the end notes to each essay should, however, help in this respect. Each essay is also prefaced by a brief introduction to its context and import.

Written at various stages in Stevenson's career, the essays emerge from very different situations and interests. Some, such as 'Child's Play' (1878) show Stevenson beginning to reflect on his childhood and its influences, crystallising his development as a writer. Others – 'A Humble Remonstrance' and 'Books Which Have Influenced Me' – form part of wider series or debates. Several were written for *Scribner's Magazine* when Stevenson was living in the icy mountains of Saranac in the late 1880s: books were hard to come by, quotations are often misremembered. Very few essays come from the later part of his life when he was producing novels and short stories at an impressive rate, was financially more secure and appeared less concerned with the mechanics of the literary process. While some of the essays reprinted here have appeared in the collected *Works* in the volume, *Essays Literary and Critical,* others are scattered through-out the Stevenson œuvre. They have been included on the grounds of the contribution they make to literary and theoretical debates about the nature of fiction, its function and the processes of producing it, both creatively and commercially. A number of significant but specific essays about major literary figures have not been included, although these have much to offer in themselves: *Familiar Studies of Men and Books* contains illuminating pieces on Whitman, Burns and Victor Hugo. The essay on 'Victor Hugo's Romances' (1874) was only excluded after much thought: although much of the discussion consists of detailed assessment of particular texts, the early parts of that essay offer a valuable outline of Stevenson's understanding of romance. One essay on a specific writer – indeed book – that has been included is 'A Gossip on a Novel of Dumas's' which reveals much about Stevenson's reading habits, in addition to representing yet another assault in the ongoing battle against realism. (As Henry James noted, Dumas and Meredith were the two writers who most influenced Stevenson; they are recurring figures in the essays.)

Although the essays are presented in chronological order, and an increasing confidence and discrimination might be discerned, it is their repeated exploration of certain key issues which holds the attention: a concern with the form and function of the novel; a compelling interest in the mechanics of reading as well as writing; a fascination with childhood and the child's imagination; and a high degree of consciousness about modes and contexts of literary production. Taken together, they also offer some sense of the literary framework in which Stevenson saw himself working, and of those writers and characters who had most impact upon him.

Realism versus romance

At the time Stevenson wrote these essays, the form and function of fiction was increasingly a subject for public debate. The very terms of the debate were, of course, contested. 'Realism', increasingly questioned by writers such as Stevenson, meant various things: an attention to life rather than art, which had resulted in the 'baggy' form of the Victorian novel; a threat to the necessary attention to structure and form in writing. Other writers, however, positioned it positively against 'Idealism', which had come to mean an adherence to outmoded literary conventions and a reluctance to engage with the modern spirit of analysis.[7] Although Stevenson himself suggested in a letter to C. W. Stoddard in 1886 that 'the famous problem of realism and idealism is one purely of detail', in several of his essays he appears to endorse or at least employ such an opposition.[8] The other polarity which structures his thinking on the subject is that of realism versus romance. Here too definitions can be problematic. The critic Peter Keating has accused Stevenson's influence of effacing any specific meanings to the term 'romance', until it became 'almost anything that wasn't realism'.[9] In 'Victor Hugo's Romances', however, Stevenson does clarify his thinking on the subject, beginning with Hugo's own assessment of *Quentin Durward*: 'Après le roman pittoresque mais prosaïque de Walter Scott il restera un autre roman à créer, plus beau et plus complet encore selon nous. C'est le roman, à la fois drame et épopée, pittoresque mais poétique, réel mais idéal, vrai mais grand, qui enchâssera Walter Scott dans Homère.'[10] Comparing Fielding with Scott, in light of the latter's move away from character towards an understanding of 'personality . . . resumed into its place in the constitution of things', Stevenson then offers Hugo's own work as advancement on this process by virtue of its self-consciousness.[11] The best romances, Stevenson suggests, are those which make a powerful artistic impression and yet offer something as simple as nature.[12] Romance, he appears to argue, is a means of embodying ideas that cannot be formulated in analytical words: 'It is not that there is anything blurred or indefinite in the impression left with us, it is just because the impression is so very definite after its own kind, that we find it hard to fit it exactly with the expressions of our philosophical speech.'[13]

Also implicit in Stevenson's apparent opposition to realism is his dislike of 'naturalism'. His role in this debate has to be understood in the context of developments within the European novel and definitions of 'naturalism' as a literary school and method evolving in France; in particular the work of Emile Zola was to have a significant, if relatively short-lived influence on debates over fiction. Although Stevenson has much of interest to say about Balzac, he positions himself against the French naturalist attention to detail and the scientific observation of determining environments, arguing instead for the significance of symbolic pattern, for the engagement of incident rather than character and for a dynamic relationship between them: 'Situation is animated with passion, passion clothed upon with situation.'[14] The picture then is a complicated one: in mapping out Stevenson's various, and at time rather contradictory, attacks on realism, it is worth remembering that his writing also attempts to recontextualise 'realism' as a theoretical term, offering a more sharply theorised analysis of what would now be called the ideological imperative of realism – that it makes itself appear all encompassing whereas in fact, he suggests in a letter to Bob, 'realism is a method, and only methodic in its consequences.'[15]

In 'A Note on Realism' (1883) he places his views very much in the context of recent changes in the debate. The opening paragraph, although a defence against the 'admission of detail' that has become the vogue, could also be read as an anticipation of *fin-de-siècle* aestheticism – principles of selection and form are central to fiction. Less opposed to earlier forms of realism, which he sees in the historical novel and the work of Scott and Balzac, he argues that their influence has become adulterated: 'a merely technical and decorative stage'. For this 'suicide of the realists' as he calls it, he blames Zola, accusing him not only of too much attention to detail, but of a cheap and sensationalist attraction to 'the rancid'. But in a more measured response than this sweeping attack, he also sets himself apart from the continuing English debate over realism versus idealism, arguing: 'All representative art, which can be said to live, is both realistic and ideal; and the realism about which we quarrel is a matter purely of externals.'[16] Resolving itself through a process of circularity and evasion, the essay returns to form as the ultimate factor: it is execution that is important and the choice of idealism's lofty whole or the immediate and particular of realism will inevitably determine the shape of the resulting work. There is, however, a danger of excess: if too much detail, the whole is lost; if attention is only on the philosophical, the work becomes 'null'. An awareness of the dangers of each should work as a corrective and yet, in the present moment, Stevenson points out, the pressure for detail is so strong that there is greater need for caution in that direction.

His ideas on the relationship between the externals of life and the nature and function of fiction are taken further in 'A Humble Remonstrance', published in 1884 in response to Henry James's essay 'The Art of Fiction' which itself engaged with issues raised by pamphlet publication of a lecture given by the novelist Walter Besant.[17] This essay, perhaps Stevenson's most sustained, measured and certainly most famous contribution to the realism debate, reveals much about contemporary arguments on the function of the novel, as well as Stevenson's own position.

Besant's lecture offered a justification for considering fiction as one of the 'Fine Arts', equal to music, painting and poetry. He also argued that, as an art, it was governed by general laws which may be laid down and taught, although he also admitted that no laws can be successfully learned by those who do not possess the 'natural and necessary gifts'. The modern novel, he suggested, offered a means of converting abstract ideas into living models because in fiction the human interest comes before everything else. In recommending that the novelist develops powers of observation, selection and dramatic presentation – 'everything in Fiction which is invented and not the result of personal experience and observation is worthless' – he advised the novelist never to go beyond personal experience.

Henry James's reply to Besant's lecture welcomed the author's arguments to an extent, noting that until recently the English novel appeared to have no theory, no conviction, no consciousness of itself: 'During the period I have alluded to there was a comfortable, good-humoured feeling abroad that a novel is a novel, as a pudding is a pudding, and that this was the end of it.' While the old suspicion that fiction was 'wicked' did not dominate to the same extent, there was still a feeling that it should not be taken too seriously. At least, he suggested, the old Evangelical suspicion had some grounding in a valid idea: that the novel does 'compete with life'. As a central tenet of his argument James claimed that, just as the painting provides a picture that is 'reality', so the novel offers 'history'. He criticised Trollope for fracturing this sense of realism in a recent work, by a digression which admitted the story was only make-believe. Agreeing with Besant that the novelist should be reputed as 'very artistic', James condemned the belief that a novel should be either instructive or amusing and that artistic preoccupations with form will somehow interfere with both these purposes.

Where James disagreed with Besant was in the idea that it is possible to say beforehand 'what sort of an affair the good novel will be'; his view was that 'the good health of an art which undertakes so immediately to reproduce life must demand that it be perfectly free.' Working through the catalogue of 'rules' that Besant had laid down, he showed that although one might not necessarily disagree, one need not assent to such a prescriptive set of guidelines. While advocating realism of a kind, he suggested that those characters and situations that strike us as most real will be those that interest us most. Writing from 'experience' may be valuable, but experience itself is never limited and never complete: 'it is an immense sensibility, a kind of huge spider-web of the finest silken threads, suspended in the chamber of consciousness and catching every air-borne particle in its tissue'. Part of his wider argument against Besant was therefore a defence of the 'organic' nature of the novel: 'A novel is a living thing, all one and continuous.' This is extended into an argument against categorising novels as either those of incident or character, novel or romance: 'What is character but the determination of incident? What is incident but the illustration of character?' Such distinctions, he suggested, may be noted by critics but have little use for producers of fiction. James also argued against the way in which Besant described the principle of selection, stating that 'Art is essentially selection, but it is a selection whose main care is to be typical, to be inclusive'. Selection should not be done on idealist or moralistic grounds. This brings him to the final, brief, discussion of Besant's ideas on the conscious moral purpose of the novel. James believed that English novelists have in fact shown diffidence and timidity in this area, and he reintroduced the question of taste: 'There is one point at which the moral sense and the artistic sense lie very near together; that is, in the light of the very obvious truth that the deepest quality of a work of art will always be the quality of the mind of the producer.'

While James challenged Besant's rather crude arguments, Stevenson, in his reply to James, questions and redefines the terms used by both men. What, he suggests, they were in fact discussing was the 'art of narrative'. Although Besant may prefer the 'art of fictitious narratives in prose' as his subject, Stevenson demonstrates the applicability of 'narrative' as a term to poetry, to drama, to biography and even to history, in which, he suggests, we can find many of the same textual features and literary strategies that are apparent in fiction. Yet rather than using this line of argument to support James in his idea that a novel has the status of history, he reverses the terms, first questioning the 'propriety' of the word 'truth' in either context and then challenging James's central proposition, that art competes with life. Literature should be seen as a reorganisation and shaping of certain elements of life. Stevenson's paradigm of art as geometry is in direct contrast to the organic images offered by James, as is his assertion that a novel exists by virtue of its immeasurable difference from life.

The second point on which he differs from James is in the idea that the choice of subject will not materially affect the work. Instead Stevenson draws a distinction between works of adventure, the novel of character and the dramatic novel. Contesting James's question, 'What is character but the determination of incident? What is incident but the illustration of character?', he proceeds to identify differences. In the novel of adventure the pleasure lies in being submerged in the story; there is little place for elaboration of character. Novels of character, by contrast, rely upon examination of (often static) characters: as a result they contain less action, as may be seen in James's own work. Finally, the dramatic novel consists not of incident but of passion, offering a more dynamic model in which there is no room for cleverness. Stevenson thus positions his approach as different from James's in its emphasis on the finished work: Stevenson is genuinely (as James purports to be) thinking of the producer of the work. He concludes the essay with a strong reminder, again at odds with both Besant and James, that the novel is not and cannot be a transcript of life.

As with all of Stevenson's critical essays, the piece gives us a sense of Stevenson's own literary influences and frame of reading. Stevenson questions the valorisation of realism which was current with certain writers of the time, but more importantly challenges James's assertion that the novel should 'compete with life'. In several other respects the essay anticipates the thinking of later theorists: in its bold challenge to fixed categories of genre and argument for the recognition of strong structural similarities between fiction, biography and even history; in Stevenson's sense of succumbing totally to the text while reading, which challenges concepts of critical objectivity but also recognises the mechanics of the reading process; and in its blurring of categories between the serious and the popular. An important contribution to a debate very much of its time, the essay also offers a thoughtful discussion of the motives, strategies and pleasures underlying the ways in which we read.

Reading as a writer and writing as a reader

In both 'A Gossip on Romance' (1882) and 'A Gossip on a Novel of Dumas's' (1887) Stevenson again engages with the pleasures of the text, but in these essays adopts a rather different strategy. In 'A Gossip on Romance', his technique is exactly that of a gossip – indulging in a casual exchange of ideas and memories, which are then resituated within a wider debate. His essay begins with the recounting of his own tastes in fiction, in particular during his childhood, all of which also point either towards books he has written or will subsequently write. This leads to an assessment of the values of those writers who have most influenced him. Likewise, 'A Gossip on a Novel of Dumas's' takes as its starting point his response to one particular work of fiction before moving on to delineate a particular view of what makes for good literature. In the latter essay, this tactic is made more vivid by the atmospheric delineation of the various locations and situations in which he read the *Vicomte*: his first encounter with the name of the author, when he reads of a character from Miss Yonge's novel chastised for reading Dumas; the first reading of a cheap pirated edition of the book itself; the re-reading in a cottage in the Pentlands in winter. Fictionalising his role as reader, while at the same time justifying his writerly interest in reading Dumas, Stevenson depicts a dynamic relationship with the text. The essay ends with him metaphorically riding off into the novel: 'Yet a sixth time, dearest d'Artagnan, we shall kidnap Monk and take horse together for Belle Isle.'[18] As Keating points out, Stevenson was a powerful advocate on the side of romance by virtue of his status as both artist and entertainer; his fiction also provided a powerful supporting voice to his cause.[19] Yet these essays go further: they are also about – and re-create – the romance of reading itself. Stevenson not only looks forward, beyond the expectation of fiction as offering immersion in characters and their moral responses to situations, to a recognition that the shape, pattern and dynamics of a novel play an equally significant role, but also never loses sight of himself as a reader. Not only is this a powerful strategy for encouraging the readers of the essay to align themselves with the author, but it also enacts the very strengths of fiction that Stevenson is advocating: the ability to create an impression that correlates to specific feelings, without dogma or detail. When we read these pieces the process of reading is both represented as active and becomes so for us: we share the pleasures of the text. The boundaries of reading and writing, the roles of writer and reader, become blurred: Stevenson suggests that 'we should gloat over a book, be rapt clean out of ourselves, and rise from the perusal, our mind filled with the busiest, kaleidoscopic dance of images, incapable of sleep or of continuous thought.'[20] And as one of his most eminent admirers, Italo Calvino, notes, this enthusiasm affects his own fiction-making: 'Stevenson himself wrote the books he would have liked to read.'[21]

Imagination and the child

Rapture of reading is also related to the raptures of imagination and creation: the processes have much in common. In several of the essays Stevenson attempts, through narrative scenario and example, to convey a sense of his own writing processes and to explore the significance of imagination. It is in the world of the child in which that rapture is most evident and most easily understood.

Childhood is highly significant to Stevenson: as Graham Balfour, his first biographer notes, he remembered his childhood more vividly than most, and wrote at considerable length about the child's imagination.[22] Balfour's *Life* quotes Stevenson remembering games with his cousin, Bob, and how they 'lived together in a purely visionary state'.[23] That visionary state becomes for Stevenson both a paradigm of what fiction should offer, and a point of entry into the workings of the creative processes, insufficiently understood: 'for the child thinks much in images, words are very live to him, phrases that imply a picture eloquent beyond their value.'[24] He also found it useful to create and re-create the image of himself as a child reader – an image which has also been seen as a strategy of evasion, an excuse to remain in the realm of the 'minor' novelists.[25]

For Stevenson the workings of the child's mind, the pleasures of creating stories and the excitement of reading are interwoven into his view of literature and his justification of romance. In 'Child's Play' (1878), the earliest essay included here, he suggest that play is of value in itself, with internal dynamics much more absorbing than the imitation of adult roles. In 'A Gossip on Romance' he returns to the notion of childhood play and what he sees as its lack of mimetic or representational qualities, observing, 'Fiction is to the grown man what play is to the child.'[26] The power of romance is likewise figurative and symbolic rather than mimetic; it allows a flexibility of the imagination and – in his description at least – serves to place the reader in an active role, recreating his or her own fancy, rather than passively absorbing detail. The final analysis of the strengths and weaknesses of Scott's fiction – his power to engage the reader with the overall narrative but the technical flaws in his style and his lack of patience in execution – are again expressed through the association of the child and romance: Scott is 'A great romantic – an idle child.'[27]

Romance, as defined in the essay, resides in 'the poetry of circumstances'. As Stevenson writes, 'The right kind of thing should fall out in the right kind of place.'[28] Place and circumstance are central features for Stevenson both as a writer and as a reader. Time and again in thinking about his fiction it is the terrain, the situation, that we remember: Jim in the apple barrel, the mournful waves around Treasure Island; Alan and David atop the rock; the streets of Soho which conceal Mr Hyde; the House of Shaws; the snowy wastes at the end of *The Master of Ballantrae*. This strength seems to derive from a child's perception of the significance of place and incident as important in themselves, rather than for their role in any larger plot. Again enacting the patterns of romance, the most significant narratives of his own childhood in these essays are powerfully located in certain resonant settings: the Pentlands, North Berwick, the streets of Edinburgh. From these very specific locations and incidents he can move into more general arguments around literary form or the nature of creativity.

This can be seen very clearly in 'The Lantern-Bearers' (1888). Writing in Saranac for *Scribner's*, childhood was again very much in his mind. As the title suggests, this essay, which revisits his early memories of holidays in North Berwick, shows a fascination with 'that small theatre of the brain which we kept lighted all night long'. Stevenson uses the fantasy world of the child, created for him and his boyhood friends by the possession of tin bull's-eyes lanterns which light their meetings at nightfall in secret places on the beach, to demonstrate the transformative power of the imagination. The children's ability to transcend and rework the banalities of the everyday gives him scope for yet another attack on the realists, who ignore fantasy and the imagination: 'There, to be sure, we find a picture of life in so far as it consists of mud and of old iron, cheap desires and cheap fears, that which we are ashamed to remember and that which we are careless whether we forget.'[29] In attacking realism, he opposes the idea that environment has a determining effect on the psyche and that the description of surfaces leads to an understanding of character: while to an outsider the boys may have appeared cold and wet, and their talk nonsense, to present it in such terms would have been 'untrue' to the warmth of their experience, another example of 'the truly haunting and truly spectral unreality of realistic books'. His alternative to this may seem vague – 'that rainbow work of fancy that clothes what is naked and seems to enoble what is base' – but such mystical imagery nevertheless offers an appropriate framework for understanding Stevenson's own literary endeavours and general philosophy: 'for no man lives in the external truth, among salts and acids, but in the warm, phantasmagoric chamber of his brain, with the painted windows and the storied walls.'[30]

Childhood again provides the inspiration for one of the most engaging essays in the volume, 'A Penny Plain and Twopence Coloured' (1884). Drawing on his experiences of buying cut-out paper toy theatres, Stevenson explores the boundaries of his childhood imagination. The essay is especially interesting in the way in which it enacts theories found elsewhere in his essays: on the romance of incident rather than character; on the fitness of place; on the inadequacy of mimesis as a concept for under-standing the working of literature or the mind. Rather, however, than weighing down this piece – which one critic at least found 'damn bad' but which others have subsequently sees as the key to his fiction – with heavy theorising, he dwells upon the play of signification which gave Skelt its continued appeal.[31] The essay rings out with lists of names – not just titles of plays and colourful characters, but the names of paint-colours themselves – crimson lake, Prussian blue, Titian and gamboge – which evoke that distant world of play. The scenery, so lovingly detailed, becomes, as Stevenson describes it, a prism through which all future experience is constructed: his first view of England is through the eyes of Skelt. The essay also explores the role of desire in motivating the drive of imagination: the final fantasy, in which Skelt himself is discovered, his plays bought up, but that treasure when attained turns to dust, operates as a metaphor of the role of the reader, endlessly desiring fulfilment of the imagination, but inevitably disappointed if gratification is no longer deferred.

'A Chapter on Dreams' (1888) shows Stevenson moving in another direction from the starting point of his childhood, this time into an exploration of his own creative processes. In keeping with the period's growing interest in psychology, he considers the relationship between dreams, our waking lives and fiction, calling into question from the first our ability to distinguish between our memories, our fantasies and our dreams – all the workings of 'the small theatre of the brain'. In this instance the symbolic anecdote deployed from his childhood is that of the nightmare. Stevenson's biographers often comment on the extraordinarily vivid nature of his dreams, and often nightmares, frequently linking the latter with the 'overrich material for night fears' provided by his nurse Cummy; this essay lists some of the worst images that would emerge for the child when 'the night-hag would have him by the throat'. Moving on to describe the dreams of a student and a young man, he picks out one of particular interest: a dream of looking down on a farmyard, in which the farmyard dog assumes the proportions in his mind of 'something hellish'. The final manifestation of horror occurs when the dog catches a fly in his paw, pops it into his mouth, turns to the sleeper and winks at him. As the sleeper is revealed as author, wondering why the sleeper 'having found so singular an incident' should be 'unable to carry the tale to a fit end', the essay moves into a consideration of the relationship between narrative artifice and the symbolic significance of dreams. The writer describes another tale, brought to him by his 'Brownies' (the name by which he refers to 'the little people who manage man's internal theatre'), a tale which he feels could not be published because of 'unmarketable elements' but which had a carefully crafted narrative structure of repetition and symmetry. While admitting he is the dreamer, he presents himself as powerless to understand the machinations of his Brownies, providing as his final example, the process of writing *The Strange Case of Dr Jekyll and Mr Hyde*.

Although the essay might be read as a whimsical effacement of authorial authority, it raises more serious questions about narrative patterning. In the tale of the Brown Dog above it also offers a striking example of Stevenson's fictional techniques, including his ability to given symbolic resonance to an incident or detail. To take *Treasure Island* as an example, the unnamed horror Jim experiences on seeing sea lions around the shore turns a detail into a symbol of uncertain terror. In 'The Lantern-Bearers' Stevenson's memories of a fisher-wife who had cut her throat, seen as a child, are likewise vividly evoked: 'it seems strange and hard that, after all these years, the poor crazy sinner should be still pilloried on her cart in the scrap-book of my memory.'[32] As commentators have noted, the power of Stevenson's writing also lies in the establishing of uncomfortable frameworks of moral collusion, based around a combination of inevitability and unease: Jim Hawkins watching Silver kill a fellow-sailor, Jim's own relationship with Billy Bones or David Balfour's with Alan Breck. Here the full horror of the dream resides in that collusive wink of dog to sleeper.

Literary production

While Stevenson might be drawn to the world of childhood, and seek to deny responsibility for his creations, he was very much aware of a changing literary market and the complicated relationship between readerly pleasures and the hierarchies of fiction.

He was writing at a time at which great changes were taking place in literary production, with circulating libraries in decline, a growth in public libraries and a decrease in the of popularity of the three-decker novel, a trend to which Stevenson himself contributed with his one-volume adventure thrillers. The role of the writer in this changing literary marketplace was also under much debate. Aside from more theoretical debates over the relationship between romance and realism, there was an ongoing argument around issues of quality in the face of an expanding readership. While earlier in the century some writers such as Wilkie Collins had viewed the expansion of readers as positive, leading to an increasingly sophisticated literary taste, others foresaw a diminution of quality through the financial pressures of having to cater to a mass market.[33] Stevenson becomes caught up in this debate through his essay 'The Morality of the Profession of Letters' (1881) in which he took issue with James Payn's contention that writers should, in order to make a living for themselves, investigate the kinds of literature in demand and produce what was required. This essay, which attempts to define the aims of writers beyond purely financial motives, was attacked by a reviewer in *The Academy* who accused him of being mistaken in his sense of the improved atmosphere of Grub Street, and ignorant of the pressures under which many writers operate.[34] In his response Stevenson refused to accept such an easy correlation between poor work and the poorest of men, and asserted that aesthetic ambition still has a part to play.

A late essay, 'Letter to a Young Gentleman Who Proposes to Embrace the Career of Art' (1888), is one of three on this subject which had clearly preoccupied Stevenson for years.[35] While the essay represents his attempts to work out his own relationship to the commercial side of publishing it has also been seen as a response to criticisms of his work, namely that his attention was directed more towards manner than matter. As William Archer observed in 1885: 'As a narrator Mr Stevenson marks the reaction against the reigning ethical school. He has somewhere given in his adhesion to a widespread heresy which proclaims narrative to be the consummate literary form . . . Put it never so speciously, this theory resolves itself in the last analysis into an assertion that incident is more important than character, action than motive, the phenomenon than the underlying cause.'[36]

In 'Letter to a Young Gentleman' Stevenson stresses the obligation of the writer to be true to himself rather than giving in to commercial pressures – or if he does so, he must recognise the necessity under which he is working. It was the image used to make this point – the artist as a Sister of Joy, someone who makes her living by a mixture of pleasure and trade – that drew criticism. Stevenson's view of the artist as prostitute, he explained to Low, had been strengthened by his reception in America, where he felt approval might be withdrawn as suddenly as it had been bestowed. Such a view did not, he argued, diminish his pleasure in writing in any sense.[37] The critic Richard le Gallienne, who believed that in the end Stevenson would be more praised as an essayist than a prose writer, admired the essay as a 'manly protest against that literary commercialism which has recently been somewhat blatant' and offered what to Stevenson appeared a helpful renegotiation of his prostitution image.[38] In a sharp review in *The Academy*, he suggested that Stevenson conflates in the figure of the prostitute the pleasures of a trade and the sale itself. If, as Stevenson suggests, the artist writes to please himself, then this is apart from the commercial transaction.[39] Stevenson responded gratefully to le Gallienne: 'I had to thank you . . . for a triumphant exposure of a paradox of my own: the literary-prostitute disappeared from view at a phrase of yours – "The essence is not in the pleasure but the sale." True: you are right, I was wrong; the author is not the whore, but the libertine; and yet I shall let the passage stand. It is an error, but it illustrated the truth for which I was contending, that literature – painting – all art, are no other than pleasures, which we turn into trades.'[40]

The Popular

Paradoxically, the other area related to questions of 'pleasure' in which Stevenson's essays can be seen to make a significant contribution is to debates around the ever-expanding world of publishing and the role of popular fiction in that context. The distinction between the serious and popular was an emerging one, although not all critics would adopt it. Some, however, like James Payn, were increasingly engaged with questions about the relationship between mainstream literature and the mass of the reading public. In a period in which anxieties about the growth of the reading public and the nature of popular publishing were multiplying, Stevenson's intervention in 'Popular Authors' is an important one. In addition to revealing further information about his childhood reading and another area of influence, it also shows him anticipating later theories about narrative desire, mass fantasies and the potential fulfilment offered in less 'canonical' texts. While mocking the productions of Stephens Hayward and Bracebridge Hemming, Stevenson gives an insight into another world of publishing quite apart from that of *belles-lettres*. With an enthusiasm and energy similar to his discussions of Skelt, he depicts the magical powers of the names and works of popular authors upon his childish imagination. Gently interrogating the already established cultural hierarchies, he questions the desire for 'upper popularity' and suggests that a writer such as himself might in some respects 'long for the penny number and the weekly woodcut.' As with 'A Gossip on a Novel of Dumas's', he brings to life his accounts of reading practices by depicting the setting for each reading experience: the wet and windy day on which his mother first read him *Macbeth*; the books found on a boyhood expedition to Neidpath Castle. The writers of such works, he suggests, returning to his theme, have no need of being praised for their talents; their 'popularity' is established in terms of the numbers they sold. He also returns to his central theme of realism: what relationship does the reader of such works perceive between the book and his or her life? Did *Tom Holt's Log* inspire someone to go to sea? Does reading about a poor heroine's romantic and financial successes in *The Young Ladies' Journal* create in the young female reader similar aspirations? It is more complicated, the essay suggests, than a crude misapprehension of the 'reality' of such fictions: for the readers 'long, not to enter into the lives of others, but to behold themselves in changed situations, ardently but impotently preconceived.' In other words, such tales offer a narrative reworking of the structures of their desires and aspirations. While others have subsequently debated the potentially radical or inherently conservative nature of this process, Stevenson begins to sketch out a patterning of readerly desire which to some extent recognises the conditions of the readers' lives and offers a model for their interactions with the text.[41] The despised popular writers 'can thus supply to the shop-girl and the shoe-black vesture cut to the pattern of their naked fancies, and furnish them with welcome scenery and properties for autobiographical romancing.'[42]

Influences

The various pleasures offered by fiction underpin Stevenson's assessment of those works which had most influence upon him, both as writer and as reader. In tracing out 'influences' as delineated in these essays, however, some caution is needed: the context of an article may shape its contents; and Stevenson's own acknowledgement of influences should not be taken too seriously. Although he accused himself of 'playing the sedulous ape', J. C. Furnas points out: 'Knowing both Stevenson and most of his models, I am well convinced that, by his late twenties, he was as near idiosyncrasy as Sterne before him, and Kipling after him.'[43]

With this in mind, his essay 'Books Which Have Influenced Me' (1887) appears in some ways to promise more than it delivers.

Written for *The British Weekly*, a predominantly religious periodical, Stevenson sets out a highly respectable – in artistic, scholarly and, to an extent, moral terms – list of influential reading; but this description of his cultural framework contains less excitement than his essays on popular authors, Dumas or Skelt. Inevitably he acknowledges fiction as the writing which has the most powerful effect, in its ability to 'clarify the lessons of life' and allow the reader to 'disengage us from ourselves': as overall good influences he cites Shakespeare and *The Pilgrim's Progress* – both extremely influential texts for almost every educated or even autodidact nineteenth-century reader – but, rather more idiosyncratically, Dumas. Moving from these three to a consideration of artistic and intellectual influences, his list is again highly respectable: Montaigne's essays, whose philosophical perspective can be discerned in 'Lay Morals'; the Gospel of St Matthew; Spencer; Lewes's *Life of Goethe*; Whitman – whom he wrote on elsewhere; the poetry of Martial and the meditations of Marcus Aurelius. Wordsworth too is rightly cited by Stevenson as a major influence and reference point for a number of writers in the period. His final mention is for Meredith's *The Egoist*: again, this is unsurprising in that Meredith was both a writer he greatly admired and a supportive friend. It is at the mention of Meredith, however, that the essay adopts a slightly different tone: as Stevenson talks about that writer's ability to engage the reader in a process of self-examination (citing his own belief – shared by others – that he was a model for the novel's central character, Willoughby Patterne), he moves with some relief, it seems, from the idea of influential writers to a consideration of the improvable reader. Indeed, the last part of the essay serves as a semi-ironic reflection on all that has gone before, as he indicates that any 'truth' in a text must be weighed and assessed by the reader, who will take from it what they wish 'and only that which suits will be assimilated'. Having freed the reader by this manoeuvre, Stevenson also frees himself from the weighty portentousness of the essay.

His enthusiasm, free from the constraints of 'respectability' and contextualised in the favoured voice of the 'gossip', is much more evident in 'A Gossip on a Novel of Dumas's'. Here he again delineates his own literary pantheon: a couple of Scott's novels; Molière, Montaigne, *The Egoist*, *The Pilgrim's Progress*, Borrow's *The Bible in Spain*, Wordsworth, Horace, Burns, Hazlitt,

Shakespeare, of course; but having established his credentials as a reader, it is to the work of Dumas, and in particular *The Vicomte de Bragelonne*, he turns. The appeal and influence of the musketeers for Stevenson are easy to comprehend. They operate as romantic and marginal figures who nevertheless succeed in influencing national histories through acts of individual endeavour. They have a clear moral code, which may contradict or work against the mores of their time but which nevertheless imbues their actions with certainty and confidence. And they most obviously represent a spirit of camaraderie and male bonding to which Stevenson was attracted. His interest in such marginal yet masculine groupings can be seen in *Treasure Island*; the figure of the romantic outsider who influences the process of history is most obvious in the character of Alan Breck in *Kidnapped*. In each of these novels, however, Stevenson balances his attraction towards such types with processes of containment: David Balfour as foil to Alan, Jim Hawkins as victim of Silver. Even the two brothers in *The Master of Ballantrae* offer oppositions between romance and sense, pleasure and stability. In his reading, however, Stevenson could enjoy to the full the pleasures offered by the musketeers, and in *The Vicomte* in particular, when the characters are ageing yet – in d'Artagnan's case at least – clinging to their youthful spirit of adventure, he could relive the excitement offered by his own imaginative play as a child. Stevenson the writer is also engaged from a more adult perspective. He is clearly interested from a technical point of view in the difficulties Dumas has with his heroines – problems closer to Stevenson's than those of his friend Meredith. But he also finds a value system that is attractive to him. Hearing much of Dumas himself in the novel, relishing that voice of a flawed humanity, he is also attracted to the older d'Artagnan and his struggles to retain a certain idealism and scope for action within a world increasingly governed by bureaucratic systems, internal politics and self-interest. His fondness for a novel which would not be the most obviously ranked as Dumas's finest becomes a means of engaging with his own moral codes.

'Some Gentlemen in Fiction' (1888), offers a less cogent negotiation between issues of morality and questions of craftsmanship. Addressing the question of what makes fictional figures memorable or convincing, the essay begins with Shakespeare. Stevenson suggests that, in the case of *Hamlet*, all is convincing except the scene with the Queen, but that the discriminating reader can choose to forget because there are certain qualities in Hamlet which constitute him a gentleman. The relationship between a character and its creator is then explored further through two opposed pairs of novelists: Fielding, who though a gentleman himself, failed to create convincing gentlemen in his fiction, is contrasted with Richardson; while in his own century, Thackeray and Dickens offer a similar comparison. Dickens had great problems in creating a gentleman, although in *Our Mutual Friend* and *A Tale of Two Cities* he succeeds to a certain extent; Thackeray on the other hand provides a notable list of gentlemanly characters. Yet the essay ends on a rather different note, a recognition perhaps of the uneasy implications of its argument, by suggesting that we should not look too closely for links between characters and their creators, because characters also belong to a historical, generic and discursive framework: 'they dwell in, they belong to, literature; convention, technical artifice, technical gusto, the mechanical necessities of the art, these are the flesh and blood with which they are invested.'[44]

It is not only Stevenson's more theoretical interventions in the romance/realism debate that place him in the context of new literary developments. 'On Some Technical Elements of Style' (1885), which attempts to analyse the determining effects of form on a piece of writing, could be related to an increasing 'professionalism' of the subject area and was certainly seen as a departure by Stevenson. 'Pathbreaking and epochmaking' were the words he used to describe it, but he recognised it would not be popular with a general readership. 'Style' of course is one area in which Stevenson was seen to excel, and in 'A Note On Realism' he had stressed that technique was as important as literary philosophies. Here he demystifies both terms, aware that in showing the 'springs and mechanism' of his art, he is 'disenchanting'. Stevenson associates literature with music, both arts of the temporal realm, and stresses its affinity with those arts which are self-sufficient, as opposed to the representative forms of sculpture, painting and acting. His emphasis on the importance of pattern, the idea of self-sufficiency – not so far removed froms self-reflexivity – and his discussion of the power of linguistic disruption, foreshadows both formalist and structuralist thinking. 'Even the derangement of phrases from their (so-called) natural order is luminous for the mind.' The essay is also significant in its attempts to find a vocabulary of criticism – whether in the metaphor of a web or of juggling oranges – as he struggles with detailed textual analysis of rhythm, phrasing and alliteration. Here Stevenson is not only writing as a writer and a reader, but also as an analytical critic, and the essay may be seen as a contribution to developments in analysis which would emerge with the growth of English Literature as a subject of academic study in the early years of the twentieth century.

The 'Modern'

Much has been written recently about the 'modern' element in Stevenson's fiction, although as early as 1885 William Archer wrote that Stevenson 'is a modern of the moderns both in his alert self-consciousness and in the particular artistic ideal which he proposes to himself.'[45] Critics, noting the impact of Stevenson upon writers such as Borges, Nabokov and Calvino, have offered analyses of what Alan Sandison calls 'a future feeling' and Tom Hubbard 'something of a modern sensibility'.[46] Using a wide range of comparisons and sources, Stevenson's fiction has been located in the context of Symbolism, Jungian and Freudian ideas on psychology, Bakhtinian concepts of carnival and a modern crisis of paternity. It has also been convincingly situated within Scottish traditions of experiment and anti-realist writing.[47] To what extent can characteristics of modernity be discerned in Stevenson's critical essays?

Certainly they offer strong evidence of Stevenson's relationship to the emerging interest in psychology, not only in the workings of the mind which so interested and attracted people such as F. W. H. Myers to his work, but also in the play of imagination, the impact of childhood on thinking and the relationship between language and feeling, structure and content. As this introduction has implied, elements of discourse theory, the breaking down of literary hierarchies, an engagement with the properties of literary language, might be heard in his arguments. The essays also appear to anticipate more recent thinking about the nature and significance of narrative desire. But if anything makes these essays 'modern' but also recognisably Stevenson's own, it is the way in which they position the reader: the reader of the essay and the reader figured in the essay are both activated; the author as writer and as part of a reading community is in continual play. In his awareness of 'readers' Stevenson may be understood in the context of anxieties expressed in his own century about the ever-expanding literary market, but he also prefigures a late twentieth-century attention to the reader in the text. For these are essays which, while illuminating Stevenson's fiction and intervening in contemporary critical debates, re-enact and remind us of the power and pleasures of reading, manifest in both theory and practice: 'The words, if the book be eloquent, should run thenceforward in our ears like the noise of breakers, and the story, if it be a story, repeat itself in a thousand coloured pictures to the eye.'[48]

Notes

1 Letter to W. H. Low, 13 March 1885 (*Letters* III, p. 40).
2 Daiches, *Stevenson and the Art of Fiction*, p. 6.
3 Furnas, *Voyage to Windward: the Life of Robert Louis Stevenson*, p. 389.
4 E. F. Benson, 'The Myth of Robert Louis Stevenson', *London Mercury* July–August, 1925, quoted in Furnas, p. 381.
5 Unsigned review, *British Quarterly Review*, July 1881, lxxiv, pp. 219–20, in Maixner, *Robert Louis Stevenson: The Critical Heritage*, p. 87.
6 William Archer, 'Robert Louis Stevenson: his Style and his Thought', *Time*, November, 1885, ii, pp. 581–91, Maixner, p. 162.
7 Such terminology had been questioned earlier by G. H. Lewes, who famously argued in the *Westminster Review*, 'Realism is thus the basis of all Art, and its antithesis is not Idealism but *Falsism*.' G. H. Lewes, *Westminster Review*, 70, 1858, pp. 488–518.
8 Letter to Charles Warren Stoddard, 13 February 1886 (*Letters* III, pp. 78–9).
9 Keating, *The Haunted Study* (1989) p. 348.
10 'In the wake of the romantic yet prosaic novel of Walter Scott there remains another novel yet to be created, and in our opinion a more beautiful and complete novel. This novel has at one and the same time elements of the epic and the theatrical, is romantic yet poetic, realist yet idealist, true yet great, and will fuse together the worlds of Walter Scott and Homer': 'Victor Hugo's Romances', *Familiar Studies of Men and Books*, Tusitala 27, p. 1.
11 Ibid., p. 6.
12 Leslie Fiedler, attempting to redefine Stevenson's reputation in light of his 'relegation' to the genre of romance, suggests that his fiction might be related to the handling of myth in modern fiction which begins with 'the outward Romance of incident, the boy's story or thriller, and moves through allegory, often elusive, to the naïve or unconscious evocation of myth.' 'RLS Revisited', *Collected Essays*, vol. 1, p. 298.
13 'Victor Hugo's Romances', *Familiar Studies of Men and Books*, Tusitala 27, p. 8.
14 'A Gossip on Romance', Tusitala 29, p. 125.

15 Letter to R. A. M. Stevenson, October 1883 (*Letters* II, p. 272).

16 'A Note on Realism', Tusitala 28, p. 70.

17 'The Art of Fiction' was delivered as a lecture by Walter Besant on 25 April 1884 and published: as 'A Lecture . . . With Notes and additions' by Chatto & Windus in 1884. Henry James, 'The Art of Fiction', *Longman's Magazine*, 4 September 1884, pp. 502–21. 'A Humble Remonstrance' *Longman's Magazine*, 5 December 1884, pp. 139–47.

18 'A Gossip on a Novel of Dumas's', Tusitala 29, p. 118.

19 Keating, *The Haunted Study*, p. 347.

20 'A Gossip on Romance', Tusitala 29, p. 119.

21 Calvino, Introduction to *I Nostri Antenati (Our Ancestors)* 1980, pp. vi-vii. I am grateful to Carol Anderson for letting me read an as yet unpublished essay on 'Stevenson and Calvino'. See also Anderson, 'No Single Key: The Fiction of Robert Louis Stevenson and Italo Calvino', 1991.

22 Stevenson, 'alike at two-and-twenty and at five-and-thirty, remembered his childhood as it is given to few grown men and women to remember' (Balfour, *Life* I, pp. 39–40).

23 Balfour, *Life* I, p. 49.

24 '*Rosa Quo Locorum*', Tusitala 30, p. 2.

25 In the essay 'Child's Play', although he talks about the incomprehensible nature of the child's world, his bewilderment emerges most strongly when talking of 'parents' and how strange they must seem. This has been seen by some as a weakness in Stevenson's writing. J. M. Barrie commented: 'He experiments too long; he is still a boy wondering what he is going to be . . .' (Furnas, p. 379). Although Barrie offers this as a criticism of his tendency to write 'minor' works of fiction, the comments are also revealing for his essays: the past is returned to as if memories of 'boyhood' will offer a model for a creative future, and the uncertainty of childhood ambitions becomes a source of potential rather than a disadvantage.

26 'A Gossip on Romance', Tusitala 29, p. 129.

27 Ibid., p. 131.

28 Ibid., p. 123.

29 'The Lantern-Bearers', Tusitala 30, p. 36.

30 Ibid., p. 39.

31 See Furnas, p. 30.

32 'The Lantern-Bearers' Tusitala 30, p. 31.

33 Collins, 'The Unknown Public', 1858.

34 Similar arguments about the changing nature of the literary milieu can be found in the debate which arose between those such as Walter Besant who welcomed the veracity of George Gissing's *New Grub Street* (1891) and others such as Andrew Lang, Stevenson's friend and champion, who accused Gissing of presenting a morbid and partial portrait of the writer's world.

35 He had submitted an essay on a similar topic to Sir Leslie Stephen at the *Cornhill* in 1878, and an essay entitled 'On the Choice of a Profession' followed 'Letter' in the collected volume of *Essays Literary and Critical*.

36 Archer, 'Robert Louis Stevenson: his Style and his Thought', Maixner, p. 162.

37 Stevenson had expressed similar sentiments in a letter to Edmund Gosse on the reception of *Prince Otto*: 'But a man is never martyred in any honest sense in the pursuit of his pleasure; and *delirium tremens* has more of the honour of the cross. We were full of the pride of life, and chose, like prostitutes, to live by a pleasure.

We should be paid if we give the pleasure we pretend to give; but why should we be honoured?' (Letter to Edmund Gosse, 2 January 1886 (*Letters* III, p. 70).

38 Le Galliennne, *The Academy*, 14 May 1892, pp. 462–4: see Maixner p. 391.
39 Further paragraphs were added to the review in 1896, in which he attempts to redefine 'pleasure'.
40 Letter to le Gallienne, 28 December 1893 (*Letters* V, p. 94).
41 For later developments of work in this area see: Frederic Jameson, *The Political Unconscious* (1981); Carolyn Steedman, *Landscape for a Good Woman* (1989) and Janice Radway, *Reading the Romance* (1987).
42 'Popular Authors', Tusitala 28, p. 31.
43 Furnas, p. 380.
44 'Some Gentlemen in Fiction', Tusitala 26, p. 110.
45 Archer, as above: see Maixner, p. 160.
46 See: Sandison, *Robert Louis Stevenson and the Appearance of Modernism*, p. 3; Tom Hubbard, *Seeking Mr Hyde: Studies in Robert Louis Stevenson, Symbolism, Myth and the Pre-Modern*, p. 20.
47 See: Anderson, 'No Single Key'; Craig, *Out of History*, ch. 3; Gifford, 'Stevenson and Scottish Fiction: The Importance of *The Master of Ballantrae*'.
48 'A Gossip on Romance', Tusita 29, p. 119.

ESSAYS

*

Child's Play

*

This essay was published in the *Cornhill Magazine* in September 1878. A well-established periodical since the 1860s, the *Cornhill* offered a mixture of articles and serialised novels. At this stage Sir Leslie Stephen was still editing the magazine, although his successor, James Payn, who took over in 1882, moved the magazine in a more popular direction. Stevenson contributed under both editors. The essay, published under Stevenson's signature, reworks material written earlier – possibly an essay of the 1870s entitled 'Children's Games', which is mentioned in 'Notes of Childhood' – and was reprinted in *Virginibus Puerisque* (1881). This version was drawn upon for 'Memoirs of Himself' (1880) and '*Rosa Quo Locorum*' (1893). A reviewer in *The Pall Mall Gazette*, 16 April 1881, picked it out as 'approaching the classical in form' (Maixner, p. 79) and even those who disliked *Virginibus Puerisque* as a whole, praised this piece.

The essay, written during the summer of 1878, at a time during which he was spending much time with Fanny at Gresz, may be usefully linked with the later essay 'The Lantern-Bearers' as representing an exploration of the processes of the imagination; it also relates to recollections of the child's creativity raised by 'A Chapter on Dreams' and 'A Penny Plain and Twopence Coloured'. As Graham Balfour, his first biographer, notes, Stevenson remembered his childhood more vividly than most, and wrote at considerable length about the life of the child's imagination. Indeed, in his later essay '*Rosa Quo Locorum*', Stevenson suggests that the child's mind should be the object of greater inquiry than it is: 'From the mind of childhood there is more history and more philosophy to be fished up than from all the printed volumes in a library' (Tusitala 30, p. 1). In his critical writing Stevenson repeatedly links the workings of the child's mind with the pleasures of creating stories and relates both to the pleasures of reading; in turn this conjunction becomes part of his defence of romance as a form. In 'Rosa Quo Locorum' again he writes: 'for the child thinks very much in images, words are very live to him, phrases that imply a picture eloquent beyond their value' (Tusitala 30, p. 2). In these words, and in this essay, Stevenson's strong inclination towards to the symbolic rather than representational nature of literature emerges.

Child's Play[1]

The regret we have for our childhood is not wholly justifiable: so much a man may lay down without fear of public ribaldry; for although we shake our heads over the change, we are not unconscious of the manifold advantages of our new state. What we lose in generous impulse, we more than gain in the habit of generously watching others; and the capacity to enjoy Shakespeare may balance a lost aptitude for playing at soldiers. Terror is gone out of our lives, moreover; we no longer see the devil in the bed-curtains nor lie awake to listen to the wind.[2] We go to school no more; and if we have only exchanged one drudgery for another (which is by no means sure), we are set free for ever from the daily fear of chastisement. And yet a great change has overtaken us; and although we do not enjoy ourselves less, at least we take our pleasure differently. We need pickles nowadays to make Wednesday's cold mutton please our Friday's appetite; and I can remember the time when to call it red venison, and tell myself a hunter's story, would have made it more palatable than the best of sauces. To the grown person, cold mutton is cold mutton all the world over; not all the mythology ever invented by man will make it better or worse to him; the broad fact, the clamant reality, of the mutton carries away before it such seductive figments. But for the child it is still possible to weave an enchantment over eatables; and if he has but read of a dish in a story-book, it will be heavenly manna to him for a week.

If a grown man does not like eating and drinking and exercise, if he is not something positive in his tastes, it means he has a feeble body and should have some medicine; but children may be pure spirits, if they will, and take their enjoyment in a world of moon-shine. Sensation does not count for so much in our first years as afterwards; something of the swaddling numbness of infancy clings about us; we see and touch and hear through a sort of golden mist. Children, for instance, are able enough to see, but they have no great faculty for looking; they do not use their eyes for the pleasure of using them, but for by-ends of their own; and the things I call to mind seeing most vividly, were not beautiful in themselves, but merely interesting or enviable to me as I thought they might be turned to practical account in play. Nor is the sense of touch so clean and poignant in children as it is in a man. If you will turn over your old memories, I think the sensations of this sort you remember will be somewhat vague, and come to not much more than a blunt, general sense of heat on summer days, or a blunt, general sense of well-being in bed. And here, of course, you will understand pleasurable sensations; for overmastering pain – the most deadly and tragical element in life, and the true commander of man's soul and body – alas! pain has its own way with all of us; it breaks in, a rude visitant, upon the fairy garden where the child wanders in a dream, no less surely than it rules upon the field of battle, or sends the immortal war-god whimpering to his father; and innocence, no more than philosophy, can protect us from this sting. As for taste, when we bear in mind the excesses of unmitigated sugar which delight a youthful palate, 'it is surely no very cynical asperity' to think taste a character of the maturer growth.[3] Smell and hearing are perhaps more developed; I remember many scents, many voices, and a great deal of spring singing in the woods. But, hearing is capable of vast improvement as a means of pleasure; and there is all the world between gaping wonderment at the jargon of birds, and the emotion with which a man listens to articulate music.

At the same time, and step by step with this increase in the definition and intensity of what we feel which accompanies our growing age, another change takes place in the sphere of intellect, by which all things are transformed and seen through theories and associations as through coloured windows. We make to ourselves day by day, out of history, and gossip, and economical speculations, and God knows what, a medium in which we walk and through which we look abroad. We study shop windows with other eyes than in our childhood, never to wonder, not always to admire, but to make and modify our little incongruous theories about life. It is no longer the uniform of a soldier that arrests our attention; but perhaps the flowing carriage of a woman, or perhaps a countenance that has been vividly stamped with passion and carries an adventurous story written in its lines. The pleasure of surprise is passed away; sugar-loaves and water-carts seem mighty tame to encounter; and we walk the streets to make romances and to sociologise. Nor must we deny that a good many of us walk them solely for the purposes of transit or in the interest of a livelier digestion. These, indeed, may look back with mingled thoughts upon their childhood, but the rest are in a better case; they know more than when they were children, they understand better, their desires and sympathies answer more nimbly to the provocation of the senses, and their minds are brimming with interest as they go about the world.

According to my contention, this is a flight to which children cannot rise. They are wheeled in perambulators or dragged about by nurses in a pleasing stupor. A vague, faint, abiding wonderment possesses them. Here and there some specially remarkable circumstance, such as a water-cart or a guardsman, fairly penetrates into the seat of thought and calls them, for half a moment, out of themselves; and you may see them, still towed forward sideways by the inexorable nurse as by a sort of destiny, but still staring at the bright object in their wake. It may be some minutes before another such moving spectacle reawakens them to the world in which they dwell. For other children, they almost invariably show some intelligent sympathy. 'There is a fine fellow making mud pies,' they seem to say; 'that I can understand, there is some sense in mud pies.' But the doings of their elders, unless where they are speakingly picturesque or recommend themselves by the quality of being easily imitable, they let them go over their heads (as we say) without the least regard. If it were not for this perpetual imitation, we should be tempted to fancy they despised us outright, or only considered us in the light of creatures brutally strong and brutally silly; among whom they condescended to dwell in obedience like a philosopher at a barbarous court. At times, indeed, they display an arrogance of disregard that is truly staggering. Once, when I was groaning aloud with physical pain, a young gentleman came into the room and nonchalantly inquired if I had seen his bow and arrow. He made no account of *my* groans, which he accepted, as he had to accept so much else, as a piece of the inexplicable conduct of his elders; and like a wise young gentleman, he would waste no wonder on the subject. Those elders, who care so little for rational enjoyment, and are even the enemies of rational enjoyment for others, he had accepted without understanding and without complaint, as the rest of us accept the scheme of the universe.

We grown people can tell ourselves a story, give and take strokes until the bucklers ring, ride far and fast, marry, fall, and die; all the while sitting quietly by the fire or lying prone in bed. This is exactly what a child cannot do, or does not do, at least, when he can find anything else. He works all with lay figures and stage properties. When his story comes to the fighting, he must rise, get something by way of a sword and have a set-to with a piece of furniture, until he is out of breath. When he comes to ride with the king's pardon, he must bestride a chair, which he will so hurry and belabour and on which he will so furiously demean himself, that the messenger will arrive, if not bloody with spurring, at least fiery red with haste. If his romance involves an accident upon a cliff, he must clamber in person about the chest of drawers and fall bodily upon the carpet, before his imagination is satisfied. Lead soldiers, dolls, all toys, in short, are in the same category and answer the same end. Nothing can stagger a child's faith; he accepts the clumsiest substitutes and can swallow the most staring incongruities. The chair he has just been besieging as a castle, or valiantly cutting to the ground as a dragon, is taken away for the accommodation of a morning visitor, and he is nothing abashed; he can skirmish by the hour with a stationary coal-scuttle; in the midst of the enchanted pleasance, he can see, without sensible shock, the gardener soberly digging potatoes for the day's dinner. He can make abstraction of whatever does not fit into his fable; and he puts his eyes into his pocket, just as we hold our noses in an unsavoury lane. And so it is, that although the ways of children cross with those of their elders in a hundred places daily, they never go in the same direction nor so much as lie in the same element. So may the telegraph wires intersect the line of the high-road, or so might a landscape painter and a bagman visit the same country, and yet move in different worlds.

People struck with these spectacles, cry aloud about the power of imagination in the young. Indeed there may be two words to that. It is, in some ways, but a pedestrian fancy that the child exhibits. It is the grown people who make the nursery stories; all the children do, is jealously to preserve the text. One out of a dozen reasons why *Robinson Crusoe* should be so popular with youth, is that it hits their level in this matter to a nicety; Crusoe was always at makeshifts and had, in so many words, to *play* at a great variety of professions; and then the book is all about tools, and there is nothing that delights a child so much. Hammers and saws belong to a province of life that positively calls for imitation. The juvenile lyrical drama, surely of the most ancient Thespian model, wherein the trades of mankind are successively simulated to the running burthen 'On a cold and frosty morning,' gives a good instance of the artistic taste in children. And this need for overt action and lay figures testifies to a defect in the child's imagination which prevents him from carrying out his novels in the privacy of his own heart. He does not yet know enough of the world and men. His experience is incomplete. That stage-wardrobe and scene-room that we call the memory is so ill-provided, that he can overtake few combinations and body out few stories, to his own content, without some external aid. He is at the experimental stage; he is not sure how one would feel in certain circumstances; to make sure, he must come as near trying it as his means permit. And so here is young heroism with a wooden sword, and mothers practice their kind vocation over a bit of jointed stick. It may be laughable enough just now; but it is these same people and these same thoughts, that not long hence, when they are on the theatre of life, will make you weep and tremble. For children think very much the same thoughts and dream the same dreams, as bearded men and marriageable women. No one is more romantic. Fame and honour, the love of young men and the love of mothers, the business man's pleasure in method, all these and others they anticipate and rehearse in their play hours. Upon us, who are further advanced and fairly dealing with the threads of destiny, they only glance from time to time to glean a hint for their own mimetic reproduction. Two children playing at soldiers are far more interesting to each other than one of the scarlet beings whom both are busy imitating. This is perhaps the greatest oddity of all. 'Art for art' is their motto; and the doings of grown folk are only interesting as the raw material for play. Not Théophile Gautier, not Flaubert, can look more callously upon life, or rate the reproduction more highly over the reality; and they will parody an execution, a deathbed, or the funeral of the young man of Nain, with all the cheerfulness in the world.[4]

The true parallel for play is not to be found, of course, in conscious art, which, though it be derived from play, is itself an abstract, impersonal thing, and depends largely upon philosophical interests beyond the scope of childhood. It is when we make castles in the air and personate the leading character in our own romances, that we return to the spirit of our first years. Only, there are several reasons why the spirit is no longer so agreeable to indulge. Nowadays, when we admit this personal element into our divagations we are apt to stir up uncomfortable and sorrowful memories, and remind ourselves sharply of old wounds. Our daydreams can no longer lie all in the air like a story in the *Arabian Nights*; they read to us rather like the history of a period in which we ourselves had taken part, where we come across many unfortunate passages and find our own conduct smartly reprimanded. And then the child, mind you, acts his parts. He does not merely repeat them to himself; he leaps, he runs, and sets the blood agog over all his body. And so his play breathes him; and he no sooner assumes a passion than he gives it vent. Alas! when we betake ourselves to our intellectual form of play, sitting quietly by the fire or lying prone in bed, we rouse many hot feelings for which we can find no outlet. Substitutes are not acceptable to the mature mind, which desires the thing itself; and even to rehearse a triumphant dialogue with one's enemy, although it is perhaps the most satisfactory piece of play still left within our reach, is not entirely satisfying, and is even apt to lead to a visit and an interview which may be the reverse of triumphant after all.

In the child's world of dim sensation, play is all in all. 'Making believe' is the gist of his whole life, and he cannot so much as take a walk except in character. I could not learn my alphabet without some suitable *mise-en-scène*, and had to act a business man in an office before I could sit down to my book. Will you kindly question your memory, and find out how much you did, work or pleasure, in good faith and soberness, and for how much you had to cheat yourself with some invention? I remember, as though it were yesterday, the expansion of spirit, the dignity and self-reliance, that came with a pair of mustachios in burnt cork, even when there was none to see. Children are even content to forego what we call the realities, and prefer the shadow to the substance. When they might be speaking intelligibly together, they chatter senseless gibberish by the hour, and are quite happy because they are making believe to speak French. I have said already how even the imperious appetite of hunger suffers itself to be gulled and led by the nose with the fag end of an old song. And it goes deeper than this: when children are together even a meal is felt as an interruption in the business of life; and they must find some imaginative sanction, and tell themselves some sort of story, to account for, to colour, to render entertaining, the simple processes of eating and drinking. What wonderful fancies I have heard evolved out of the pattern upon tea-cups! – from which there followed a code of rules and a whole world of excitement, until tea-drinking began to take rank as a game. When my cousin and I took our porridge of a morning, we had a device to enliven the course of the meal.[5] He ate his with sugar, and explained it to be a country continually buried under snow. I took mine with milk, and explained it to be a country suffering gradual inundation. You can imagine us exchanging bulletins; how here was an island still unsubmerged, here a valley not yet covered with snow; what inventions were made; how his population lived in cabins on perches and travelled on stilts, and how mine was always in boats; how the interest grew furious, as the last corner of safe ground was cut off on all sides and grew smaller every moment; and how, in fine, the food was of altogether secondary importance, and might even have been nauseous, so long as we seasoned it with these dreams. But perhaps the most exciting moments I ever had over a meal, were in the case of calves' feet jelly. It was hardly possible not to believe – and you may be sure, so far from trying, I did all I could to favour the illusion – that some part of it was hollow, and that sooner or later my spoon would lay open the secret tabernacle of the golden rock. There, might some miniature *Red Beard* await his hour; there, might one find the treasures of the *Forty Thieves*, and bewildered Cassim beating about the walls. And so I quarried on slowly, with bated breath, savouring the interest. Believe me, I had little palate left for the jelly; and though I preferred the taste when I took cream with it, I used often to go without, because the cream dimmed the transparent fractures.

Even with games, this spirit is authoritative with right-minded children. It is thus that hide-and-seek has so pre-eminent a sovereignty, for it is the wellspring of romance, and the actions and the excitement to which it gives rise lend themselves to almost any sort of fable. And thus cricket, which is a mere matter of dexterity, palpably about nothing and for no end, often fails to satisfy infantile craving. It is a game, if you like, but not a game of play. You cannot tell yourself a story about cricket; and the activity it calls forth can be justified on no rational theory. Even football, although it admirably simulates the tug and the ebb and flow of battle, has presented difficulties to the mind of young sticklers after verisimilitude; and I knew at least one little boy who was mightily exercised about the presence of the ball, and had to spirit himself up, whenever he came to play, with an elaborate story of enchantment, and take the missile as a sort of talisman bandied about in conflict between two Arabian nations.

To think of such a frame of mind, is to become disquieted about the bringing up of children. Surely they dwell in a mythological epoch, and are not the contemporaries of their parents. What can they think of them? what can they make of these bearded or petticoated giants who look down upon their games? who move upon a cloudy Olympus, following unknown designs apart from rational enjoyment? who profess the tenderest solicitude for children, and yet every now and again reach down out of their altitude and terribly vindicate the prerogatives of age? Off goes the child, corporally smarting, but morally rebellious. Were there ever such unthinkable deities as parents? I would give a great deal to know what, in nine cases out of ten, is the child's unvarnished feeling. A sense of past cajolery; a sense of personal attraction, at best very feeble; above all, I should imagine, a sense of terror for the untried residue of mankind: go to make up the attraction that he feels. No wonder, poor little heart, with such a weltering world in front of him, if he clings to the hand he knows! The dread irrationality of the whole affair, as it seems to children, is a thing we are all too ready to forget. 'Oh, why,' I remember passionately wondering, 'why can we not all be happy and devote ourselves to play?' And when children do philosophise, I believe it is usually to very much the same purpose.

One thing, at least, comes very clearly out of these considerations; that whatever we are to expect at the hands of children, it should not be any peddling exactitude about matters of fact. They walk in a vain show, and among mists and rainbows; they are passionate after dreams and unconcerned about realities; speech is a difficult art not wholly learned and there is nothing in their own tastes or purposes to teach them what we mean by abstract truthfulness. When a bad writer is inexact, even if he can look back on half a century of years, we charge him with incompetence and not with dishonesty. And why not extend the same allowance to imperfect speakers? Let a stockbroker be dead stupid about poetry, or a poet inexact in the details of business, and we excuse them heartily from blame. But show us a miserable, unbreeched, human entity, whose whole profession it is to take a tub for a fortified town and a shaving-brush for the deadly stiletto, and who passes three-fourths of his time in a dream and the rest in open self-deception, and we expect him to be as nice upon a matter of fact as a scientific expert bearing evidence. Upon my heart, I think it less than decent. You do not consider how little the child sees, or how swift he is to weave what he has seen into bewildering fiction; and that he cares no more for what you call truth, than you for a gingerbread dragoon.

I am reminded, as I write, that the child is very inquiring as to the precise truth of stories. But indeed this is a very different matter, and one bound up with the subject of play, and the precise amount of playfulness, or playability, to be looked for in the world. Many such burning questions must arise in the course of nursery education. Among the fauna of this planet, which already embraces the pretty soldier and the terrifying Irish beggarman, is, or is not, the child to expect a Bluebeard or a Cormoran?[6] Is he, or is he not, to look out for magicians, kindly and potent? May he, or may he not, reasonably hope to be cast away upon a desert island, or turned to such diminutive proportions that he can live on equal terms with his lead soldiery, and go a cruise in his own toy schooner? Surely all these are practical questions to a neophyte entering upon life with a view to play. Precision upon such a point, the child can understand. But if you merely ask him of his past behaviour, as to who threw such a stone, for instance, or struck such and such a match; or whether he had looked into a parcel or gone by a forbidden path – why, he can see no moment in the inquiry, and it is ten to one, he has already half forgotten and half bemused himself with subsequent imaginings.

It would be easy to leave them in their native cloudland, where they figure so prettily – pretty like flowers and innocent like dogs. They will come out of their gardens soon enough, and have to go into offices and the witness-box. Spare them yet a while, O conscientious parent! Let them doze among their playthings yet a little! for who knows what a rough, war-faring existence lies before them in the future?

The Morality of the Profession of Letters

✳

Written during Stevenson's first season in Davos (1881), when he was often too ill to do much serious work, and also felt depressed, this essay was a response in part to James Payn's essay 'Penny Fiction' (*Nineteenth Century*, 1881), which argued that writers had to meet the demands of their expanding public, rather than trying to educate their tastes. It appeared in the highly respected literary journal, the *Fortnightly Review* in April 1881. Stevenson's article, characterised by what J. C. Furnas calls a 'relative pomposity' caused by lack of stimulation, was intended to contribute to a debate over the profession of literature. In the 1880s the rapid expansion of market forces was bringing about dramatic changes in literary production and Stevenson himself had contributed to the popularity of one-volume adventure stories and thrillers, as opposed to the older triple-decker format.

In addition to serialised novels, the *Fortnightly Review*, of which G. H. Lewes was the first editor, and which was edited from 1867–82 by John Morley, published articles on a wide variety of topics. A reviewer of this particular issue in *The Academy* – a highly influential but rather more conventional periodical – described (9 April 1881) how the *Fortnightly*'s varied contents included an instalment by Herbert Spencer of *The Principles of Sociology*; an example of the new biology from Sir John Lubbock; and Stevenson's essay, in which 'the manner is exquisitely light and graceful, and the matter naught.' This reviewer went on to accuse Stevenson of writing as if the financial pressures of Grub Street were a thing of the past, and argued that Stevenson's 'cunningly wrought optimism' will not help writers who have to give up their time to the acquiring of 'filthy lucre whereon to keep body and soul together.'

Stevenson replied to *The Academy* in a letter published on 7 May 1881, suggesting that he was well aware of the nature of Grub Street, but still believed that writers could rise in a profession. He was also, he claimed, reluctant to believe that the worst kind of work produced in Grub Street was inevitably the product of the poorest of men. He ends his letter with a jibe at the critic, noting that the reviewer has persuaded him 'that the influence of literature lies chiefly in single and striking expressions, since not even a critic seems able to observe both the end and the beginning of an article so short as mine.'

The Morality of the Profession of Letters[1]

The profession of letters has been lately debated in the public prints; and it has been debated, to put the matter mildly, from a point of view that was calculated to surprise high-minded men, and bring a general contempt on books and reading. Some time ago, in particular, a lively, pleasant, popular writer devoted an essay, lively and pleasant like himself, to a very encouraging view of the profession.[2] We may be glad that his experience is so cheering, and we may hope that all others, who deserve it, shall be as handsomely rewarded; but I do not think we need be at all glad to have this question, so important to the public and ourselves, debated solely on the ground of money. The salary in any business under heaven is not the only, nor indeed the first, question. That you should continue to exist is a matter for your own consideration; but that your business should be first honest, and second useful, are points in which honour and morality are concerned. If the writer to whom I refer succeeds in persuading a number of young persons to adopt this way of life with an eye set singly on the livelihood, we must expect them in their works to follow profit only, and we must expect in consequence, if he will pardon me the epithets, a slovenly, base, untrue, and empty literature. Of that writer himself I am not speaking: he is diligent, clean and pleasing; we all owe him periods of entertainment, and he has achieved an amiable popularity which he has adequately deserved. But the truth is, he does not, or did not when he first embraced it, regard his profession from this purely mercenary side. He went into it, I shall venture to say, if not with any noble design, at least in the ardour of a first love; and he enjoyed its practice long before he paused to

calculate the wage. The other day an author was complimented on a piece of work, good in itself and exceptionally
good for him, and replied, in terms unworthy of a
commercial traveller, that as the book was not briskly selling
he did not give a copper farthing for its merit. It must not be
supposed that the person to whom this answer was addressed
received it as a profession of faith; he knew, on the other
hand, that it was only a whiff of irritation; just as we know,
when a respectable writer talks of literature as a way of life,
like shoemaking, but not so useful, that he is only debating
one aspect of a question, and is still clearly conscious of a
dozen others more important in themselves and more central
to the matter in hand. But while those who treat literature in
this penny-wise and virtue-foolish spirit are themselves truly
in possession of a better light, it does not follow that the
treatment is decent, or improving, whether for themselves or
others. To treat all subjects in the highest, the most
honourable, and the pluckiest spirit, consistent with the
fact, is the first duty of a writer. If he be well paid, as I am
glad to hear he is, this duty becomes the more urgent, the
neglect of it the more disgraceful. And perhaps there is no
subject on which a man should speak so gravely as that
industry, whatever it may be, which is the occupation or
delight of his life; which is his tool to earn or serve with; and
which, if it be unworthy, stamps himself as a mere incubus of
dumb and greedy bowels on the shoulders of labouring
humanity. On that subject alone even to force the note
might lean to virtue's side. It is to be hoped that a numerous
and enterprising generation of writers will follow and surpass
the present one; but it would be better if the stream were
stayed, and the roll of our old honest English books were
closed, than that esurient book-makers should continue and
debase a brave tradition, and lower, in their own eyes, a
famous race.[3] Better that our serene temples were deserted
than filled with trafficking and juggling priests.

There are two just reasons for the choice of any way of life:
the first is inbred taste in the chooser; the second some high
utility in the industry selected. Literature, like any other art,
is singularly interesting to the artist; and, in a degree peculiar
to itself among the arts, it is useful to mankind. These are
sufficient justifications for any young man or woman who

adopts it as the business of his life. I shall not say much about the wages. A writer can live by his writing. If not so luxuriously as by other trades, then less luxuriously. The nature of the work he does all day will more affect his happiness than the quality of his dinner at night. Whatever be your calling and however much it brings you in the year, you could still, you know, get more by cheating. We all suffer ourselves to be too much concerned about a little poverty; but such considerations should not move us in the choice of that which is to be the business and justification of so great a portion of our lives; and like the missionary, the patriot, or the philosopher, we should all choose that poor and brave career in which we can do the most and best for mankind. Now Nature, faithfully followed, proves herself a careful mother. A lad, for some liking to the jingle of words, betakes himself to letters for his life; by-and-by, when he learns more gravity, he finds that he has chosen better than he knew; that if he earns little, he is earning it amply; that if he receives a small wage, he is in a position to do considerable services; that it is in his power, in some small measure to protect the oppressed and to defend the truth. So kindly is the world arranged, such great profit may arise from a small degree of human reliance on oneself, and such, in particular, is the happy star of this trade of writing, that it should combine pleasure and profit to both parties, and be at once agreeable, like fiddling, and useful, like good preaching.

This is to speak of literature at its highest; and with the four great elders who are still spared to our respect and admiration, with Carlyle, Ruskin, Browning, and Tennyson before us, it would be cowardly to consider it at first in any lesser aspect.[4] But while we cannot follow these athletes, while we may none of us, perhaps, be very vigorous, very original, or very wise, I still contend that, in the humblest sort of literary work, we have it in our power either to do great harm or great good. We may seek merely to please; we may seek, having no higher gift, merely to gratify the idle nine days' curiosity of our contemporaries; or we may essay, however feebly, to instruct. In each of these we shall have to deal with that remarkable art of words which, because it is the dialect of life, comes home so easily and powerfully to the minds of men; and since that is so, we contribute, in each of these branches, to build up the sum of sentiments and appreciations which goes by the name of Public Opinion or Public Feeling. The total of a nation's reading, in these days of daily papers, greatly modifies the total of the nation's speech; and the speech and reading, taken together, form the efficient educational medium of youth. A good man or woman may keep a youth some little while in clearer air; but the contemporary atmosphere is all-powerful in the end on the average of mediocre characters. The copious Corinthian baseness of the American reporter or the Parisian *chroniqueur*, both so lightly readable, must exercise an incalculable influence for ill; they touch upon all subjects, and on all with the same ungenerous hand; they begin the consideration of all, in young and unprepared minds, in an unworthy spirit; on all, they supply some pungency for dull people to quote.[5] The mere body of this ugly matter overwhelms the rare utterances of good men; the sneering, the selfish, and the cowardly are scattered in broad sheets on every table, while the antidote, in small volumes, lies unread upon the shelf.[6] I have spoken of the American and the French, not because they are so much baser, but so much more readable, than the English; their evil is done more effectively, in America for the masses, in French for the few that care to read; but with us as with them, the duties of literature are daily neglected, truth daily perverted and suppressed, and grave subjects daily degraded in the treatment. The journalist is not reckoned an important officer; yet judge of the good he might do, the harm he does; judge of it by one instance only: that when we find two journals on the reverse sides of politics each, on the same day, openly garbling a piece of news for the interest of its own party, we smile at the discovery (no discovery now!) as over a good joke and pardonable stratagem. Lying so open is scarce lying, it is true, but one of the things that we profess to teach our young is a respect for truth; and I cannot think this piece of education will be crowned with any great success, so long as some of us practise and the rest openly approve of public falsehood.

There are two duties incumbent upon any man who enters on the business of writing: truth to the fact and a good spirit in the treatment. In every department of literature, though so low as hardly to deserve the name, truth to the fact is of importance to the education and comfort of mankind, and so hard to preserve, that the faithful trying to do so will lend some dignity to the man who tries it. Our judgements are based upon two things: first, upon the original preferences of our soul; but, second, upon the mass of testimony to the nature of God, man, and the universe which reaches us, in divers manners, from without. For the most part these divers manners are reducible to one, all that we learn of past times and much that we learn of our own reaching us through the medium of books or papers, and even he who cannot read learning from the same source at second-hand and by the report of him who can. Thus the sum of the contemporary knowledge or ignorance of good and evil is, in large measure, the handiwork of those who write. Those who write have to see that each man's knowledge is, as near as they can make it, answerable to the facts of life; that he shall not suppose himself an angel or a monster; nor take this world for a hell; nor be suffered to imagine that all rights are concentred in his own caste or country, or all veracities in his own parochial creed. Each man should learn what is within him, that he may strive to mend; he must be taught what is without him, that he may be kind to others. It can never be wrong to tell him the truth; for, in his disputable state, weaving as he goes his theory of life, steering himself, cheering or reproving others, all facts are of the first importance to his conduct; and even if a fact shall discourage or corrupt him, it is still best that he should know it; for it is in this world as it is, and not in a world made easy by educational suppressions, that he must win his way to shame or glory. In one word, it must always be foul to tell what is false; and it can never be safe to suppress what is true. The very fact that you omit may be the fact which somebody was wanting, for one man's meat is another man's poison, and I have known a person who was cheered by the perusal of *Candide*.[7] Every fact is a part of that great puzzle we must set together; and none that comes directly in a writer's path but has some nice relations, unperceivable by him, to the totality and bearing of the subject under hand. Yet there are certain classes of fact eternally more necessary than others, and it is with these that literature must first bestir itself. They are not hard to distinguish, nature once more easily leading us; for the necessary, because the efficacious, facts are those which are most interesting to the natural mind of man. Those which are coloured, picturesque, human, and rooted in morality, and those, on the other hand, which are clear, indisputable, and a part of science, are alone vital in importance, seizing by their interest, or useful to communicate. So far as the writer merely narrates, he should principally tell of these. He should tell of the kind and wholesome and beautiful elements of our life; he should tell unsparingly of the evil and sorrow of the present, to move us with instances; he should tell of wise and good people in the past, to excite us by example; and of these he should tell soberly and truthfully, not glossing faults, that we may neither grow discouraged with ourselves nor exacting to our neighbours. So the body of contemporary literature, ephemeral and feeble in itself, touches in the minds of men the springs of thought and kindness, and supports them (for those who will go at all are easily supported) on their way to what is true and right. And if, in any degree, it does so now, how much more might it do so if the writers chose! There is not a life in all the records of the past but, properly studied, might lend a hint and a help to some contemporary. There is not a juncture in to-day's affairs but some useful word may yet be said of it. Even the reporter has an office, and, with clear eyes and honest language, may unveil injustices, and point the way to progress. And for a last word: in all narration there is only one way to be clever, and that is to be exact. To be vivid is a secondary quality which must presuppose the first; for vividly to convey a wrong impression is only to make failure conspicuous.

But a fact may be viewed on many sides; it may be chronicled with rage, tears, laughter, indifference, or admiration, and by each of these the story will be transformed to something else. The newspapers that told of the return of our representatives from Berlin, even if they had not differed as to the facts, would have sufficiently differed by their spirits; so that the one description would have been a second ovation, and the other a prolonged insult.[8] The subject makes but a trifling part of any piece of literature and the view of the writer is itself a fact more important because less disputable than the others. Now this spirit in which a subject is regarded, important in all kinds of literary work, becomes all-important in works of fiction, meditation, or rhapsody for there it not only colours but itself chooses the facts; not only modifies but shapes the work. And hence, over the far larger proportion of the field of literature, the health or disease of the writer's mind or momentary humour forms not only the leading feature of his work, but is, at bottom, the only thing he can communicate to others. In all works of art, widely speaking, it is first of all the author's attitude that is narrated, though in the attitude there be implied a whole experience and a theory of life. An author who has begged the question and reposes in some narrow faith cannot, if he would, express the whole or even many of the sides of this various existence; for, his own life being maim, some of them are not admitted in his theory, and were only dimly and unwillingly recognised in his experience. Hence the smallness, the triteness, and the inhumanity in works of merely sectarian religion; and hence we find equal although unsimilar limitation in works inspired by the spirit of the flesh or the despicable taste for high society. So that the first duty of any man who is to write is intellectual. Designedly or not, he has so far set himself up for a leader of the minds of men; and he must see that his own mind is kept supple, charitable, and bright. Everything but prejudice should find a voice through him; he should see the good in all things; where he has even a fear that he does not wholly understand, there he should be wholly silent; and he should recognise from the first that he has only one tool in his workshop, and that tool is sympathy.[9]

The second duty, far harder to define, is moral. There are a thousand different humours in the mind, and about each of them, when it is uppermost, some literature tends to be deposited. Is this to be allowed? Not certainly in every case, and yet perhaps in more than rigourists would fancy. It were to be desired that all literary work, and chiefly works of art, issued from sound, human, healthy, and potent impulses, whether grave or laughing, humorous, romantic or religious. Yet it cannot be denied that some valuable books are partially insane; some, mostly religious, partially inhuman; and very many tainted with morbidity and impotence. We do not loathe a masterpiece although we gird against its blemishes. We are not, above all, to look for faults, but merits. There is no book perfect, even in design; but there are many that will delight, improve, or encourage the reader. On the one hand, the Hebrew psalms are the only religious poetry on earth; yet they contain sallies that savour rankly of the man of blood. On the other hand, Alfred de Musset had a poisoned and a contorted nature; I am only quoting that generous and frivolous giant, old Dumas, when I accuse him of a bad heart; yet when the impulse under which he wrote was purely creative, he could give us works like *Carmosine* or *Fantasia*, in which the last note of the romantic comedy seems to have been found again to touch and please us.[10] When Flaubert wrote *Madame Bovary*, I believe he thought chiefly of a somewhat morbid realism; and behold! the book turned in his hands into a masterpiece of appalling morality. But the truth is, when books are conceived under a great stress, with a soul of ninefold power, nine times heated and electrified by effort, the conditions of our being are seized with such an ample grasp, that, even should the main design be trivial or base, some truth and beauty cannot fail to be expressed. Out of the strong comes forth sweetness; but an ill thing poorly done is an ill thing top and bottom. And so this can be no encouragement to knock-kneed, feeble-wristed scribes, who must take their business conscientiously or be ashamed to practise it.

Man is imperfect; yet, in his literature, he must express himself and his own views and preferences; for to do anything else is to do a far more perilous thing than to risk being immoral; it is to be sure of being untrue. To ape a sentiment, even a good one, is to travesty a sentiment; that will not be helpful. To conceal a sentiment, if you are sure you hold it, is to take a liberty with truth. There is probably no point of view possible to a sane man but contains some truth and, in the true connection, might be profitable to the race. I am not afraid of the truth, if any one could tell it me, but I am afraid of parts of it impertinently uttered. There is a time to dance and a time to mourn; to be harsh as well as to be sentimental; to be ascetic as well as to glorify the appetites; and if a man were to combine all these extremes into his work, each in its place and proportion, that work would be the world's masterpiece of morality, as well as of art.[11] Partiality is immorality; for any book is wrong that gives a misleading picture of the world and life. The trouble is that the weakling must be partial; the work of one proving dank and depressing; of another, cheap and vulgar; of a third, epileptically sensual; of a fourth, sourly ascetic. In literature as in conduct, you can never hope to do exactly right. All you can do is to make as sure as possible; and for that there is but one rule. Nothing should be done in a hurry that can be done slowly. It is no use to write a book and put it by for nine or even ninety years; for in the writing you will have partly convinced yourself; the delay must precede any beginning; and if you meditate a work of art, you should first long roll the subject under the tongue to make sure you like the flavour, before you brew a volume that shall taste of it from end to end; or if you propose to enter on the field of controversy, you should first have thought upon the question under all conditions, in health as well as in sickness, in sorrow as well as in joy. It is this nearness of examination necessary for any true and kind writing, that makes practice of the art a prolonged and noble education for the writer.

There is plenty to do, plenty to say, or to say over again, in the meantime. Any literary work which conveys faithful facts or pleasing impressions is a service to the public. It is even a service to be thankfully proud of having rendered. The slightest novels are a blessing to those in distress, not chloroform itself a greater. Our fine old sea-captain's life was justified when Carlyle soothed his mind with *The King's Own* or *Newton Forster*.[12] To please is to serve; and so far from its being difficult to instruct while you amuse, it is difficult to do the one thoroughly without the other. Some part of the writer or his life will crop out in even a vapid book; and to read a novel that was conceived with any force is to multiply experience and to exercise the sympathies. Every article, every piece of verse, every essay, every *entre-filet*, is destined to pass, however swiftly, through the minds of some portion of the public, and to colour, however transiently, their thoughts.[13] When any subject falls to be discussed, some scribbler on a paper has the invaluable opportunity of beginning its discussion in a dignified and human spirit; and if there were enough who did so in our public press, neither the public nor the Parliament would find it in their minds to drop to meaner thoughts. The writer has the chance to stumble, by the way, on something pleasing, something interesting, something encouraging, were it only to a single reader. He will be unfortunate, indeed, if he suit no one. He has the chance, besides, to stumble on something that a dull person shall be able to comprehend; and for a dull person to have read anything, and, for that once, comprehended it, makes a marking epoch in his education.

Here, then, is work worth doing and worth trying to do well. And so, if I were minded to welcome any great accession to our trade, it should not be from any reason of a higher wage, but because it was a trade which was useful in a very great and in a very high degree; which every honest tradesman could make more serviceable to mankind in his single strength; which was difficult to do well and possible to do better every year; which called for scrupulous thought on the part of all who practised it, and hence became a perpetual education to their nobler natures; and which, pay it as you please, in the large majority of the best cases will still be underpaid. For surely at this time of the day in the nineteenth century, there is nothing that an honest man should fear more timorously than getting and spending more than he deserves.

A Gossip on Romance

✳

This essay, completed in February 1882, is central to any understanding of Stevenson's theories about literature and, according to William Archer, another of those articles which make up Stevenson's 'literary confession of faith'. While in correspondence Stevenson played down the significance of the piece, describing it as 'light' and 'chatty', and stating that the issues will be more fully explored 'if I ever do my book on Art and Literature' (February 1882, *Letters* II, p. 185), the essay serves two important functions. First, it offered him a chance to explore the theme, which he returned to again and again at this time, of the relationship between realism and romance, and to delineate his own place in this contested area. Secondly, the passion and enthusiasm of the piece, poured into the selection of details, provides the reader with a fascinating description of Stevenson's own framework of reference from his reading. Here we find him recalling books which had shaped his childhood memories of fiction, relating those to the way in which certain places and topics suggest to him material for his own writing, and from this highly personal starting point delving into an exploration of what draws any reader into a fiction. As a result the piece moves from throwaway references to the work of Dumas, Thackeray, Trollope and Meredith, to a detailed stylistic analysis of the strengths and weaknesses of Scott's fiction.

On reading this essay Gerard Manley Hopkins saw a clear link between the definition it offered of romance: 'which is fictitious history, consists of event, of incident', and Stevenson's fiction: 'His own stories are written on this principle: they are very good and he has all the gifts a writer of fiction should have, including those he holds unessential, as characterisation, and at first you notice no more than an ordinary well told story, but on looking back in the light of this doctrine you see that the persons illustrate the incident or strain of incidents, the plot, *the story*, not the story and incidents the persons' (Maixner, p. 123, letter of 15 August 1883). Indeed, much of the essay could be read as Stevenson staking a claim, demanding a particular appreciation for the aims of his own novels, but it moves beyond that to a more theoretical – although as he acknowledges – 'gossipy' assessment of the particular pleasures afforded by the reading of fiction in general. 'Gossip', however, is not simply a disclaimer of serious intent: it also carries connotations of play, of the association of incident and idea, which is essential to any understanding of Stevenson's concept of literature.

In the essay Stevenson advocates writing which does not become over-engaged with issues of moral relativism; those he believes to be more suitable for drama. Fiction should aim for more, he suggests, than in-depth delineation of character. His position here should, of course, be situated within contemporary debates over the nature of realism and idealism, the moral role of literature and the growing influence of French Naturalism. Yet the essay offers more than a defence of romance against new literary trends. In the early parts of the essay, in which the writer advocates the necessary fitness of events and places – 'the right kind of thing should fall out in the right kind of place' – Stevenson not only points to one of the most obvious strengths in his fiction, the evocation of place, but also suggests that in his writings moral schemes are worked out through a system of mapping, offering a symbolic universe of values, but one which is not necessarily related to the everyday negotiations of 'conduct'.

A Gossip on Romance[1]

In anything fit to be called by the name of reading, the process itself should be absorbing and voluptuous; we should gloat over a book, be rapt clean out of ourselves, and rise from the perusal, our mind filled with the busiest, kaleidoscopic dance of images, incapable of sleep or of continuous thought. The words, if the book be eloquent, should run thenceforward in our ears like the noise of breakers, and the story, if it be a story, repeat itself in a thousand coloured pictures to the eye. It was for this last pleasure that we read so closely, and loved our books so dearly, in the bright, troubled period of boyhood. Eloquence and thought, character and conversation, were but obstacles to brush aside as we dug blithely after a certain sort of incident, like a pig for truffles. For my part, I liked a story to begin with an old wayside inn where, 'towards the close of the year 17 –, several gentlemen in three-cocked hats were playing bowls.'[2] A friend of mine preferred the Malabar coast in a storm, with a ship beating to windward, and a scowling fellow of Herculean proportions striding along the beach; he, to be sure, was a pirate. This was further afield than my home-keeping fancy loved to travel, and designed altogether for a larger canvas than the tales that I affected. Give me a highwayman and I was full to the brim; a Jacobite would do, but the highwayman was my favourite dish. I can still hear that merry clatter of the hoofs along the moonlit lane; night and the coming of day are still related in my mind with the doings of John Rann or Jerry Abershaw; and the words 'postchaise', the 'great North road', 'ostler', and 'nag' still sound in my ears like poetry.[3] One and all, at least, and each with his particular fancy, we read story-books in childhood, not for eloquence or character or thought, but for some quality of the brute incident. That quality was not mere bloodshed or wonder. Although each of these was welcome in its place, the charm for the sake of which we read depended on something different from either. My elders used to read novels aloud; and I can still remember four different passages which I heard, before I was ten, with the same keen and lasting pleasure. One I discovered long afterwards to be the admirable opening of *What Will He Do With It*: it was no wonder I was pleased with that.[4] The other three still remain unidentified. One is a little vague; it was about a dark, tall house at night, and people groping on the stairs by the light that escaped from the open door of a sickroom.[5] In another, a lover left a ball, and went walking in a cool, dewy park, whence he could watch the lighted windows and the figures of the dancers as they moved. This was the most sentimental impression I think I had yet received, for a child is somewhat deaf to the sentimental. In the last, a poet, who had been tragically wrangling with his wife, walked forth on the sea-beach on a tempestuous night and witnessed the horrors of a wreck.[6] Different as they are, all these early favourites have a common note – they have all a touch of the romantic.

Drama is the poetry of conduct, romance the poetry of
circumstance. The pleasure that we take in life is of two sorts
– the active and the passive. Now we are conscious of a great
command over our destiny; anon we are lifted up by
circumstance, as by a breaking wave, and dashed we know
not how into the future. Now we are pleased by our conduct,
anon merely pleased by our surroundings. It would be hard to
say which of these modes of satisfaction is the more effective,
but the latter is surely the more constant. Conduct is three
parts of life, they say; but I think they put it high.[7] There is a
vast deal in life and letters both which is not immoral, but
simply a-moral; which either does not regard the human will
at all, or deals with it in obvious and healthy relations; where
the interest turns, not upon what a man shall choose to do,
but on how he manages to do it; not on the passionate slips
and hesitations of the conscience, but on the problems of the
body and of the practical intelligence, in clean, open-air
adventure, the shock of arms or the diplomacy of life. With
such material as this it is impossible to build a play, for the
serious theatre exists solely on moral grounds, and is a
standing proof of the dissemination of the human conscience. But it is possible to build, upon this ground, the
most joyous of verses, and the most lively, beautiful, and
buoyant tales.

One thing in life calls for another; there is a fitness in
events and places. The sight of a pleasant arbour puts it in
our mind to sit there. One place suggests work, another
idleness, a third early rising and long rambles in the dew.
The effect of night, of any flowing water, of lighted cities, of
the peep of day, of ships, of the open ocean, calls up in the
mind an army of anonymous desires and pleasures. Something, we feel, should happen; we know not what, yet we
proceed in quest of it. And many of the happiest hours of life
fleet by us in this vain attendance on the genius of the place
and moment. It is thus that tracts of young fir, and low rocks
that reach into deep soundings, particularly torture and
delight me. Something must have happened in such places,
and perhaps ages back, to members of my race; and when I
was a child I tried in vain to invent appropriate games for
them, as I still try, just as vainly, to fit them with the proper
story. Some places speak distinctly. Certain dank gardens cry

aloud for a murder; certain old houses demand to be haunted; certain coasts are set apart for shipwreck. Other spots again seem to abide their destiny, suggestive and impenetrable, 'miching mallecho'.[8] The inn at Burford Bridge, with its arbours and green garden and silent, eddying river – though it is known already as the place where Keats wrote some of his *Endymion* and Nelson parted from his Emma – still seems to wait the coming of the appropriate legend.[9] Within these ivied walls, behind these old green shutters, some further business smoulders, waiting for its hour. The old Hawes Inn at the Queen's Ferry makes a similar call upon my fancy. There it stands, apart from the town, beside the pier, in a climate of its own, half inland, half marine – in front, the ferry bubbling with the tide and the guardship swinging to her anchor; behind, the old garden with the trees. Americans seek it already for the sake of Lovel and Oldbuck who dined there at the beginning of *The Antiquary*.[10] But you need not tell me – that is not all; there is some story, unrecorded or not yet complete, which must express the meaning of that inn more fully. So it is with names and faces; so it is with incidents that are idle and inconclusive in themselves, and yet seem like the beginning of some quaint romance, which the all-careless author leaves untold. How many of these romances have we not seen determined at their birth; how many people have met us with a look of meaning in their eye, and sunk at once into trivial acquaintances; to how many places have we not drawn near, with express intimations – 'here my destiny awaits me' – and we have but dined there and passed on! I have lived both at the Hawes and Burford in a perpetual flutter, on the heels, as it seemed, of some adventure that should justify the place; but though the feeling had me to bed at night and called me again at morning in one unbroken round of pleasure and suspense, nothing befell me in either worth remark. The man or the hour had not yet come; but some day, I think, a boat shall put off from the Queen's Ferry, fraught with a dear cargo, and some frosty night a horseman, on a tragic errand, rattle with his whip upon the green shutters of the inn at Burford.[11]

Now, this is one of the natural appetites with which any lively literature has to count. The desire for knowledge, I had almost added the desire for meat, is not more deeply seated than this demand for fit and striking incident. The dullest of clowns tells, or tries to tell, himself a story, as the feeblest of children uses invention in his play; and even as the imaginative grown person, joining in the game, at once enriches it with many delightful circumstances, the great creative writer shows us the realisation and the apotheosis of the day-dreams of common men. His stories may be nourished with the realities of life, but their true mark is to satisfy the nameless longings of the reader, and to obey the ideal laws of the day-dream. The right kind of thing should fall out in the right kind of place; the right kind of thing should follow; and not only the characters talk aptly and think naturally, but all the circumstances in a tale answer one to another like notes in music. The threads of a story come from time to time together and make a picture in the web; the characters fall from time to time into some attitude to each other or to nature, which stamps the story home like an illustration. Crusoe recoiling from the footprint, Achilles shouting over against the Trojans, Ulysses bending the great bow, Christian running with his fingers in his ears, these are each culminating moments in the legend, and each has been printed on the mind's eye for ever. Other things we may forget; we may forget the words, although they are beautiful; we may forget the author's comment, although perhaps it was ingenious and true; but these epoch-making scenes, which put the last mark of truth upon a story and fill up, at one blow, our capacity for sympathetic pleasure, we so adopt into the very bosom of our mind that neither time nor tide can efface or weaken the impression. This, then, is the plastic part of literature: to embody character, thought, or emotion in some act or attitude that shall be remarkably striking to the mind's eye.[12] This is the highest and hardest thing to do in words; the thing which, once accomplished, equally delights the schoolboy and the sage, and makes, in its own right, the quality of epics. Compared with this, all other purposes in literature, except the purely lyrical or the purely philosophic, are bastard in nature, facile of execution, and feeble in result. It is one thing to write about the inn at Burford, or to describe scenery with the word-painters; it is quite another to seize on the heart of the suggestion and make a country famous with a legend. It is one thing to remark and to dissect, with the most cutting logic, the complications of life, and of the human spirit; it is quite another to give them body and blood in the story of Ajax or of Hamlet. The first is literature, but the second is something besides, for it is likewise art.

English people of the present day are apt, I know not why, to look somewhat down on incident, and reserve their admiration for the clink of teaspoons and the accents of the curate.[13] It is thought clever to write a novel with no story at all, or at least with a very dull one. Reduced even to the lowest terms, a certain interest can be communicated by the art of narrative; a sense of human kinship stirred; and a kind of monotonous fitness, comparable to the words and air of 'Sandy's Mull', preserved among the infinitesimal occurrences recorded.[14] Some people work, in this manner, with even a strong touch. Mr Trollope's inimitable clergymen naturally arise to the mind in this connection. But even Mr Trollope does not confine himself to chronicling small beer. Mr Crawley's collision with the Bishop's wife, Mr Melnotte dallying in the deserted banquet-room, are typical incidents, epically conceived, fitly embodying a crisis.[15] Or again look at Thackeray. If Rawdon Crawley's blow were not delivered, *Vanity Fair* would cease to be a work of art. That scene is the chief ganglion of the tale; and the discharge of energy from Rawdon's fist is the reward and consolation of the reader. The end of *Esmond* is a yet wider excursion from the author's customary fields; the scene at Castlewood is pure Dumas; the great and wily English borrower has here borrowed from the great, unblushing French thief; as usual, he has borrowed admirably well, and the breaking of the sword rounds off the best of all his books with a manly, martial note.[16] But perhaps nothing can more strongly illustrate the necessity for marking incident than to compare the living fame of *Robinson Crusoe* with the discredit of *Clarissa Harlowe*.[17] *Clarissa* is a book of a far more startling import, worked out, on a great canvas, with inimitable courage and unflagging art. It contains wit, character, passion, plot, conversations full of spirit and insight, letters sparkling with unstrained humanity; and if the death of the heroine be somewhat frigid and artificial, the last days of the hero strike the only note of what we now call Byronism, between the Elizabethans and Byron himself. And yet a little story of a shipwrecked sailor, with not a tenth part of the style nor a thousandth part of the wisdom, exploring none of the arcana of humanity and deprived of the perennial interest of love, goes on from edition to edition, ever young, while *Clarissa* lies upon the shelves unread. A friend of mine, a Welsh blacksmith, was twenty-five years old and could neither read nor write, when he heard a chapter of *Robinson* read aloud in a farm kitchen. Up to that moment he had sat content, huddled in his ignorance, but he left that farm another man. There were day-dreams, it appeared, divine day-dreams, written and printed and bound, and to be bought for money and enjoyed at pleasure. Down he sat that day, painfully learned to read Welsh, and returned to borrow the book. It had been lost, nor could he find another copy but one that was in English. Down he sat once more, learned English, and at length, and with entire delight, read *Robinson*. It is like the story of a love-chase. If he had heard a letter from *Clarissa*, would he have been fired with the same chivalrous ardour? I wonder. Yet *Clarissa* has every quality that can be shown in prose, one alone excepted – pictorial or picture-making romance. While *Robinson* depends, for the most part and with the overwhelming majority of its readers, on the charm of circumstance.

In the highest achievements of the art of words, the dramatic and the pictorial, the moral and romantic interest, rise and fall together by a common and organic law. Situation is animated with passion, passion clothed upon with situation. Neither exists for itself, but each inheres indissolubly with the other. This is high art; and not only the highest art possible in words, but the highest art of all, since it combines the greatest mass and diversity of the elements of truth and pleasure. Such are epics, and the few prose tales that have the epic weight. But as from a school of works, aping the creative, incident and romance are ruthlessly discarded, so may character and drama be omitted or subordinated to romance. There is one book, for example, more generally loved than Shakespeare, that captivates in childhood, and still delights in age – I mean the *Arabian Nights* – where you shall look in vain for moral or for intellectual interest.[18] No human face or voice greets us among that wooden crowd of kings and genies, sorcerers and beggarmen. Adventure, on the most naked terms, furnishes forth the entertainment and is found enough. Dumas approaches perhaps nearest of any modern to these Arabian authors in the purely material charm of some of his romances. The early part of *Monte Cristo*, down to the finding of the treasure, is a piece of perfect storytelling; the man never breathed who shared these moving incidents without a tremour; and yet Faria is a thing of packthread and Dantès little more than a name. The sequel is one long-drawn error, gloomy, bloody, unnatural and dull; but as for these early chapters, I do not believe there is another volume extant where you can breathe the same unmingled atmosphere of romance. It is very thin and light, to be sure, as on a high mountain; but it is brisk and clear and sunny in proportion.[19] I saw the other day, with envy, an old and a very clever lady setting forth on a second or third voyage into *Monte Cristo*. Here are stories which powerfully affect the reader, which can be reperused at any age, and where the characters are no more than puppets. The bony fist of the showman visibly propels them; their springs are an open secret; their faces are of wood, their bellies filled with bran; and yet we thrillingly partake of their adventures. And the point may be illustrated still further. The last interview between Lucy and Richard Feveril is pure drama; more than that, it is the strongest scene, since Shakespeare, in the English tongue.[20] Their first meeting by the river, on the other hand, is pure romance; it has nothing to do with character; it might happen to any other boy and maiden, and be none the less delightful for the change. And yet I think he would be a bold man who should choose between these passages. Thus, in the same book, we may have two scenes, each capital in its order: in the one, human passion, deep calling unto deep, shall utter its genuine voice; in the second, according circumstances, like instruments in tune, shall build up a trivial but desirable incident, such as we love to prefigure for ourselves; and in the end, in spite of the critics, we may hesitate to give the preference to either. The one may ask more genius – I do not say it does; but at least the other dwells as clearly in the memory.

True romantic art, again, makes a romance of all things. It reaches into the highest abstraction of the ideal; it does not refuse the most pedestrian realism. *Robinson Crusoe* is as realistic as it is romantic; both qualities are pushed to an extreme, and neither suffers. Nor does romance depend upon the material importance of the incidents. To deal with strong and deadly elements, banditti, pirates, war and murder, is to conjure with great names, and, in the event of failure, to double the disgrace. The arrival of Haydn and Consuelo at the Canon's villa is a very trifling incident; yet we may read a dozen boisterous stories from beginning to end, and not receive so fresh and stirring an impression of adventure.[21] It was the scene of Crusoe at the wreck, if I remember rightly, that so bewitched my blacksmith. Nor is the fact surprising. Every single article the castaway recovers from the hulk is 'a joy for ever' to the man who reads of them. They are the things that should be found, and the bare enumeration stirs the blood. I found a glimmer of the same interest the other day in a new book, *The Sailor's Sweetheart*, by Mr Clark Russell.[22] The whole business of the brig *Morning Star* is very rightly felt and spiritedly written; but the clothes, the books and the money satisfy the reader's mind like things to eat. We are dealing here with the old cut-and-dry, legitimate interest of treasure trove. But even treasure trove can be made dull. There are few people who have not groaned under the plethora of goods that fell to the lot of the *Swiss Family Robinson*, that dreary family.[23] They found article after article, creature after creature, from milk kine to pieces of ordnance, a whole consignment; but no informing taste had presided over the selection, there was no smack or relish in the invoice; and these riches left the fancy cold. The box of goods in Verne's *Mysterious Island* is another case in point: there was no gusto and no glamour about that; it might have come from a shop.[24] But the two hundred and seventy-eight Australian sovereigns on board the *Morning Star* fell upon me like a surprise that I had expected; whole vistas of secondary stories, besides the one in hand, radiated forth from that discovery, as they radiate from a striking particular in life; and I was made for the moment as happy as a reader has the right to be.

To come at all at the nature of this quality of romance, we

must bear in mind the peculiarity of our attitude to any art. No art produces illusion; in the theatre we never forget that we are in the theatre; and while we read a story, we sit wavering between two minds, now merely clapping our hands at the merit of the performance, now condescending to take an active part in fancy with the characters. This last is the triumph of romantic story-telling: when the reader consciously plays at being the hero, the scene is a good scene. Now in character-studies the pleasure that we take is critical; we watch, we approve, we smile at incongruities, we are moved to sudden heats of sympathy with courage, suffering or virtue. But the characters are still themselves, they are not us; the more clearly they are depicted, the more widely do they stand away from us, the more imperiously do they thrust us back into our place as a spectator. I cannot identify myself with Rawdon Crawley or with Eugène de Rastignac, for I have scarce a hope or fear in common with them.[25] It is not character but incident that woos us out of our reserve. Something happens as we desire to have it happen to ourselves; some situation, that we have long dallied with in fancy, is realised in the story with enticing and appropriate details. Then we forget the characters; then we push the hero aside; then we plunge into the tale in our own person and bathe in fresh experience; and then, and then only, do we say we have been reading a romance. It is not only pleasurable things that we imagine in our day-dreams; there are lights in which we are willing to contemplate even the idea of our own death; ways in which it seems as if it would amuse us to be cheated, wounded or calumniated. It is thus possible to construct a story, even of tragic import, in which every incident, detail and trick of circumstance shall be welcome to the reader's thoughts. Fiction is to the grown man what play is to the child; it is there that he changes the atmosphere and tenor of his life; and when the game so chimes with his fancy that he can join in it with all his heart, when it pleases him with every turn, when he loves to recall it and dwells upon its recollection with entire delight, fiction is called romance.

Walter Scott is out and away the king of the romantics. *The Lady of the Lake* has no indisputable claim to be a poem beyond the inherent fitness and desirability of the tale.[26] It is just such a story as a man would make up for himself, walking, in the best health and temper, through just such scenes as it is laid in. Hence it is that a charm dwells undefinable among these slovenly verses, as the unseen cuckoo fills the mountains with his note; hence, even after we have flung the book aside, the scenery and adventures remain present to the mind, a new and green possession, not unworthy of that beautiful name, *The Lady of The Lake*, or that direct, romantic opening – one of the most spirited and poetical in literature – 'The stag at eve had drunk his fill.' The same strength and the same weaknesses adorn and disfigure the novels. In that ill-written, ragged book, *The Pirate*, the figure of Cleveland – cast up by the sea on the resounding foreland of Dunrossness – moving, with the blood on his hands and the Spanish words on his tongue, among the simple islanders – singing a serenade under the window of his Shetland mistress – is conceived in the very highest manner of romantic invention.[27] The words of his song, 'Through groves of palm,' sung in such a scene and by such a lover, clench, as in a nutshell, the emphatic contrast upon which the tale is built. In *Guy Mannering*, again, every incident is delightful to the imagination; and the scene when Harry Bertram lands at Ellangowan is a model instance of romantic method.[28]

> 'I remember the tune well,' he says, 'though I cannot guess what should at present so strongly recall it to my memory.' He took his flageolet from his pocket and played a simple melody. Apparently the tune awoke the corresponding associations of a damsel . . . She immediately took up the song –
>
> 'Are these the links of Forth, she said
> Or are they the crooks of Dee,
> Or the bonny woods of Warroch Head
> That I so fain would see?'
>
> 'By heaven!' said Bertram, 'it is the very ballad.'

On this quotation two remarks fall to be made. First, as an instance of modern feeling for romance, this famous touch of the flageolet and the old song is selected by Miss Braddon for omission. Miss Braddon's idea of a story, like Mrs. Todgers's idea of a wooden leg, were something strange to have expounded.[29] As a matter of personal experience, Meg's appearance to old Mr Bertram on the road, the ruins of Derncleugh, the scene of the flageolet, and the Dominie's recognition of Harry, are the four strong notes that continue to ring in the mind after the book is laid aside. The second point is still more curious. The reader will observe a mark of excision in the passage as quoted by me. Well, here is how it runs in the original: 'A damsel, who, close behind a fine spring about half-way down the descent, and which had once supplied the castle with water, was engaged in bleaching linen.' A man who gave in such copy would be discharged from the staff of a daily paper. Scott has forgotten to prepare the reader for the presence of the 'damsel'; he has forgotten to mention the spring and its relation to the ruin; and now, face to face with his omission, instead of trying back and starting fair, crams all this matter, tail foremost, into a single shambling sentence. It is not merely bad English, or bad style; it is abominably bad narrative besides.

Certainly the contrast is remarkable; and it is one that throws a strong light upon the subject of this paper. For here we have a man of the finest creative instinct, touching with perfect certainty and charm the romantic junctures of his story; and we find him utterly careless, almost, it would seem, incapable, in the technical matter of style, and not only frequently weak, but frequently wrong in points of drama. In character parts, indeed, and particularly in the Scotch, he was delicate, strong and truthful; but the trite, obliterated features of too many of his heroes have already wearied two generations of readers. At times his characters will speak with something far beyond propriety – with a true heroic note; but on the next page they will be wading wearily forward with an ungrammatical and undramatic rigmarole of words. The man who could conceive and write the character of Elspeth of the Craigburnfoot, as Scott has conceived and written it, had not only splendid romantic, but splendid tragic gifts.[30] How comes it, then, that he could so often fob us off with languid, inarticulate twaddle?

It seems to me that the explanation is to be found in the very quality of his surprising merits. As his books are play to the reader, so were they play to him. He conjured up the romantic with delight, but he had hardly patience to describe it. He was a great daydreamer, a seer of fit and beautiful and humorous visions, but hardly a great artist; hardly, in the manful sense, an artist at all. He pleased himself, and so he pleases us. Of the pleasures of his art he tasted fully; but of its toils and vigils and distresses never man knew less. A great romantic – an idle child.

A Note on Realism

✳

The question of realism had exercised Stevenson's imagination for some time before his famous exchange with Henry James on the subject. Although he stated in a letter to his cousin that he regarded realism as 'a mere question of method', his argument in this essay clearly relates both to his whole philosophy of fiction and to his admiration or dislike of certain authors. 'A Note on Realism' found an ideal home in *The Magazine of Art* which concerned itself with issues of literary and visual aesthetics. Edited by Stevenson's friend W. E. Henley in the 1880s, it has been seen as a manifestation of a new kind of journalism – appreciations written by Oxbridge-educated young men. Henley not only used the magazine to defend the controversial figure of Rodin but also promoted a striking new art critic, Stevenson's cousin, R. A. M. Stevenson. It is to Bob that Stevenson describes the piece: 'I have written a breathless note on Realism for Henley; a fifth part of the subject hurriedly touched, which will show you how my thoughts are driving' (October 1883, *Letters* II, pp. 270–2). The letter goes on to draw useful analogies with the visual arts, returning to the idea, which appears in more developed form in 'A Humble Remonstrance', that literature – and the other arts – involves not just observation of detail but also selection and construction into a valid form: 'These temples of art are, as you say, inaccessible to the realistic climber.'

In the essay itself Stevenson draws upon architecture and painting as a means of illustrating his points on the construction of fiction; here he might be seen to prefigure Modernists such as Virginia Woolf, who also discuss the shape and design of their writing in visual terms. Although his advocacy of 'idealism' as a form of art which follows the aesthetic of 'pleasing' the reader may sound old-fashioned, his questioning of the power attributed to realism has a more forward-looking tone: to Bob he writes: 'I want you to help me get people to understand that realism is only a method, and only methodic in its consequences.' Using Balzac, whom he had been reading at this time, as the central example in his argument, he begins to set out a position which will find its fullest expression in 'A Humble Remonstrance' and his debate with Henry James.

A Note on Realism[1]

Style is the invariable mark of any master; and for the student who does not aspire so high as to be numbered with the giants, it is still the one quality in which he may improve himself at will. Passion, wisdom, creative force, the power of mystery or colour, are allotted in the hour of birth, and can be neither learned nor simulated. But the just and dexterous use of what qualities we have, the proportion of one part to another and to the whole, the elision of the useless, the accentuation of the important, and the preservation of a uniform character from end to end – these, which taken together constitute technical perfection, are to some degree within the reach of industry and intellectual courage. What to put in and what to leave out; whether some particular fact be organically necessary or purely ornamental; whether, if it be purely ornamental, it may not weaken or obscure the general design; and finally, whether, if we decide to use it we should do so grossly and notably or in some conventional disguise: are questions of plastic style continually re-arising.[2] And the sphinx that patrols the highways of executive art has no more unanswerable riddle to propound.

In literature (from which I must draw my instances) the great change of the past century has been effected by the admission of detail. It was inaugurated by the romantic Scott; and at length, by the semi-romantic Balzac and his more or less wholly unromantic followers, bound like a duty on the novelist.[3] For some time it signified and expressed a more ample contemplation of the conditions of man's life; but it has recently (at least in France) fallen into a merely technical and decorative stage, which it is, perhaps, still too harsh to call survival.[4] With a movement of alarm, the wiser or more timid begin to fall a little back from these extremities; they begin to aspire after a more naked, narrative articulation; after the succinct, the dignified and the poetic; and as a means to this, after a general lightening of this baggage of detail. After Scott we beheld the starveling story – once, in the hands of Voltaire, as abstract or parable – begin to be pampered upon facts.[5] The introduction of these details developed a particular ability of hand; and that ability, childishly indulged, has led to the works that amaze us now on a railway journey. A man of the unquestionable force of M. Zola spends himself on technical successes. To afford a popular flavour and attract the mob, he adds a steady current of what I may be allowed to call the rancid. That is exciting to the moralist; but what more particularly interests the artist is this tendency of the extremity of detail, when followed as a principle, to degenerate into mere *feux-de-joie* of literary tricking. The other day even M. Daudet was to be heard babbling of audible colours and visible sounds.[6]

This odd suicide of one branch of the realists may serve to remind us of the fact which underlies a very dusty conflict of the critics. All representative art, which can be said to live, is both realistic and ideal; and the realism about which we quarrel is a matter purely of externals. It is no especial cultus of nature and veracity, but a mere whim of veering fashion that has made us turn our back upon the larger, more various, and more romantic art of yore. A photographic exactitude in dialogue is now the exclusive fashion; but even in the ablest hands it tells us no more – I think it even tells us less – than Molière, wielding his artificial medium, has told to us all and to all time of Alceste or Orgon, Dorine or Chrysale.[7] The historical novel is forgotten. Yet truth to the conditions of man's nature and the conditions of man's life, the truth of literary art, is free of the ages. It may be told us in a carpet comedy, in a novel of adventure, or a fairy-tale. The scene may be pitched in London, on the sea-coast of Bohemia or away on the mountains of Beulah.[8] And by an odd and luminous accident, if there is any page of literature calculated to awake the envy of M. Zola, it must be that *Troilus and Cressida* which Shakespeare, in a spasm of unmanly anger with the world, grafted on the heroic story of the siege of Troy.[9]

This question of realism, let it be then clearly understood, regards not in the least degree the fundamental truth, but only the technical method, of a work of art. Be as ideal or as abstract as you please, you will be none the less veracious; but if you be weak, you run the risk of being tedious and inexpressive; and if you be very strong and honest, you may chance upon a masterpiece.

A work of art is first cloudily conceived in the mind; during the period of gestation it stands more clearly forward from these swaddling mists, puts on expressive lineaments, and becomes at length that most faultless, but also, alas! that incommunicable product of the human mind, a perfected design. On the approach to execution all is changed. The artist must now step down, don his working clothes, and become the artisan. He now resolutely commits his airy conception, his delicate Ariel, to the touch of matter; he must decide, almost in a breath, the scale, the style, the spirit, and the particularity of execution of his whole design.[10]

The engendering idea of some works is stylistic; a technical preoccupation stands them instead of some robuster principle of life. And with these the execution is but play; for the stylistic problem is resolved beforehand, and all large originality of treatment wilfully foregone. Such are the verses, intricately designed, which we have learned to admire, with a certain smiling admiration at the hands of Mr Lang and Mr Dobson; such, too, are those canvases where dexterity or even breadth of plastic style takes the place of pictorial nobility of design.[11] So, it may be remarked, it was easier to begin to write *Esmond* than *Vanity Fair*, since, in the first, the style was dictated by the nature of the plan; and Thackeray, a man probably of some indolence of mind, enjoyed and got good profit of this economy of effort.[12] But the case is exceptional. Usually in all works of art that have been conceived from within outwards, and generously nourished from the author's mind, the moment in which he begins to execute is one of extreme perplexity and strain. Artists of indifferent energy and an imperfect devotion to their own ideal make this ungrateful effort once for all and, having formed a style, adhere to it through life. But those of a higher order cannot rest content with a process which, as they continue to employ it, must infallibly degenerate toward the academic and the cut-and-dried. Every fresh work in which they embark is the signal for a fresh engagement of the whole forces of their mind; and the changing views which accompany the growth of their experience are marked by still more sweeping alterations in the manner of their art. So that criticism loves to dwell upon and distinguish the varying periods of a Raphael, a Shakespeare, or a Beethoven.

It is, then, first of all, at this initial and decisive moment when execution is begun, and thenceforth only in a less degree, that the ideal and the real do indeed, like good and evil angels, contend for the direction of the work. Marble, paint, and language, the pen, the needle, and the brush, all have their grossnesses, their ineffable impotences, their hours, if I may so express myself, of insubordination. It is the work and it is a great part of the delight of any artist to contend with these unruly tools, and now by brute energy, now by witty expedient, to drive and coax them to effect his will. Given these means, so laughably inadequate, and given the interest, the intensity, and the multiplicity of the actual sensation whose effect he is to render with their aid, the artist has one main and necessary resource which he must, in every case and upon any theory, employ. He must, that is, suppress much and omit more. He must omit what is tedious or irrelevant, and suppress what is tedious and necessary. But such facts as, in regard to the main design, subserve a variety of purposes, he will perforce and eagerly retain. And it is the mark of the very highest order of creative art to be woven exclusively of such. There, any fact that is registered is contrived a double or a treble debt to pay, and is at once an ornament in its place and a pillar in the main design. Nothing would find room in such a picture that did not serve, at once, to complete the composition, to accentuate the scheme of colour, to distinguish the planes of distance, and to strike the note of the selected sentiment; nothing would be allowed in such a story that did not, at the same time, expedite the progress of the fable, build up the characters, and strike home the moral or the philosophical design. But this is unattainable. As a rule, so far from building the fabric of our works exclusively with these, we are thrown into a rapture if we think we can muster a dozen or a score of them, to be the plums of our confection. And hence, in order that the canvas may be filled or the story proceed from point to point, other details must be admitted. They must be admitted, alas! upon a doubtful title; many without marriage robes. Thus any work of art, as it proceeds toward completion, too often – I had almost written always – loses in force and poignancy of main design. Our little air is swamped and dwarfed among hardly relevant orchestration; our little passionate story drowns in a deep sea of descriptive eloquence or slipshod talk.

But again, we are rather more tempted to admit those particulars which we know we can describe; and hence those most of all which, having been described very often, have grown to be conventionally treated in the practice of our art. These we choose, as the mason chooses the acanthus to adorn his capital, because they come naturally to the accustomed hand. The old stock incidents and accessories, tricks of workmanship and schemes of composition (all being admirably good, or they would long have been forgotten) haunt and tempt our fancy, offer us ready-made but not perfectly appropriate solutions for any problem that arises, and wean us from the study of nature and the uncompromising practice of art.[13] To struggle, to face nature, to find fresh solutions, and give expression to facts which have not yet been adequately or not yet elegantly expressed, is to run a little upon the danger of extreme self-love. Difficulty sets a high price upon achievement; and the artist may easily fall into the error of the French naturalists, and consider any fact as welcome to admission if it be the ground of brilliant handiwork; or, again, into the error of the modern landscape-painter, who is apt to think that difficulty overcome and science well displayed can take the place of what is, after all, the one excuse and breath of art – charm. A little further, and he will regard charm in the light of an unworthy sacrifice to prettiness, and the omission of a tedious passage as an infidelity to art.

We have now the matter of this difference before us. The idealist, his eye singly fixed upon the greater outlines, loves rather to fill up the interval with detail of the conventional order, briefly touched, soberly suppressed in tone, courting neglect. But the realist, with a fine intemperance, will not suffer the presence of anything so dead as a convention; he shall have all fiery, all hot-pressed from nature, all charactered and notable, seizing the eye. The style that befits either of these extremes, once chosen, brings with it its necessary disabilities and dangers. The immediate danger of the realist is to sacrifice the beauty and significance of the whole to local dexterity, or, in the insane pursuit of completion, to immolate his readers under facts; but he comes in the last resort, and as his energy declines, to discard all design, abjure all choice, and, with scientific thoroughness, steadily to communicate matter which is not worth learning. The danger of the idealist is, of course, to become merely null and lose all grip of fact, particularity, or passion.

We talk of bad and good. Everything, indeed, is good which is conceived with honesty and executed with communicative ardour. But though on neither side is dogmatism fitting, and though in every case the artist must decide for himself, and decide afresh and yet afresh for each succeeding work and new creation; yet one thing may be generally said, that we of the last quarter of the nineteenth century, breathing as we do the intellectual atmosphere of our age, are more apt to err upon the side of realism than to sin in quest of the ideal. Upon that theory it may be well to watch and correct our own decisions, always holding back the hand from the least appearance of irrelevant dexterity, and resolutely fixed to begin no work that is not philosophical, passionate, dignified, happily mirthful, or, at the last and least, romantic in design.

'A Penny Plain and Twopence Coloured'

✳

Skelt's Juvenile Drama, which is the subject of this essay, was created by Skelt, the illustrator of popular figures from the world of melodrama, packaged in magazine form with illustrations of characters and sets, and used as children's model toy theatres. The first English toy theatre sheets were issued by William West in 1811 and became extremely popular: they provided drawings of actors, scenery and props from successful contemporary plays, suitable for cutting-out and mounting on cardboard. Sheets could be bought for 'a penny plain or twopence coloured', the colouring in the latter being done by hand. Stevenson was given his version of the toy theatre when he was six. In his cousin Bob, he found a equally enthusiastic player. For Stevenson, 'Skelt' came to mean the workings of the romantic and fantastical imagination (Maixner, p. 137 and *Letters* II, p. 305) and 'Skeltery' to refer to a certain kind of melodrama.

In this vividly evocative essay, published in *The Magazine of Art* (April 1884), Stevenson describes scenes from his childhood and recreates the world of Victorian melodrama, through a litany of extraordinary characters and titles; but he also makes considerable claims for the extent to which Skelt structured his imagination over the subsequent years. The critics have agreed: J. C. Furnas draws upon the argument advanced in 'Penny Plain' – that while the purchase and colouring of the illustrations was exciting, the performance itself was an anti-climax – as an explanation for Stevenson's lack of success as a playwright. G. K. Chesterton suggested that Skelt was an important element in shaping both Stevenson's writing and its reception: 'he did not appeal to Imperialism or Socialism or Scotland: he appealed to Skelt' (Chesterton, pp. 49–51). Tom Hubbard, offering a Bakhtinian analysis of Stevenson's fiction, comments: 'His attraction to carnival . . . began in the north' (Hubbard, p. 33). As with other essays, however, this piece of writing not only analyses the power of the carnivalesque world upon the imagination but recreates that hold for the reader.

'A Penny Plain and Twopence Coloured'[1]

These words will be familiar to all students of Skelt's Juvenile Drama. That national monument, after having changed its name to Park's, to Webb's, to Redington's, and last of all to Pollock's, has now become, for the most part, a memory.[2] Some of its pillars, like Stonehenge, are still afoot, the rest clean vanished. It may be the Museum numbers a full set; and Mr Ionides perhaps, or else her gracious Majesty, may boast their great collections; but to the plain private person they are become, like Raphaels, unattainable.[3] I have, at different times, possessed 'Aladdin', 'The Red Rover', 'The Blind Boy', 'The Old Oak Chest', 'The Wood Daemon', 'Jack Sheppard', 'The Miller and his Men', 'Der Freischütz', 'The Smuggler', 'The Forest of Bondy', 'Robin Hood', 'The Waterman', 'Richard I', 'My Poll and my Partner Joe', 'The Inchcape Bell' (imperfect), and 'Three-Fingered Jack, the Terror of Jamaica'; and I have assisted others in the illumination of 'The Maid of the Inn' and 'The Battle of Waterloo'.[4] In this roll-call of stirring names you read the evidences of a happy childhood; and though not half of them are still to be procured of any living stationer, in the mind of their once happy owner all survive, kaleidoscopes of changing pictures, echoes of the past.

There stands, I fancy, to this day (but now how fallen!) a certain stationer's shop at a corner of the wide thoroughfare that joins the city of my childhood with the sea. When, upon any Saturday, we made a party to behold the ships, we passed that corner and since in those days I loved a ship as a man loves Burgundy or daybreak, this of itself had been enough to hallow it. But there was more than that. In the Leith Walk window, all the year round, there stood displayed a theatre in working order, with a forest 'set', a 'combat', and a few 'robbers carousing' in the slides; and below and about, dearer tenfold to me! the plays themselves, those budgets of romance, lay tumbled one upon another. Long and often have I lingered there with empty pockets. One figure, we shall say, was visible in the first plate of characters, bearded, pistol in hand, or drawing to his ear the clothyard arrow; I would spell the name: was it Macaire, or Long Tom Coffin, or Grindoff, 2d dress? O, how I would long to see the rest! how – if the name by chance were hidden – I would wonder in what play he figured, and what immortal legend justified his attitude and strange apparel! And then to go within, to announce yourself as an intending purchaser, and, closely watched, be suffered to undo those bundles and breathlessly devour those pages of gesticulating villains, epileptic combats, bosky forests, palaces and war-ships, frowning fortresses and prison vaults – it was a giddy joy. That shop, which was dark and smelt of Bibles, was a loadstone rock for all that bore the name of boy. They could not pass it by, nor, having entered, leave it. It was a place besieged; the shopmen, like the Jews rebuilding Salem, had a double task. They kept us at the stick's end, frowned us down, snatched each play out of our hand ere we were trusted with another; and, increditable as it may sound, used to demand of us upon our entrance, like banditti, if we came with money or with empty hand. Old Mr Smith himself, worn out with my eternal vacillation, once swept the treasures from before me, with the cry: 'I do not believe, child, that you are an intending purchaser at all!' These were the dragons of the garden; but for such joys of paradise we could have faced the Terror of Jamaica himself. Every sheet we fingered was another lightning glance into obscure, delicious story; it was like wallowing in the raw stuff of story-books. I know nothing to compare with it save now and then in dreams, when I am privileged to read in certain unwrit stories of adventure, from which I awake to find the world all vanity. The *crux* of Buridan's donkey was as nothing to the uncertainty of the boy as he handled and lingered and doated on these bundles of delight; there was a physical pleasure in the sight and touch of them which he would jealously prolong; and when at length the deed was done, the play selected, and the impatient shopman had brushed the rest into the grey portfolio, and the boy was forth again, a little late for dinner, the lamps springing into light in the blue winter's even, and 'The Miller', or 'The Rover', or some kindred drama clutched against his side – on what gay feet he ran, and how he laughed aloud in exultation![5] I can hear that laughter still. Out of all the years of my life, I can recall but one home-coming to compare with these, and that was on the night when I brought back with me the *Arabian Entertainments* in the fat, old, double-columned volume with the prints. I was just well into the story of the Hunchback, I remember, when my clergyman-grandfather (a man we counted pretty stiff) came in behind me. I grew blind with terror. But instead of ordering the book away, he said he envied me. Ah, well he might!

The purchase and the first half-hour at home, that was the summit. Thenceforth the interest declined by little and little. The fable, as set forth in the play-book, proved to be not worthy of the scenes and characters: what fable would not? Such passages as: 'Scene 6. The Hermitage. Night set scene. Place back of scene 1, No. 2, at back of stage and hermitage, Fig. 2, out of set piece, R. H. in a slanting direction' – such passages, I say, though very practical, are hardly to be called good reading. Indeed, as literature, these dramas did not much appeal to me. I forget the very outline of the plots. Of 'The Blind Boy', beyond the fact that he was a most injured prince and once, I think, abducted, I know nothing. And 'The Old Oak Chest', what was it all about? that proscript (1st dress), that prodigious number of banditti, that old woman with the broom, and the magnificent kitchen in the third act (was it in the third?) – they are all fallen in a deliquium, swim faintly in my brain, and mix and vanish.

I cannot deny that joy attended the illumination; nor can I quite forgive that child who, wilfully foregoing pleasure, stoops to 'twopence coloured'. With crimson lake (hark to the sound of it – crimson lake! the horns of elf-land are not richer on the ear) – with crimson lake and Prussian blue a certain purple is to be compounded which, for cloaks especially, Titian could not equal. The latter colour with gamboge, a hated name although an exquisite pigment, supplied a green of such a savoury greenness that today my heart regrets it. Nor can I recall without a tender weakness the very aspect of the water where I dipped my brush. Yes, there was pleasure in the painting. But when all was painted, it is needless to deny it, all was spoiled. You might, indeed, set up a scene or two to look at; but to cut the figures out was simply sacrilege; nor could any child twice court the tedium, the worry, and the long-drawn disenchantment of an actual performance. Two days after the purchase the honey had been sucked. Parents used to complain; they thought I wearied of my play. It was not so: no more than a person can be said to have wearied of his dinner when he leaves the bones and dishes; I had got the marrow of it and said grace.

Then was the time to turn to the back of the play-book and to study that enticing double file of names, where poetry, for the true child of Skelt, reigned happy and glorious like her Majesty the Queen. Much as I have travelled in these realms of gold, I have yet seen, upon that map or abstract, names of El Dorados that still haunt the ear of memory, and are still but names.[6] 'The Floating Beacon' – why was that denied me? or 'The Wreck Ashore'? 'Sixteen-String-Jack', whom I did not even guess to be a highwayman, troubled me awake and haunted my slumbers; and there is one sequence of three from that enchanted calendar that I still at times recall, like a loved verse of poetry: 'Lodoiska', 'Silver Palace', 'Echo of Westminster Bridge'.[7] Names, bare names, are surely more to children than we poor, grown-up, obliterated fools remember.

The name of Skelt itself has always seemed a part and parcel of the charm of his productions. It may be different with the rose, but the attraction of this paper drama sensibly declined when Webb had crept into the rubric: a poor cuckoo, flaunting in Skelt's nest. And now we have reached Pollock, sounding deeper gulfs. Indeed, this name of Skelt appears so stagey and piratic, that I will adopt it boldly to design these qualities. Skeltery, then, is a quality of much art. It is even to be found, with reverence be it said, among the works of nature. The stagey is its generic name; but it is an old, insular, home-bred staginess; not French, domestically British; not of to-day, but smacking of O. Smith, Fitzball, and the great age of melodrama: a peculiar fragrance haunting it; uttering its unimportant message in a tone of voice that has the charm of fresh antiquity.[8] I will not insist upon the art of Skelt's purveyors. These wonderful characters that once so thrilled our soul with their bold attitude, array of deadly engines and incomparable costume, to-day look somewhat pallidly; the extreme hard favour of the heroine strikes me, I had almost said with pain; the villain's scowl no longer thrills me like a trumpet; and the scenes themselves, those once unparalleled landscapes, seem the efforts of a prentice hand. So much of fault we find; but on the other side the impartial critic rejoices to remark the presence of a great unity of gusto; of those direct clap-trap appeals, which a man is dead and buriable when he fails to answer; of the footlight glamour, the ready-made, bare-faced, transpontine picturesque, a thing not one with cold reality, but how much dearer to the mind!

The scenery of Skeltdom – or, shall we say, the kingdom of Transpontus? – had a prevailing character.[9] Whether it set forth Poland as in 'The Blind Boy', or Bohemia with 'The Miller and his Men' or Italy with 'The Old Oak Chest', still it was Transpontus. A botanist could tell it by the plants. The hollyhock was all pervasive, running wild in deserts; the dock was common, and the bending reed; and overshadowing these were poplar, palm, potato tree, and Quercus Skeltica – brave growths. The caves were all embowelled in the Surreyside formation; the soil was all betrodden by the light pump of T. P. Cooke.[10] Skelt, to be sure, had yet another, an oriental string: he held the gorgeous cast in fee; and in the new quarter of Hyères, say, in the garden of the Hotel des Iles d'Or, you may behold these blessed visions realised.[11] But on these I will not dwell; they were an outwork; it was in the occidental scenery that Skelt was all himself. It had a strong flavour of England; it was a sort of indigestion of England and drop-scenes, and I am bound to say was charming. How the roads wander, how the castle sits upon the hill, how the sun eradiates from behind the cloud, and how the congregated clouds themselves uproll, as stiff as bolsters! Here is the cottage interior, the usual first flat, with the cloak upon the nail, the rosaries of onions, the gun and powder-horn and corner-cupboard; here is the inn (this drama must be nautical, I foresee Captain Luff and Bold Bob Bowsprit) with the red curtain, pipes, spittoons, and eight-day clock; and there again is that impressive dungeon with the chains, which was so dull to colour. England, the hedgerow elms, the thin brick houses, windmills, glimpses of the navigable Thames – England, when at last I came to visit it, was only Skelt made evident: to cross the border was, for

the Scotsman, to come home to Skelt; there was the inn-sign
and there the horse-trough, all foreshadowed in the faithful
Skelt. If, at the ripe age of fourteen years, I bought a certain
cudgel, got a friend to load it, and thenceforward walked the
tame ways of the earth my own ideal, radiating pure romance
– still I was but a puppet in the hand of Skelt; the original of
that regretted bludgeon, and surely the antitype of all the
bludgeon kind, greatly improved from Cruikshank, had
adorned the hand of Jonathan Wild, pl. 1.[12] 'This is
mastering me,' as Whitman cries, upon some lesser
provocation. What am I? what are life, art, letters, the
world, but what my Skelt has made them? He stamped
himself upon my immaturity. The world was plain before I
knew him, a poor penny world; but soon it was all coloured
with romance. If I go to the theatre to see a good old
melodrama, 'tis but Skelt a little faded. If I visit a bold scene
in nature, Skelt would have been bolder; there had been
certainly a castle on that mountain, and the hollow tree –
that set piece – I seem to miss it in the foreground. Indeed,
out of this cut-and-dry, dull, swaggering, obtrusive and
infantile art, I seem to have learned the very spirit of my life's
enjoyment; met there the shadows of the characters I was to
read about and love in a late future; got the romance of 'Der
Freischütz' long ere I was to hear of Weber or the mighty
Formes; acquired a gallery of scenes and characters with
which, in the silent theatre of the brain, I might enact all
novels and romances; and took from these rude cuts an
enduring and transforming pleasure.[13] Reader – and
yourself?[14]

A word of moral: it appears that B. Pollock, late J.
Redington, No. 73 Hoxton Street, not only publishes
twenty-three of these old stage favourites, but owns the
necessary plates and displays a modest readiness to issue
other thirty-three. If you love art, folly, or the bright eyes of
children, speed to Pollock's, or to Clarke's of Garrick Street.
In Pollock's list of publicanda I perceive a pair of my ancient
aspirations: 'Wreck Ashore' and 'Sixteen-String Jack'; and I
cherish the belief that when these shall see once more the
light of day, B. Pollock will remember this apologist. But,
indeed, I have a dream at times that is not all a dream. I seem
to myself to wander in a ghostly street – E. W., I think, the

postal district – close below the fool's-cap of St. Paul's, and yet within easy hearing of the echo of the Abbey bridge. There in a dim shop, low in the roof and smelling strong of glue and footlights, I find myself in quaking treaty with great Skelt himself, the aboriginal, all dusty from the tomb. I buy, with what a choking heart – I buy them all, all but the pantomimes; I pay my mental money, and go forth; and lo! the packets are dust.

A Humble Remonstrance

✳

'A Humble Remonstrance' appeared in *Longman's Magazine* of December 1884, in response to a previous piece by Henry James, 'The Art of Fiction', published in *Longman's* in September 1884, which was in itself a reply to a pamphlet publication of a lecture on 'The Art of Fiction' given by the novelist Walter Besant on 25 April 1884. The dialogue between James and Stevenson is of particular importance on three accounts: first, it gave both writers the opportunity to express their own ideas on the nature and role of fiction and its relationship to life and to the other arts; secondly, the two pieces represent important contributions to existing debates on the state of the novel which had become increasingly heated in the 1880s, with writers dividing into particular schools, such as French scientific realists and American moralists; and thirdly, it established a long-lasting and warm friendship between the two men.

Stevenson included the essay in *Memories and Portraits* (1887), because he saw its themes as a continuation of the arguments on realism and romance to be found in 'A Gossip on Romance', written in 1882. Some very slight changes in punctuation were made in the reprinting, but only one phrase was altered significantly. In the second version, on which this text is based, he also added comments on an intervention made in the debate by the American novelist W. D. Howells who, unlike Henry James, was neither an admirer nor a friend of Stevenson's.

Following the publication of 'A Humble Remonstrance' in *Longman's*, James promised in a letter to Stevenson that he would continue the debate but such a dialogue was not forthcoming for public consumption. Nevertheless, the issues raised by the piece clearly preoccupied both men in their private correspondence. Stevenson was delighted with the reference made by James to his own work and in his first private letter of response wrote: 'I am rejoiced indeed to hear you speak so kindly of my work; rejoiced and surprised. I seem to myself a very rude, left-handed countryman; not fit to be read, far less complimented, by a man so accomplished, so adroit, so craftsmanlike as you' (8 December 1884, *Letters* III, p. 24). And as he claimed in a letter to W. H. Low in March: 'Anyway the controversy is amusing to see' (*Letters* III, p. 40).

James was equally courteous. Even at the first exchange he admitted they did not fundamentally disagree: 'we agree, I think, much more than we disagree.' Moreover, his reply to Stevenson conveys the level of enjoyment he derived from the exchange: 'It's a luxury in this immoral age, to encounter some one who *does* write – who is really acquainted with that lovely art. . . . I want to . . . thank you for so much that is suggestive and felicitous in your remarks – justly felt and brilliantly said. They are full of these things, and the current of your admirable style floats pearls and diamonds' (5 December 1884). James's own delight in Stevenson's fiction emerged again in a piece he wrote for *Century Magazine* in 1888 (which greatly pleased Stevenson) and in his very personal discussion of Stevenson's character and work prompted by the appearance of Colvin's edition of the *Letters* in 1899.

A Humble Remonstrance[1]

I

We have recently enjoyed a quite peculiar pleasure: hearing, in some detail, the opinions, about the art they practise, of Mr Walter Besant and Mr Henry James; two men certainly of very different calibre: Mr James so precise of outline, so cunning of fence, so scrupulous of finish, and Mr Besant so genial, so friendly, with so persuasive and humorous a vein of whim: Mr James the very type of the deliberate artist, Mr Besant the impersonation of good nature.[2] That such doctors should differ will excite no great surprise; but one point in which they seem to agree fills me, I confess, with wonder. For they are both content to talk about the 'art of fiction'; and Mr Besant, waxing exceedingly bold, goes on to oppose this so-called 'art of fiction' to the 'art of poetry'. By the art of poetry he can mean nothing but the art of verse, an art of handicraft, and only comparable with the art of prose. For that heat and height of sane emotion which we agree to call by the name of poetry, is but a libertine and vagrant quality; present, at times, in any art, more often absent from them all; too seldom present in the prose novel, too frequently absent from the ode and epic. Fiction is in the same case; it is no substantive art, but an element which enters largely into all the arts but architecture. Homer, Wordsworth, Phidias, Hogarth, and Salvini, all deal in fiction; and yet I do not suppose that either Hogarth or Salvini, to mention but these two, entered in any degree into the scope of Mr Besant's interesting lecture or Mr James's charming essay.[3] The art of fiction, then, regarded as a definition, is both too ample and too scanty. Let me suggest another; let me suggest that what both Mr James and Mr Besant had in view was neither more nor less than the art of narrative.

But Mr Besant is anxious to speak solely of 'the modern English novel', the stay and bread-winner of Mr Mudie; and in the author of the most pleasing novel on that roll, *All Sorts and Conditions of Men*, the desire is natural enough.[4] I can conceive then, that he would hasten to propose two additions, and read thus: the art of *fictitious* narrative *in prose*.

Now the fact of the existence of the modern English novel is not to be denied; materially, with its three volumes, leaded type, and gilded lettering, it is easily distinguishable from other forms of literature; but to talk at all fruitfully of any branch of art, it is needful to build our definitions on some more fundamental ground than binding. Why, then, are we to add 'in prose'? The *Odyssey* appears to me the best of romances; *The Lady of the Lake* to stand high in the second order; and Chaucer's tales and prologues to contain more of the matter and art of the modern English novel than the whole treasury of Mr Mudie.[5] Whether a narrative be written in blank verse or the Spenserian stanza, in the long period of Gibbon or the chipped phrase of Charles Reade, the principles of the art of narrative must be equally observed.[6] The choice of a noble and swelling style in prose affects the problem of narration in the same way, if not to the same degree, as the choice of measured verse; for both imply a closer synthesis of events, a higher key of dialogue, and a more picked and stately strain of words. If you are to refuse

Don Juan, it is hard to see why you should include *Zanoni* or
(to bracket works of very different value) *The Scarlet Letter*;
and by what discrimination are you to open your doors to
The Pilgrim's Progress and close them on *The Faery Queen?*[7]
To bring things closer home, I will here propound to Mr
Besant a conundrum. A narrative called *Paradise Lost* was
written in English verse by one John Milton; what was it
then? It was next translated by Chateaubriand into French
prose; and what was it then? Lastly, the French translation
was, by some inspired compatriot of George Gilfillan (and of
mine) turned bodily into an English novel; and, in the name
of clearness, what was it then?[8]

But, once more, why should we add 'fictitious'? The reason
why is obvious. The reason why not, if something more
recondite, does not want for weight. The art of narrative, in
fact, is the same, whether it is applied to the selection and
illustration of a real series of events or of an imaginary series.
Boswell's *Life of Johnson* (a work of cunning and inimitable
art) owes its success to the same technical manoeuvres as (let
us say) *Tom Jones*: the clear conception of certain characters
of man, the choice and presentation of certain incidents out
of a great number that offered, and the invention (yes,
invention) and preservation of a certain key in dialogue.[9] In
which these things are done with the more art – in which
with the greater air of nature – readers will differently judge.
Boswell's is, indeed, a very special case, and almost a generic;
but it is not only in Boswell, it is in every biography with any
salt of life, it is in every history where events and men, rather
than ideas, are presented – in Tacitus, in Carlyle, in
Michelet, in Macaulay – that the novelist will find many of
his own methods most conspicuously and adroitly handled.[10]
He will find besides that he, who is free – who has the right
to invent or steal a missing incident, who has the right, more
precious still, of wholesale omission – is frequently defeated,
and, with all his advantages, leaves a less strong impression of
reality and passion. Mr James utters his mind with a
becoming fervour on the sanctity of truth to the novelist;
on a more careful examination truth will seem a word of very
debateable propriety, not only for the labours of the novelist,
but for those of the historian. No art – to use the daring
phrase of Mr James – can successfully 'compete with life'; and

the art that seeks to do so is condemned to perish *montibus aviis*.[11] Life goes before us, infinite in complication; attended by the most various and surprising meteors; appealing at once to the eye, to the ear, to the mind – the seat of wonder, to the touch – so thrillingly delicate, and to the belly – so imperious when starved. It combines and employs in its manifestation the method and material, not of one art only, but of all the arts. Music is but an arbitrary trifling with a few of life's majestic chords; painting is but a shadow of its pageantry of light and colour; literature does but drily indicate that wealth of incident, of moral obligation, of virtue, vice, action, rapture and agony, with which it teems. To 'compete with life', whose sun we cannot look upon, whose passions and diseases waste and slay us – to compete with the flavour of wine, the beauty of the dawn, the scorching of fire, the bitterness of death and separation – here is, indeed, a projected escalade of heaven; here are, indeed, labours for a Hercules in a dress coat, armed with a pen and a dictionary to depict the passions, armed with a tube of superior flake-white to paint the portrait of the insufferable sun. No art is true in this sense: none can 'compete with life': not even history, built indeed of indisputable facts, but these facts robbed of their vivacity and sting; so that even when we read of the sack of a city or the fall of an empire, we are surprised, and justly commend the author's talent, if our pulse be quickened. And mark, for a last differentia, that this quickening of the pulse is, in almost every case, purely agreeable; that these phantom reproductions of experience, even at their most acute, convey decided pleasure; while experience itself, in the cockpit of life, can torture and slay.

What, then, is the object, what the method, of an art, and what the source of its power? The whole secret is that no art does 'compete with life'. Man's one method, whether he reasons or creates, is to half-shut his eyes against the dazzle and confusion of reality.[12] The arts, like arithmetic and geometry, turn away their eyes from the gross, coloured and mobile nature at our feet, and regard instead a certain figmentary abstraction. Geometry will tell us of a circle, a thing never seen in nature; asked about a green circle or an iron circle, it lays its hand upon its mouth. So with the arts.

Painting, ruefully comparing sunshine and flake-white, gives up truth of colour, as it had already given up relief and movement; and instead of vying with nature, arranges a scheme of harmonious tints. Literature, above all in its most typical mood, the mood of narrative, similarly flees the direct challenge and pursues instead an independent and creative aim. So far as it imitates at all, it imitates not life but speech: not the facts of human destiny, but the emphasis and the suppressions with which the human actor tells of them. The real art that dealt with life directly was that of the first men who told their stories round the savage camp-fire.[13] Our art is occupied, and bound to be occupied, not so much in making stories true as in making them typical; not so much in capturing the lineaments of each fact, as in marshalling all of them towards a common end. For the welter of impressions, all forcible but all discreet, which life presents, it substitutes a certain artificial series of impressions, all indeed most feebly represented, but all aiming at the same effect, all eloquent of the same idea, all chiming together like consonant notes in music or like the graduated tints in a good picture. From all its chapters, from all its pages, from all its sentences, the well-written novel echoes and re-echoes its one creative and controlling thought; to this must every incident and character contribute; the style must have been pitched in unison with this; and if there is anywhere a word that looks another way, the book would be stronger, clearer, and (I had almost said) fuller without it. Life is monstrous, infinite, illogical, abrupt and poignant; a work of art, in comparison, is neat, finite, self-contained, rational, flowing and emasculate. Life imposes by brute energy, like inarticulate thunder; art catches the ear, among the far louder noises of experience, like an air artificially made by a discreet musician. A proposition of geometry does not compete with life; and a proposition of geometry is a fair and luminous parallel for a work of art. Both are reasonable, both untrue to the crude fact; both inhere in nature, neither represents it. The novel, which is a work of art, exists, not by its resemblances to life, which are forced and material, as a shoe must still consist of leather, but by its immeasurable difference from life, which is designed and significant, and is both the method and the meaning of the work.

The life of man is not the subject of novels, but the inexhaustible magazine from which subjects are to be selected; the name of these is legion; and with each new subject – for here again I must differ by the whole width of heaven from Mr James – the true artist will vary his method and change the point of attack. That which was in one case an excellence, will become a defect in another; what was the making of one book, will in the next be impertinent or dull. First each novel, and then each class of novels, exists by and for itself. I will take, for instance, three main classes, which are fairly distinct: first, the novel of adventure, which appeals to certain almost sensual and quite illogical tendencies in man; second, the novel of character, which appeals to our intellectual appreciation of man's foibles and mingled and inconstant motives; and third, the dramatic novel, which deals with the same stuff as the serious theatre, and appeals to our emotional nature and moral judgment.

And first for the novel of adventure. Mr James refers, with singular generosity of praise, to a little book about a quest for hidden treasure; but he lets fall, by the way, some rather startling words.[14] In this book he misses what he calls the 'immense luxury' of being able to quarrel with his author. The luxury, to most of us, is to lay by our judgment, to be submerged by the tale as by a billow, and only to awake, and begin to distinguish and find fault, when the piece is over and the volume laid aside. Still more remarkable is Mr James's reason. He cannot criticise the author, as he goes, 'because', says he, comparing it with another work, '*I have been a child, but I have never been on a quest for buried treasure.*' Here is, indeed, a wilful paradox; for if he has never been on a quest for buried treasure, it can be demonstrated that he has never been a child. There never was a child (unless Master James) but has hunted gold, and been a pirate, and a military commander, and a bandit of the mountains; but has fought, and suffered shipwreck and prison, and imbrued its little hands in gore, and gallantly retrieved the lost battle, and triumphantly protected innocence and beauty. Elsewhere in his essay Mr James has protested with excellent reason against too narrow a conception of experience; for the born artist, he contends, the 'faintest hints of life' are converted into revelations; and it will be found true, I believe, in a majority of cases, that the artist writes with more gusto and effect of those things which he has only wished to do, than of those which he has done. Desire is a wonderful telescope, and Pisgah the best observatory.[15] Now, while it is true that neither Mr James nor the author of the work in question has ever, in the fleshly sense, gone questing after gold, it is probable that both have ardently desired and fondly imagined the details of such a life in youthful day-dreams; and the author, counting upon that, and well aware (cunning and low-minded man!) that this class of interest, having been frequently treated, finds a readily accessible and beaten road to the sympathies of the reader, addressed himself throughout to the building up and circumstantiation of this boyish dream. Character to the boy is a sealed book; for him, a pirate is a beard, a pair of wide trousers and a liberal complement of pistols.[16] The author, for the sake of circumstantiation and because he was himself more or less grown up, admitted character, within certain limits, into his design; but only within certain limits. Had the same puppets figured in a scheme of another sort, they had been drawn to very different purpose; for in this elementary novel of adventure, the characters need to be presented with but one class of qualities – the warlike and formidable. So as they appear insidious in deceit and fatal in the combat, they have served their end. Danger is the matter with which this class of novel deals; fear, the passion with which it idly trifles; and the characters are portrayed only so far as they realise the sense of danger and provoke the sympathy of fear.[17] To add more traits, to be too clever, to start the hare of moral or intellectual interest while we are running the fox of material interest, is not to enrich but to stultify your tale. The stupid reader will only be offended, and the clever reader lose the scent.

The novel of character has this difference from all others: that it requires no coherency of plot, and for this reason, as in the case of *Gil Blas*, it is sometimes called the novel of adventure.[18] It turns on the humours of the persons represented; these are, to be sure, embodied in incidents, but the incidents themselves, being tributary, need not march in a progression; and the characters may be statically shown. As they enter, so they may go out; they must be consistent, but they need not grow. Here Mr James will recognise the note of much of his own work: he treats, for the most part, the statics of character, studying it at rest or only gently moved; and, with his usual delicate and just artistic instinct, he avoids those stronger passions which would deform the attitudes he loves to study, and change his sitters from the humorists of ordinary life to the brute forces and bare types of more emotional moments. In his recent *Author of Beltraffio*, so just in conception, so nimble and neat in workmanship, strong passion is indeed employed; but observe that it is not displayed.[19] Even in the heroine the working of the passion is suppressed; and the great struggle, the true tragedy, the *scène-à-faire*, passes unseen behind the panels of a locked door. The delectable invention of the young visitor is introduced, consciously or not, to this end: that Mr James, true to his method, might avoid the scene of passion. I trust no reader will suppose me guilty of undervaluing this little masterpiece. I mean merely that it belongs to one marked class of novel, and that it would have been very differently conceived and treated had it belonged to that other marked class, of which I now proceed to speak.

I take pleasure in calling the dramatic novel by that name, because it enables me to point out by the way a strange and peculiarly English misconception. It is sometimes supposed that the drama consists of incident. It consists of passion, which gives the actor his opportunity; and that passion must progressively increase, or the actor, as the piece proceeded, would be unable to carry the audience from a lower to a higher pitch of interest and emotion. A good serious play must therefore be founded on one of the passionate *cruces* of life, where duty and inclination come nobly to the grapple; and the same is true of what I call, for that reason, the dramatic novel. I will instance a few worthy specimens, all of our own day and language; Meredith's *Rhoda Fleming*, that wonderful and painful book, long out of print, and hunted for at bookstalls like an Aldine; Hardy's *Pair of Blue Eyes*, and two of Charles Reade's, *Griffith Gaunt* and *The Double Marriage*, originally called *White Lies*, and founded (by an accident quaintly favourable to my nomenclature) on a play by Maquet, the partner of the great Dumas.[20] In this kind of novel the closed door of *The Author of Beltraffio* must be broken open; passion must appear upon the scene and utter its last word; passion is the be-all and the end-all, the plot and the solution, the protagonist and the *deus ex machina* in one. The characters may come anyhow upon the stage: we do not care; the point is, that, before they leave it, they shall become transfigured and raised out of themselves by passion. It may be part of the design to draw them with detail; to depict a full-length character, and then behold it melt and change in the furnace of emotion. But there is no obligation of the sort; nice portraiture is not required; and we are content to accept mere abstract types, so they be strongly and sincerely moved. A novel of this class may be even great, and yet contain no individual figure; it may be great, because it displays the workings of the perturbed heart and the impersonal utterance of passion; and with an artist of the second class it is, indeed, even more likely to be great, when the issue has thus been narrowed and the whole force of the writer's mind directed to passion alone. Cleverness again, which has its fair field in the novel of character, is debarred all entry upon this more solemn theatre. A far-fetched motive, an ingenious evasion of the issue, a witty instead of a passionate turn, offend us like an insincerity. All should be plain, all straightforward to the end. Hence it is that, in *Rhoda Fleming*, Mrs Lovel raises such resentment in the reader; her motives are too flimsy, her ways are too equivocal, for the weight and strength of her surroundings.[21] Hence the hot indignation of the reader when Balzac, after having begun the *Duchesse de Langeais* in terms of strong if somewhat swollen passion, cuts the knot by the derangement of the hero's clock.[22] Such personages and incidents belong to the novel of character; they are out of place in the high society of the passions; when the passions are introduced in art at their full height, we look to see them, not baffled and impotently striving, as in life, but towering above circumstance and acting substitutes for fate.

And here I can imagine Mr James, with his lucid sense, to intervene. To much of what I have said he would apparently demur; in much he would, somewhat impatiently, acquiesce. It may be true; but it is not what he desired to say or to hear said. He spoke of the finished picture and its worth when done; I, of the brushes, the palette, and the north light. He uttered his views in the tone and for the ear of good society; I, with the emphasis and technicalities of the obtrusive student. But the point, I may reply, is not merely to amuse the public, but to offer helpful advice to the young writer. And the young writer will not so much be helped by genial pictures of what an art may aspire to at its highest, as by a true idea of what it must be on the lowest terms. The best that we can say to him is this: Let him choose a motive, whether of character or passion; carefully construct his plot so that every incident is an illustration of the motive, and every property employed shall bear to it a near relation of congruity or contrast; avoid a sub-plot, unless, as sometimes in Shakespeare, the sub-plot be a reversion or complement of the main intrigue; suffer not his style to flag below the level of the argument; pitch the key of conversation, not with any thought of how men talk in parlours, but with a single eye to the degree of passion he may be called on to express; and allow neither himself in the narrative nor any character in the course of the dialogue, to utter one sentence that is not part and parcel of the business of the story or the discussion of the problem involved. Let him not regret if this shortens his book; it will be better so; for to add irrelevant matter is not to lengthen but to bury. Let him not mind if he miss a thousand qualities, so that he keeps unflaggingly in pursuit of the one he has chosen. Let him not care particularly if he miss the tone of conversation, the pungent material detail of the day's manners, the reproduction of the atmosphere and the environment. These elements are not essential: a novel may be excellent, and yet have none of them; a passion or a character is so much the better depicted as it rises clearer from material circumstance. In this age of the particular, let him remember the ages of the abstract, the great books of the past, the brave men that lived before Shakespeare and before Balzac. And as the root of the whole matter, let him bear in mind that his novel is not a transcript of life, to be judged by its exactitude; but a simplification of some side or point of life, to stand or fall by its significant simplicity. For although, in great men, working upon great motives, what we observe and admire is often their complexity, yet underneath appearances the truth remains unchanged: that simplification was their method, and that simplicity is their excellence.[23]

II

Since the above was written another novelist has entered repeatedly the lists of theory: one well worthy of mention, Mr W. D. Howells; and none ever couched a lance with narrower convictions.[24] His own work and those of his pupils and masters singly occupy his mind; he is the bondslave, the zealot of his school; he dreams of an advance in art like what there is in science; he thinks of past things as radically dead; he thinks a form can be outlived: a strange immersion in his own history; a strange forgetfulness of the history of the race! Meanwhile, by a glance at his own works (could he see them with the eager eyes of his readers) much of this illusion would be dispelled. For while he holds all the poor little orthodoxies of the day – no poorer and no smaller than those of yesterday or to-morrow, poor and small, indeed, only so far as they are exclusive – the living quality of much that he has done is of a contrary, I had almost said of a heretical, complexion. A man, as I read him, of an originally strong romantic bent – a certain glow of romance still resides in many of his books, and lends them their distinction. As by accident he runs out and revels in the exceptional; and it is then, as often as not, that his reader rejoices – justly, as I contend. For in all this excessive eagerness to be centrally human, is there not one central human thing that Mr Howells is too often tempted to neglect: I mean himself? A poet, a finished artist, a man in love with the appearances of life, a cunning reader of the mind, he has other passions and aspirations than those he loves to draw. And why should he suppress himself and do such reverence to the Lemuel Barkers?[25] The obvious is not of necessity the normal; fashion rules and deforms; the majority fall tamely into the contemporary shape, and thus attain, in the eyes of the true observer, only a higher power of insignificance; and the danger is lest, in seeking to draw the normal, a man should draw the null, and write the novel of society instead of the romance of man.

On Some Technical Elements of
Style in Literature

✳

Writing to Henley in the winter of 1884, Stevenson described how he had written: 'a long and peculiarly solemn paper on the technical elements of style. It is pathbreaking and epochmaking; but I do not think the public will be readily convoked to its perusal' (*Letters* III, pp. 29–30). It was this essay which he described to W. H. Low in March 1885 as constituting a start upon 'my Treatise on the Art of Literature' (*Letters* III, pp. 39–40). Balfour describes the essay, written in Bournemouth, as 'the work of five days in bed', and a follow-up to 'A Humble Remonstrance'. He continues:

> At the time it was ill-received and generally misunderstood: it is, however, the result of long and close study; and it is a singularly suggestive inquiry into a subject which has always been considered too vague and difficult for analysis, at any rate since the classical writers on rhetoric, whom Stevenson had never read. (*Life* II, p. 11)

Stevenson even intended to follow this with a series of lectures to be delivered in London in 1886, to students of art.

It is true that the essay lacks the engagement with readerly pleasures to be found in many of the other pieces in the volume; as Stevenson acknowledges he is 'pulling the musical cart to pieces'. Nevertheless it shows Stevenson writing as writer and – as his biographer, J. C. Furnas points out – the essay depends upon someone knowing at least a little about writing in order to understand its argument. Although Balfour noted that Stevenson had not read classical writers on rhetoric, it is difficult not to detect some influence of earlier ideas on rhetoric. As in other essays, the visual arts provides the closest model for technique, but Stevenson also uses music and, more strikingly, the effects of a conjurer or juggler, to offer a paradigm for the creation of textual impact. This last image, with its emphasis on play and illusion, also points to that 'modern' sensibility, that self-consciousness of effect, critics have observed in Stevenson's fiction. In its detailed technicality it might also be seen to prefigure a new kind of literary criticism.

On Some Technical Elements of Style in Literature[1]

There is nothing more disenchanting to man than to be shown the springs and mechanism of any art. All our arts and occupations lie wholly on the surface; it is on the surface that we perceive their beauty, fitness, and significance; and to pry below is to be appalled by their emptiness and shocked by the coarseness of the strings and pulleys. In a similar way, psychology itself, when pushed to any nicety, discovers an abhorrent baldness, but rather from the fault of our analysis than from any poverty native to the mind. And perhaps in aesthetics the reason is the same: those disclosures which seem fatal to the dignity of art seem so perhaps only in the proportion of our ignorance; and those conscious and unconscious artifices which it seems unworthy of the serious artist to employ were yet, if we had the power to trace them to their springs, indications of a delicacy of the sense finer than we conceive, and hints of ancient harmonies in nature. This ignorance at least is largely irremediable. We shall never learn the affinities of beauty, for they lie too deep in nature and too far back in the mysterious history of man. The amateur, in consequence, will always grudgingly receive details of method, which can be stated but never can wholly be explained; nay, on the principle laid down in *Hudibras* that

> Still the less they understand,
> The more they admire the sleight-of-hand.[2]

many are conscious at each new disclosure of a diminution in the ardour of their pleasure. I must therefore warn that well-known character, the general reader, that I am here embarked upon a most distasteful business: taking down the picture from the wall and looking on the back; and, like the inquiring child, pulling the musical cart to pieces.

1. *Choice of Words* – The art of literature stands apart from among its sisters, because the material in which the literary artist works is the dialect of life; hence, on the one hand, a strange freshness and immediacy of address to the public mind, which is ready prepared to understand it; but hence, on the other, a singular limitation. The sister arts enjoy the use of a plastic and ductile material, like the modeller's clay; literature alone is condemned to work in mosaic with finite and quite rigid words. You have seen these blocks, dear to the nursery: this one a pillar, that a pediment, a third a window or a vase. It is with blocks of just such arbitrary size and figure that the literary architect is condemned to design the palace of his art. Nor is this all; for since these blocks, or words, are the acknowledged currency of our daily affairs, there are here possible none of those suppressions by which other arts obtain relief, continuity, and vigour: no hieroglyphic touch, no smoothed impasto, no inscrutable shadow, as in painting; no blank wall, as in architecture; but every word, phrase, sentence, and paragraph must move in a logical progression, and convey a definite conventional import.

Now the first merit which attracts in the pages of a good writer, or the talk of a brilliant conversationalist, is the apt choice and contrast of the words employed. It is, indeed, a strange art to take these blocks, rudely conceived for the purpose of the market or the bar, and by tact of application touch them to the finest meanings and distinctions; restore to them their primal energy, wittily shift them to another issue, or make of them a drum to rouse the passions. But though this form of merit is without doubt the most sensible and seizing, it is far from being equally present in all writers. The effect of words in Shakespeare, their singular justice, significance, and poetic charm, is different, indeed, from the effect of words in Addison or Fielding. Or, to take an example nearer home, the words in Carlyle seem electrified into an energy of lineament, like the faces of men furiously moved; whilst the words in Macaulay, apt enough to convey his meaning, harmonious enough in sound, yet glide from the memory like undistinguished elements in a general effect.

But the first class of writers have no monopoly of literary merit. There is a sense in which Addison is superior to Carlyle; a sense in which Cicero is better than Tacitus, in which Voltaire excels Montaigne: it certainly lies not in the choice of words; it lies not in the interest or value of the matter; it lies not in force of intellect, of poetry, or of humour.[3] The three first are but infants to the three second; and yet each, in a particular point of literary art, excels his superior in the whole. What is that point?

2. *The Web* – Literature, although it stands apart by reason of the great destiny and general use of its medium in the affairs of men, is yet an art like other arts. Of these we may distinguish two great classes: those arts, like sculpture, painting, acting, which are representative, or as used to be said very clumsily, imitative; and those, like architecture, music, and the dance, which are self-sufficient, and merely presentative.[4] Each class, in right of this distinction, obeys principles apart; yet both may claim a common ground of existence, and it may be said with sufficient justice that the motive and end of any art whatever, is to make a pattern; a pattern, it may be, of colours, of sounds, of changing attitudes, geometrical figures, or imitative lines; but still a pattern. That is the plane on which these sisters meet; it is by this that they are arts; and if it be well they should at times forget their childish origin, addressing their intelligence to virile tasks, and performing unconsciously that necessary function of their life, to make a pattern, it is still imperative that the pattern shall be made.

Music and literature, the two temporal arts, contrive their pattern of sounds in time; or, in other words, of sounds and pauses. Communication may be made in broken words, the business of life be carried on with substantives alone; but that is not what we call literature; and the true business of the literary artist is to plait or weave his meaning, involving it around itself so that each sentence, by successive phrases, shall first come into a kind of knot, and then, after a moment of suspended meaning, solve and clear itself. In every properly constructed sentence there should be observed this knot or hitch; so that (however delicately) we are led to foresee, to expect, and then to welcome the successive phrases. The pleasure may be heightened by an element of surprise, as, very grossly, in the common figure of the antithesis, or, with much greater subtlety, where an antithesis is first suggested and then deftly evaded. Each phrase, besides, is to be comely in itself; and between the implication and the evolution of the sentence there should be a satisfying equipoise of sound; for nothing more often disappoints the ear than a sentence solemnly and sonorously prepared, and hastily and weakly finished. Nor should the balance be too striking and exact, for the one rule is to be infinitely various; to interest, to disappoint, to surprise, and yet still to gratify; to be ever changing, as it were, the stitch, and yet still to give the effect of an ingenious neatness.

The conjuror juggles with two oranges, and our pleasure in beholding him springs from this, that neither is for an instant overlooked or sacrificed. So with the writer. His pattern, which is to please the supersensual ear, is yet addressed, throughout and first of all, to the demands of logic. Whatever be the obscurities, whatever the intricacies of the argument, the neatness of the fabric must not suffer, or the artist has been proved unequal to his design. And, on the other hand, no form of words must be selected, no knot must be tied among the phrases, unless knot and word be precisely what is wanted to forward and illuminate the argument; for to fail in this is to swindle in the game. The genius of prose rejects the *cheville* no less emphatically than the laws of verse; and the *cheville*, I should perhaps explain to some of my readers, is any meaningless or very watered phrase employed to strike a balance in the sound. Pattern and argument live in each other; and it is by the brevity, clearness, charm, or emphasis of the second, that we judge the strength and fitness of the first.

Style is synthetic; and the artist, seeking, so to speak, a peg to plait about, takes up at once two or more elements or two or more views of the subject in hand; combines, implicates, and contrasts them; and while, in one sense, he was merely seeking an occasion for the necessary knot, he will be found, in the other, to have greatly enriched the meaning, or to have transacted the work of two sentences in the space of one. In the change from the successive shallow statements of the old chronicler to the dense and luminous flow of highly synthetic narrative, there is implied a vast amount of both philosophy and wit. The philosophy we clearly see, recognising in the synthetic writer a far more deep and stimulating view of life, and a far keener sense of the generation and affinity of events. The wit we might imagine to be lost, but it is not so, for it is just that wit, these perpetual nice contrivances, these difficulties overcome, this double purpose attained, these two oranges kept simultaneously dancing in the air, that, consciously or not, afford the reader his delight. Nay, and this wit, so little recognised, is the necessary organ of that philosophy which we so much admire. That style is therefore the most perfect, not, as fools say, which is the most natural, for the most natural is the disjointed babble of the chronicler; but which attains the highest degree of elegant and pregnant implication unobstrusively; or if obtrusively, then with the greatest gain to sense and vigour. Even the derangement of the phrases from their (so-called) natural order is luminous for the mind; and it is by the means of such designed reversal that the elements of a judgement may be most pertinently marshalled, or the stages of a complicated action most perspicuously bound into one.

The web, then, or the pattern: a web at once sensuous and logical, an elegant and pregnant texture: that is style, that is the foundation of the art of literature. Books indeed continue to be read, for the interest of the fact or fable, in which this quality is poorly represented, but still it will be there. And, on the other hand, how many do we continue to peruse and re-peruse with pleasure whose only merit is the elegance of texture? I am tempted to mention Cicero, and since Mr Anthony Trollope is dead, I will.[5] It is a poor diet for the mind, a very colourless and toothless 'criticism of life' but we enjoy the pleasure of a most intricate and dexterous pattern, every stitch a model at once of elegance and of good sense; and the two oranges, even if one of them be rotten, kept dancing with inimitable grace.

Up to this moment I have had my eye mainly upon prose; for though in verse also the implication of the logical texture is a crowning beauty, yet in verse it may be dispensed with. You would think that here was a death-blow to all I have been saying; and, far from that, it is but a new illustration of the principle involved. For if the versifier is not bound to weave a pattern of his own, it is because another pattern has been formally imposed upon him by the laws of verse. For that is the essence of a prosody. Verse may be rhythmical; it may be merely alliterative; it may, like the French, depend wholly on the (quasi) regular recurrence of the rhyme; or, like the Hebrew, it may consist in the strangely fanciful device of repeating the same idea. It does not matter on what principle the law is based, so it be a law. It may be pure convention; it may have no inherent beauty; all that we have a right to ask of any prosody is, that it shall lay down a pattern for the writer, and that what it lays down shall be neither too easy nor too hard. Hence it comes that it is much easier for men of equal facility to write fairly pleasing verse than reasonably interesting prose; for in prose the pattern itself has to be invented, and the difficulties first created before they can be solved. Hence, again, there follows the peculiar greatness of the true versifier: such as Shakespeare, Milton, and Victor Hugo, whom I place beside them as versifier merely, not as poet. These not only knit and knot the logical texture of the style with all the dexterity and strength of prose; they not only fill up the pattern of the verse with infinite variety and sober wit; but they give us, besides, a rare and special pleasure, by the art, comparable to that of counterpoint, with which they follow at the same time, and now contrast, and now combine, the double pattern of the texture and the verse. Here the sounding line concludes; a little further on, the well-knit sentence; and yet a little further, and both will reach their solution on the same ringing syllable. The best that can be offered by the best writer of prose is to show us the development of the idea and the stylistic pattern proceed hand in hand, sometimes by an obvious and triumphant effort, sometimes with a great air of ease and nature. The writer of verse, by virtue of conquering another difficulty, delights us with a new series of triumphs. He follows three purposes where his rival followed only two; and the change is of precisely the same nature as that from melody to harmony. Or if you prefer to return to the juggler, behold him now, to the vastly increased enthusiasm of the spectators, juggling with three oranges instead of two. Thus it is: added difficulty, added beauty; and the pattern, with every fresh element, becoming more interesting in itself.

Yet it must not be thought that verse is simply an addition; something is lost as well as something gained; and there remains plainly traceable, in comparing the best prose with the best verse, a certain broad distinction of method in the web. Tight as the versifier may draw the knot of logic, yet for the ear he still leaves the tissue of the sentence floating somewhat loose. In prose, the sentence turns upon a pivot, nicely balanced, and fits into itself with an obtrusive neatness like a puzzle. The ear remarks and is singly gratified by this return and balance; while in verse it is all diverted to the measure. To find comparable passages is hard; for either the versifier is hugely the superior of the rival, or, if he be not, and still persist in his more delicate enterprise, he falls to be as widely his inferior. But let us select them from the pages of the same writer, one who was ambidexter; let us take, for instance, Rumour's Prologue to the Second Part of *Henry IV*, a fine flourish of eloquence in Shakespeare's second manner, and set it side by side with Falstaff's praise of sherris, act iv. scene i.; or let us compare the beautiful prose spoken throughout by Rosalind and Orlando; compare for example, the first speech of all, Orlando's speech to Adam, with what passage it shall please you to select – the Seven Ages from the same play, or even such a stave of nobility as Othello's farewell to war; and still you will be able to perceive, if you have an ear for that class of music, a certain superior degree of organisation in the prose; a compacter fitting of the parts; a balance in the swing and the return as of a throbbing pendulum.[6] We must not, in things temporal, take from those who have little, the little that they have; the merits of prose are inferior, but they are not the same; it is a little kingdom, but an independent.

3. *Rhythm of the Phrase* – Some way back, I used a word which still awaits an application. Each phrase, I said, was to be comely; but what is a comely phrase? In all ideal and material points, literature, being a representative art, must look for analogies to painting and the like; but in what is technical and executive, being a temporal art, it must seek for them in music. Each phrase of each sentence, like an air or a recitative in music, should be so artfully compounded out of long and short, out of accented and unaccented, as to gratify the sensual ear. And of this the ear is the sole judge. It

is impossible to lay down laws. Even in our accentual and rhythmic language no analysis can find the secret of the beauty of a verse; how much less then, of those phrases, such as prose is built of, which obey no law but to be lawless and yet to please? The little that we know of verse (and for my part I owe it all to my friend Professor Fleeming Jenkin) is, however, particularly interesting in the present connection.[7] We have been accustomed to describe the heroic line as five iambic feet, and to be filled with pain and confusion whenever, as by the conscientious schoolboy, we have heard our own description put in practice.

All níght/the dréad/less Àn/gel ùn/pursúed,

goes the schoolboy; but though we close our ears, we cling to our definition, in spite of its proved and naked insufficiency.[8] Mr Jenkin was not so easily pleased, and readily discovered that the heroic line consisted of four groups, or, if you prefer the phrase, contains four pauses:

All night/the dreadless/angel/unpursued.

Four groups, each practically uttered as one word: the first, in this case, an iamb; the second, an amphibrachys; the third, a trochee; and the fourth, an amphimacer; and yet our schoolboy, with no other liberty but that of inflicting pain, had triumphantly scanned it as five iambs. Perceive, now, this fresh richness of intricacy in the web; this fourth orange, hitherto unremarked, but still kept flying with the others. What had seemed to be one thing it now appears is two; and, like some puzzle in arithmetic, the verse is made at the same time to read in fives and to read in fours.

But again, four is not necessary. We do not, indeed, find verses in six groups, because there is not room for six in the ten syllables; and we do not find verses of two, because one of the main distinctions of verse from prose resides in the comparative shortness of the group; but it is even common to find verses of three. Five is the one forbidden number; because five is the number of the feet; and if five were chosen, the two patterns would coincide, and that opposition which is the life of verse would instantly be lost. We have here a clue to the effect of polysyllables, above all in Latin, where they are so common and make so brave an architecture in the verse; for the polysyllable is a group of Nature's making. If but some Roman would return from Hades (Martial, for choice), and tell me by what conduct of the voice these thundering verses should be uttered – '*Aut Lacedaemonium Tarentum*' for a case in point – I feel as if I should enter at last into the full enjoyment of the best of human verses.[9]

But, again, the five feet are all iambic, or supposed to be; by the mere count of syllables the four groups cannot be all iambic; as a question of elegance, I doubt if any one of them requires to be so; and I am certain that for choice no two of them should scan the same. The singular beauty of the verse analysed above is due, so far as analysis can carry us, part, indeed, to the clever repetition of L, D, and N, but part to this variety of scansion in the groups. The groups which, like the bar in music, break up the verse for utterance, fall uniambically; and in declaiming a so-called iambic verse, it may so happen that we never utter one iambic foot. And yet to this neglect of the original beat there is a limit.

Athens, the eye of Greece, mother of arts,

is, with all its eccentricities, a good heroic line; for though it scarcely can be said to indicate the beat of the iamb, it certainly suggests no other measure to the ear.[10] But begin

Mother Athens, eye of Greece,

or merely 'Mother Athens,' and the game is up, for the trochaic beat has been suggested. The eccentric scansion of the groups is an adornment; but as soon as the original beat has been forgotten, they cease implicitly to be eccentric. Variety is what is sought; but if we destroy the original mould, one of the terms of this variety is lost, and we fall back on sameness. Thus, both as to the arithmetical measure of the verse, and the degree of regularity in scansion, we see the laws of prosody to have one common purpose: to keep alive the opposition of two schemes simultaneously followed; to keep them notably apart, though still coincident; and to balance them with such judicial nicety before the reader, that neither shall be unperceived and neither signally prevail.

The rule of rhythm in prose is not so intricate. Here, too, we write in groups, or phrases, as I prefer to call them, for the prose phrase is greatly longer and is much more nonchalantly uttered than the group in verse; so that not only is there a greater interval of continuous sound between the pauses, but, for that very reason, word is linked more readily to word by a more summary enunciation. Still, the phrase is the strict analogue of the group, and successive phrases, like successive groups, must differ openly in length and rhythm. The rule of scansion in verse is to suggest no measure but the one in hand; in prose, to suggest no measure at all. Prose must be rhythmical, and it may be as much so as you will; but it must not be metrical. It may be anything, but it must not be verse. A single heroic line may very well pass and not disturb the somewhat larger stride of the prose style; but one following another will produce an instant impression of poverty, flatness, and disenchantment. The same lines delivered with the measured utterance of verse would perhaps seem rich in variety. By the more summary enunciation proper to prose, as to a more distant vision, these niceties of difference are lost. A whole verse is uttered as one phrase; and the ear is soon wearied by a succession of groups identical in length. The prose writer, in fact, since he is allowed to be so much less harmonious, is condemned to a perpetually fresh variety of movement on a larger scale, and must never disappoint the ear by the trot of an accepted metre. And this obligation is the third orange with which he has to juggle, the third quality which the prose writer must work into his pattern of words. It may be thought perhaps that this is a quality of ease rather than a fresh difficulty; but such is the inherently rhythmical strain of the English language, that the bad writer – and must I take for example that admired friend of my boyhood, Captain Reid? – the inexperienced writer, as Dickens in his earlier attempts to be impressive, and the jaded writer, as any one may see for himself, all tend to fall at once into the production of bad blank verse.[11] And here it may be pertinently asked, Why bad? And I suppose it might be enough to answer that no man ever made good verse by accident, and that no verse can ever sound otherwise than trivial when uttered with the delivery of prose. But we can go beyond such answers. The weak side of verse is the regularity of the beat, which in itself is decidedly less impressive than the movement of the nobler prose; and it is just into this weak side, and this alone, that our careless writer falls. A peculiar density and mass consequent on the nearness of the pauses is one of the chief good qualities of verse; but this our accidental versifier, still following after the swift gait and large gestures of prose, does not so much as aspire to imitate. Lastly, since he remains unconscious that he is making verse at all, it can never occur to him to extract those effects of counterpoint and opposition which I have referred to as the final grace and justification of verse, and, I may add, of blank verse in particular.

4. *Contents of the Phrase* – Here is a great deal of talk about rhythm – and naturally; for in our canorous language, rhythm is always at the door. But it must not be forgotten that in some languages this element is almost, if not quite, extinct, and that in our own it is probably decaying. The even speech of many educated Americans sounds the note of danger. I should see it go with something as bitter as despair, but I should not be desperate. As in verse no element, not even rhythm, is necessary, so, in prose also, other sorts of beauty will arise and take the place and play the part of those that we outlive. The beauty of the expected beat in verse, the beauty in prose of its larger and more lawless melody, patent as they are to English hearing, are already silent in the ears of our next neighbours; for in France the oratorical accent and the pattern of the web have almost or altogether succeeded to their places; and the French prose writer would be astounded at the labours of his brother across the Channel, and how a good quarter of his toil, above all *invita Minerva*, is to avoid writing verse.[12] So wonderfully far apart have races wandered in spirit, and so hard it is to understand the literature next door!

Yet French prose is distinctly better than English; and French verse, above all while Hugo lives, it will not do to place upon one side. What is more to our purpose, a phrase or a verse in French is easily distinguishable as comely or uncomely. There is then another element of comeliness hitherto overlooked in this analysis: the contents of the phrase. Each phrase in literature is built of sounds, as each phrase in music consists of notes. One sound suggests, echoes, demands, and harmonises with another; and the art of rightly using these concordances is the final art in literature. It used to be a piece of good advice to all writers to avoid alliteration; and the advice was sound in so far as it prevented daubing. None the less for that, was it abominable nonsense, and the mere raving of those blindest of the blind who will not see. The beauty of the contents of a phrase, or of a sentence, depends implicitly upon alliteration and upon assonance. The vowel demands to be repeated; the consonant demands to be repeated; and both cry aloud to be perpetually varied. You may follow the adventures of a letter through any passage that has particularly pleased you; find it, perhaps, denied awhile, to tantalise the ear; find it fired again at you in a whole broadside; or find it pass into congenerous sounds, one liquid or labial melting away into another. And you will find another and much stranger circumstance. Literature is written by and for two senses: a sort of internal ear, quick to perceive 'unheard melodies', and the eye, which directs the pen and deciphers the printed phrase.[13] Well, even as there are rhymes for the eye, so you will find that there are assonances and alliterations; that where an author is running the open A, deceived by the eye and our strange English spelling, he will often show a tenderness for the flat A, and that where he is running a particular consonant, he will not improbably rejoice to write it down even when it is mute or bears a different value.

Here, then, we have a fresh pattern – a pattern, to speak grossly, of letters – which makes the fourth preoccupation of the prose writer, and the fifth of the versifier. At times it is very delicate and hard to perceive, and then perhaps most excellent and winning (I say perhaps); but at times again the elements of this literal melody stand more boldly forward and usurp the ear. It becomes, therefore, somewhat a matter of conscience to select examples; and as I cannot very well ask the reader to help me, I shall do the next best by giving him the reason or the history of each selection. The two first, one in prose, one in verse, I chose without previous analysis, simply as engaging passages that had long re-echoed in my ear.

> I cannot praise a fugitive and cloistered virtue, unexercised and unbreathed, that never sallies out and sees her adversary, but slinks out of the race where that immortal garland is to be run for, not without dust and heat.[14]

Down to 'virtue,'the current S and R are both announced and repeated unobstrusively, and by way of a grace-note that almost inseparable group PVF is given entire.[15] The next phrase is a period of repose, almost ugly in itself, both S and R still audible, and B given as the last fulfilment of PVF. In the next four phrases, from 'that never' down to 'run for', the mask is thrown off, and, but for a slight repetition of the F and V, the whole matter turns, almost too obtrusively, on S and R; first S coming to the front, and then R. In the concluding phrase all these favourite letters, and even the flat A, a timid preference for which is just perceptible, are discarded at a blow and in a bundle; and to make the break more obvious, every word ends with a dental, and all but one with T, for which we have been cautiously prepared since the beginning. The singular dignity of the first clause, and this hammer-stroke of the last, go far to make the charm of this exquisite sentence. But it is fair to own that S and R are used a little coarsely.

In Xanadu did Kubla Khan	(KĂNDL)
A stately pleasure dome decree,	(KDLSR)
Where Alph the sacred river ran,	(KĂNDLSR)
Through caverns measureless to man,	(KĂNLSR)
Down to a sunless sea.[16]	(NDLS)

Here I have put the analysis of the main group alongside the lines; and the more it is looked at, the more interesting it will seem. But there are further niceties. In lines two and four, the current S is most delicately varied with Z. In line three, the current flat A is twice varied with the open A, already suggested in line two, and both times ('where' and 'sacred') in conjunction with the current R. In the same line F and V (a harmony in themselves, even when shorn of their comrade P) are admirably contrasted. And in line four there is a marked subsidiary M, which again was announced in line two. I stop from weariness, for more might yet be said.

My next example was recently quoted from Shakespeare as an example of the poet's colour sense. Now, I do not think literature has anything to do with colour, or poets anyway the better of such a sense; and I instantly attacked this passage, since 'purple' was the word that had so pleased the writer of the article, to see if there might not be some literary reason for its use. It will be seen that I succeeded amply; and I am bound to say I think the passage exceptional in Shakespeare – exceptional, indeed, in literature; but it was not I who chose it.

> The BARrge she sat iN, like a BURnished throNe
> BURNT oN the water: the POOP was beatEN gold,
> PURPle the sails and so PUR*Fumed that   *per
> The wiNds were love-sick with them*[17]

It may be asked why I have put the F of 'perfumèd' in capitals; and I reply, because this change from P to F is the completion of that from B to P, already so adroitly carried out. Indeed, the whole passage is a monument of curious ingenuity; and it seems scarce worth while to indicate the subsidiary S, L, and W. In the same article, a second passage from Shakespeare was quoted, once again as an example of his colour sense:

> A mole cinque-spotted like the crimson drops
> I' the bottom of a cowslip.[18]

It is very curious, very artificial, and not worth while to analyse at length: I leave it to the reader. But before I turn my back on Shakespeare, I should like to quote a passage, for my own pleasure, and for a very model of every technical art:

> But in the wind and tempest of her frown,
>   W.P.V.F. (st) (ow)

Distinction with a loud and powerful fan,
W.P.F. (st) (ow) L.
Puffing at all, winnows the light away;
W.P.F.L.
And what hath mass and matter by itself ᴜ
W.F.L.M.A̤.
Lies rich in virtue and unmingled.[19]
V.L.M.

From these delicate and choice writers I turned with some curiosity to a player of the big drum – Macaulay. I had in hand the two-volume edition, and I opened at the beginning of the second volume. Here was what I read:

> The violence of revolutions is generally proportioned to the degree of the maladministration which has produced them. It is therefore not strange that the government of Scotland, having been during many years greatly more corrupt than the government of England, should have fallen with a far heavier ruin. The movement against the last king of the house of Stuart was in England conservative, in Scotland destructive. The English complained not of the law, but of the violation of the law.[20]

This was plain-sailing enough; it was our old friend PVF, floated by the liquids in a body; but as I read on, and turned the page, and still found PVF with his attendant liquids, I confess my mind misgave me utterly. This could be no trick of Macaulay's; it must be the nature of the English tongue. In a kind of despair, I turned halfway through the volume; and coming upon his lordship dealing with General Cannon, and fresh from Claverhouse and Killiecrankie, here, with elucidative spelling, was my reward:

> Meanwhile the disorders of Kannon's Kamp went on inKreasing. He Kalled a Kouncil of war to Konsider what Kourse it would be advisable to take. But as soon as the Kouncil had met, a preliminary Kuestion was raised. The army was almost eKsKlusively a Highland army. The recent viKtory had been won eKsKlusively

by Highland warriors. Great chiefs who had brought siKs or Seven hundred *f*ighting men into the *f*ield did not think it *f*air that they should be out-*v*oted by gentlemen *f*rom Ireland, and *f*rom the Low Kountries, who bore indeed King James's Kommission, and were Kalled Kolonels and Kaptains, but who were Kolonels without regiments and Kaptains without Kompanies.[21]

A moment of FV in all this world of K's! It was not the English language, then, that was an instrument of one string, but Macaulay that was an incomparable dauber.

It was probably from this barbaric love of repeating the same sound, rather than from any design of clearness, that he acquired his irritating habit of repeating words; I say the one rather than the other, because such a trick of the ear is deeper-seated and more original in man than any logical consideration. Few writers, indeed, are probably conscious of the length to which they push this melody of letters. One, writing very diligently, and only concerned about the meaning of his words and the rhythm of his phrases, was struck into amazement by the eager triumph with which he cancelled one expression to substitute another. Neither changed the sense; both being monosyllables, neither could affect the scansion; and it was only by looking back on what he had already written that the mystery was solved: the second word contained an open A, and for nearly half a page he had been riding that vowel to the death.

In practice, I should add, the ear is not always so exacting; and ordinary writers, in ordinary moments, content themselves with avoiding what is harsh, and here and there, upon a rare occasion, buttressing a phrase, or linking two together, with a patch of assonance or a momentary jingle of alliteration. To understand how constant is this preoccupation of good writers, even where its results are least obtrusive, it is only necessary to turn to the bad. There, indeed, you will find cacophony supreme, the rattle of incongruous consonants only relieved by the jaw-breaking hiatus, and whole phrases not to be articulated by the powers of man.

Conclusion – We may now briefly enumerate the elements of style. We have, peculiar to the prose writer, the task of keeping his phrases large, rhythmical, and pleasing to the ear, without ever allowing them to fall into the strictly metrical: peculiar to the versifier, the task of combining and contrasting his double, treble, and quadruple pattern, feet and groups, logic and metre – harmonious in diversity: common to both, the task of artfully combining the prime elements of language into phrases that shall be musical in the mouth; the task of weaving their argument into a texture of committed phrases and of rounded periods – but this particularly binding in the case of prose: and, again common to both, the task of choosing apt, explicit, and communicative words. We begin to see now what an intricate affair is any perfect passage; how many faculties, whether of taste or pure reason, must be held upon the stretch to make it; and why, when it is made, it should afford us so complete a pleasure. From the arrangement of according letters, which is altogether arabesque and sensual, up to the architecture of the elegant and pregnant sentence, which is a vigorous act of the pure intellect, there is scarce a faculty in man but has been exercised. We need not wonder, then, if perfect sentences are rare, and perfect pages rarer.

Books Which Have Influenced Me

*

The essay, first published in May 1887 as part of a series in a mainly religious periodical, *The British Weekly*, has often been quoted as a source for Stevenson's early reading experiences, although the rather 'serious' nature of the texts cited might have been influenced by the tone of the journal. *The British Weekly*, subtitled 'A Journal of Social and Christian Progress', had been running this series for some time; Stevenson's contribution was the eighth. The essay offers a contrast with other writings, such as 'Popular Authors' and 'A Penny Plain and Twopence Coloured', which suggest rather different patterns for his early imaginative life, placing more emphasis on popular texts. It does nevertheless sketch out a pattern of Stevenson's intellectual development in his youth, and provides a useful map of those writers he wished to emulate in his own work. His literary 'hierarchies' did, however, undergo some reassessments over the years.

Books Which Have Influenced Me[1]

The Editor has somewhat insidiously laid a trap for his correspondents, the question put appearing at first so innocent, truly cutting so deep. It is not, indeed, until after some reconnaissance and review that the writer awakes to find himself engaged upon something in the nature of autobiography, or, perhaps worse, upon a chapter in the life of that little, beautiful brother whom we once all had, and whom we have all lost and mourned, the man we ought to have been, the man we hoped to be. But when word has been passed (even to an editor), it should, if possible, be kept; and if sometimes I am wise and say too little, and sometimes weak and say too much, the blame must lie at the door of the person who entrapped me.

The most influential books, and the truest in their influence, are works of fiction. They do not pin the reader to a dogma which he must afterwards discover to be inexact; they do not teach him a lesson which he must afterwards unlearn. They repeat, they rearrange, they clarify the lessons of life; they disengage us from ourselves, they constrain us to the acquaintance of others; and they show us the web of experience, not as we can see it for ourselves, but with a singular change – that monstrous, consuming *ego* of ours being, for the nonce, struck out. To be so, they must be reasonably true to the human comedy; and any work that is so serves the turn of instruction. But the course of our education is answered best by those poems and romances where we breathe a magnanimous atmosphere of thought and meet generous and pious characters. Shakespeare has served me best. Few living friends have had upon me an influence so strong for good as Hamlet or Rosalind. The last character, already well beloved in the reading, I had the good fortune to see, I must think, in an impressionable hour, played by Mrs Scott Siddons.[2] Nothing has ever more moved, more delighted, more refreshed me; nor has the influence quite passed away. Kent's brief speech over the dying Lear had a great effect upon my mind, and was the burthen of my reflections for long, so profoundly, so touchingly generous did it appear in sense, so overpowering in expression. Perhaps my dearest and best friend outside of Shakespeare is d'Artagnan – the elderly d'Artagnan of the *Vicomte de Bragelonne*.[3] I know not a more human soul, nor, in his way, a finer; I shall be very sorry for the man who is so much of a pedant in morals that he cannot learn from the Captain of Musketeers. Lastly, I must name the *Pilgrim's Progress*, a book that breathes of every beautiful and valuable emotion.[4]

But of works of art little can be said; their influence is profound and silent, like the influence of nature; they mould by contact; we drink them up like water, and are bettered, yet know not how. It is in books more specifically didactic that we can follow out the effect, and distinguish and weigh and compare. A book which has been very influential upon me fell early into my hands, and so may stand first, though I think its influence was only sensible later on, and perhaps still keeps growing, for it is a book not easily outlived; the

Essais of Montaigne.[5] That temperate and genial picture of life is a great gift to place in the hands of persons of today; they will find in these smiling pages a magazine of heroism and wisdom, all of an antique strain; they will have their 'linen decencies' and excited orthodoxies fluttered, and will (if they have any gift of reading) perceive that these have not been fluttered without some excuse and ground of reason; and (again if they have any gift of reading) they will end by seeing that this old gentleman was in a dozen ways a finer fellow, and held in a dozen ways a nobler view of life than they or their contemporaries.

The next book, in order of time, to influence me, was the New Testament, and in particular the Gospel according to St. Matthew. I believe it would startle and move any one if they could make a certain effort of imagination and read it freshly like a book, not droningly and dully like a portion of the Bible. Any one would then be able to see in it those truths which we are all courteously supposed to know and all modestly refrain from applying. But upon this subject it is perhaps better to be silent.

I come next to Whitman's *Leaves of Grass*, a book of singular service, a book which tumbled the world upside down for me, blew into space a thousand cobwebs of genteel and ethical illusion, and, having thus shaken my tabernacle of lies, set me back again upon a strong foundation of all the original and manly virtues.[6] But it is, once more, only a book for those who have the gift of reading. I will be very frank – I believe it is so with all good books except, perhaps, fiction. The average man lives, and must live, so wholly in convention, that gunpowder charges of the truth are more apt to discompose than to invigorate his creed. Either he cries out upon blasphemy and indecency, and crouches the closer round that little idol of part-truths and part-conveniences which is the contemporary deity, or he is convinced by what is new, forgets what is old, and becomes truly blasphemous and indecent himself. New truth is only useful to supplement the old; rough truth is only wanted to expand, not to destroy, our civil and often elegant conventions. He who cannot judge had better stick to fiction and the daily papers. There he will get little harm, and, in the first at least, some good.

Close upon the back of my discovery of Whitman, I came under the influence of Herbert Spencer.[7] No more persuasive rabbi exists, and few better. How much of his vast structure will bear the touch of time, how much is clay and how much brass, it were too curious to inquire. But his words, if dry, are always manly and honest; there dwells in his pages a spirit of highly abstract joy, plucked naked like an algebraic symbol but still joyful; and the reader will find there a *caput-mortuum* of piety, with little indeed of its loveliness, but with most of its essentials; and these two qualities make him a wholesome, as his intellectual vigour makes him a bracing, writer.[8] I should be much of a hound if I lost my gratitude to Herbert Spencer.

Goethe's Life, by Lewes, had a great importance for me when it first fell into my hands – a strange instance of the partiality of man's good and man's evil.[9] I know no one whom I less admire than Goethe; he seems a very epitome of the sins of genius, breaking open the doors of private life and wantonly wounding friends, in that crowning offence of *Werther*, and in his own character a mere pen-and-ink Napoleon, conscious of the rights and duties of superior talents as a Spanish inquisitor was conscious of the rights and duties of his office.[10] And yet in his fine devotion to his art, in his honest and serviceable friendship for Schiller, what lessons are contained! Biography, usually so false to its office, does here for once perform for us some of the work of fiction, reminding us, that is, of the truly mingled tissue of man's nature, and how huge faults and shining virtues cohabit and persevere in the same character. History serves us well to this effect, but in the originals not in the pages of the popular epitomiser, who is bound, by the very nature of his task, to make us feel the difference of epochs instead of the essential identity of man, and even in the originals only to those who can recognise their own human virtues and defects in strange forms often inverted, and under strange names often interchanged. Martial is a poet of no good repute and it gives a man new thoughts to read his works dispassionately, and find in this unseemly jester's serious passages the image of a kind, wise, and self-respecting gentleman.[11] It is customary, I suppose, in reading Martial, to leave out these pleasant verses; I never heard of them, at least, until I found them for myself; and this partiality is one among a thousand things that help to build up our distorted and hysterical conception of the great Roman Empire.

This brings us by a natural transition to a very noble book – the *Meditations* of Marcus Aurelius.[12] The dispassionate gravity, the noble forgetfulness of self, the tenderness of others, that are there expressed and were practised on so great a scale in the life of its writer, make this book a book quite by itself. No one can read it and not be moved. Yet it scarcely or rarely appeals to the feelings – those very mobile, those not very trusty parts of man. Its address lies further back: its lesson comes more deeply home; when you have read, you carry away with you a memory of the man himself; it is as though you had touched a loyal hand, looked into brave eyes, and made a noble friend; there is another bond on you thenceforward, binding you to life and to the love of virtue.

Wordsworth should perhaps come next. Every one has been influenced by Wordsworth, and it is hard to tell precisely how. A certain innocence, a rugged austerity of joy, a sight of the stars, 'the silence that is in the lonely hills', something of the cold thrill of dawn, cling to his work and give it a particular address to what is best in us.[13] I do not know that you learn a lesson; you need not – Mill did not – agree with any one of his beliefs; and yet the spell is cast.[14] Such are the best teachers: a dogma learned is only a new error – the old one was perhaps as good; but a spirit communicated is a perpetual possession. These best teachers climb beyond teaching to the plane of art; it is themselves, and what is best in themselves, that they communicate.

I should never forgive myself if I forgot *The Egoist*.[15] It is art, if you like, but it belongs purely to didactic art, and from all the novels I have read (and I have read thousands) stands in a place by itself. Here is a Nathan for the modern David; here is a book to send the blood into men's faces.[16] Satire, the angry picture of human faults, is not great art; we can all be angry with our neighbour; what we want is to be shown, not his defects, of which we are too conscious, but his merits, to which we are too blind. And *The Egoist* is a satire; so much must be allowed; but it is a satire of a singular quality, which tells you nothing of that obvious mote, which is engaged from first to last with that invisible beam. It is yourself that is hunted down; these are your own faults that are dragged into the day and numbered, with lingering relish, with cruel cunning and precision. A young friend of Mr Meredith's (as I have the story) came to him in an agony. 'This is too bad of you,' he cried. 'Willoughby is me!' 'No, my dear fellow,' said the author; 'he is all of us.'[17] I have read *The Egoist* five or six times myself, and I mean to read it again; for I am like the young friend of the anecdote – I think Willoughby an unmanly but a very serviceable exposure of myself.

I suppose, when I am done, I shall find that I have forgotten much that was most influential, as I see already I have forgotten Thoreau, and Hazlitt whose paper 'On the Spirit of Obligations' was a turning-point in my life, and Penn whose little book of aphorisms had a brief but strong effect on me, and Mitford's *Tales of Old Japan* wherein I learned for the first time the proper attitude of any rational man to his country's laws – a secret found, and kept, in the Asiatic islands.[18] That I should commemorate all is more than I can hope or the Editor could ask. It will be more to the point, after having said so much upon improving books, to say a word or two about the improvable reader. The gift of reading, as I have called it, is not very common, nor very generally understood. It consists, first of all, in a vast intellectual endowment – a free grace, I find I must call it – by which a man rises to understand that he is not punctually right, nor those from whom he differs absolutely wrong. He may hold dogmas; he may hold them passionately; and he may know that others hold them but coldly, or hold them differently, or hold them not at all. Well, if he has the gift of reading, these others will be full of meat for him. They will see the other side of propositions and the other side of virtues. He need not change his dogma for that, but he may change his reading of that dogma, and he must supplement and correct his deductions from it. A human truth, which is always very much a lie, hides as much of life as it displays. It is men who hold another truth, or, as it seems to us, perhaps, a dangerous lie, who can extend our restricted field of knowledge, and rouse our drowsy consciences. Something that seems quite new, or that seems insolently false or very dangerous, is the test of a reader. If he tries to see what it means, what truth excuses it, he has the gift, and let him read. If he is merely hurt, or offended, or exclaims upon his author's folly, he had better take to the daily papers; he will never be a reader.

And here, with the aptest illustrative force, after I have laid down my part-truth, I must step in with its opposite. For, after all, we are vessels of a very limited content. Not all men can read all books; it is only in a chosen few that any man will find his appointed food; and the fittest lessons are the most palatable, and make themselves welcome to the mind. A writer learns this early, and it is his chief support; he goes on unafraid, laying down the law; and he is sure at heart that most of what he says is demonstrably false, and much of a mingled strain, and some hurtful, and very little good for service; but he is sure besides that when his words fall into the hands of any genuine reader, they will be weighed and winnowed, and only that which suits will be assimilated; and when they fall into the hands of one who cannot intelligently read, they come there quite silent and inarticulate, falling upon deaf ears, and his secret is kept as if he had not written.

A Gossip on a Novel of Dumas's

*

This essay was written in the spring of 1887, and included in *Memories and Portraits*. Stevenson had been interested in Dumas, however, for a long time, and made frequent references to him in other essays on fiction and in letters. Indeed Henry James once commented: 'It is, indeed, my impression that he prefers the author of *The Three Musketeers* to any novelists except Mr George Meredith. I should go so far as to suspect that his ideal of the delightful work of fiction would be the adventures of Monte Cristo related by the author of *Richard Feverel*.' ('Robert Louis Stevenson', *Century Magazine*, April 1888, written in 1887 and shown to Stevenson in the autumn.) Stevenson himself admitted to Henley: 'Dumas I have read and re-read too often' (*Letters* III, p. 8). Dumas himself, the prolific writer, the man who lived life to the full, the prodigious spendthrift, clearly appealed to Stevenson, and he was keen to see this life done justice in a good biography, as his advice to Henley on this subject suggest (*Letters* III, p. 162). The amazing energy of Dumas, in both literary production and style, was also attractive to him.

Interestingly, it is neither *The Three Musketeers* nor *The Count of Monte Cristo*, the author's best-known works, that Stevenson makes the subject of his essay, but *The Vicomte de Bragelonne*, the third in the musketeers series, and the one which witnesses the death of Athos and Porthos. Obviously aware that this may be a surprising choice, not only in relation to the rest of Dumas's *oeuvre* but as the novel which he had read more times than any other, Stevenson presents a strong defence of the text through two strategies: he gives a detailed account of the pleasures it offers, placing this in the context of more general remarks about what it is that attracts readers to novels, but he also argues that the novel offers an enlightening model of morality. Making his appeal on both grounds even stronger is the romantic atmosphere he creates in the essay by detailing his own experiences of reading specific chapters and incidents.

William Archer, in a review of 1887 in the *Pall Mall Gazette*, linked this essay with 'A Gossip on Romance' and 'A Humble Remonstrance' as making up Stevenson's 'literary confession of faith' (Maixner, p. 288). Although it takes a single novel, little read today, as its starting point, the piece still offers considerable insights into both the literary and moral codes by which Stevenson operated.

A Gossip on a Novel of Dumas's[1]

The books that we re-read the oftenest are not always those that we admire the most; we choose and we revisit them for many and various reasons, as we choose and revisit human friends. One or two of Scott's novels, Shakespeare, Molière, Montaigne, *The Egoist*, and the *Vicomte de Bragelonne*, form the inner circle of my intimates.[2] Behind these comes a good troop of dear acquaintants; *The Pilgrim's Progress* in the front rank, *The Bible in Spain* not far behind.[3] There are besides a certain number that look at me with reproach as I pass them by on my shelves: books that I once thumbed and studied: houses which were once like home to me, but where I now rarely visit. I am on these sad terms (and blush to confess it) with Wordsworth, Horace, Burns and Hazlitt. Last of all, there is the class of book that has its hour of brilliancy – glows, sings, charms, and then fades again into insignificance until the fit return. Chief of those who thus smile and frown on me by turns, I must name Virgil and Herrick, who, were they but 'Their sometime selves the same throughout the year,' must have stood in the first company with the six names of my continual literary intimates.[4] To these six, incongruous as they seem, I have long been faithful, and hope to be faithful to the day of death. I have never read the whole of Montaigne, but I do not like to be long without reading some of him, and my delight in what I do read never lessens. Of Shakespeare I have read all but *Richard III*, *Henry VI*, *Titus Andronicus*, and *All's Well That Ends Well*; and these, having already made all suitable endeavour, I now know that I shall never read – to make up for which unfaithfulness I could read much of the rest for ever. Of Molière – surely the next greatest name of Christendom – I could tell a very similar story; but in a little corner of a little essay these princes are too much out of place, and I prefer to pay my fealty and pass on. How often I have read *Guy Mannering*, *Rob Roy*, or *Redgauntlet*, I have no means of guessing, having begun young.[5] But it is either four or five times that I have read *The Egoist*, and either five or six that I have read the *Vicomte de Bragelonne*.[6]

Some, who would accept the others, may wonder that I should have spent so much of this brief life of ours over a work so little famous as the last. And, indeed, I am surprised myself; not at my own devotion, but the coldness of the world. My acquaintance with the *Vicomte* began, somewhat indirectly, in the year of grace 1863, when I had the advantage of studying certain illustrated dessert plates in a hotel at Nice.[7] The name of d'Artagnan in the legends I already saluted like an old friend, for I had met it the year before in a work of Miss Yonge's.[8] My first perusal was in one of those pirated editions that swarmed at that time out of Brussels, and ran to such a troop of neat and dwarfish volumes. I understood but little of the merits of the book; my strongest memory is of the execution of d'Eyméric and Lyodot – a strange testimony to the dulness of a boy, who could enjoy the rough-and-tumble in the Place de Grève, and forget d'Artagnan's visits to the two financiers.[9] My next reading was in winter-time, when I lived alone upon the Pentlands.[10] I would return in the early night from one of my patrols with the shepherd; a friendly face would meet me in the door, a friendly retriever scurry upstairs to fetch my slippers; and I would sit down with the *Vicomte* for a long, silent, solitary lamplight evening by the fire. And yet I know not why I call it silent, when it was enlivened with such a clatter of horse-shoes, and such a rattle of musketry, and such a stir of talk; or why I call those evenings solitary in which I gained so many friends. I would rise from my book and pull the blind aside, and see the snow and the glittering hollies chequer a Scotch garden, and the winter moonlight brighten the white hills. Thence I would turn again to that crowded and sunny field of life in which it was so easy to forget myself, my cares, and my surroundings: a place busy as a city, bright as a theatre, thronged with memorable faces, and sounding with delightful speech. I carried the thread of that epic into my slumbers, I woke with it unbroken, I rejoiced to plunge into the book again at breakfast, it was with a pang that I must lay it down and turn to my own labours; for no part of the world has ever seemed to me so charming as these pages, and not even my friends are quite so real, perhaps quite so dear, as d'Artagnan.

Since then I have been going to and fro at very brief intervals in my favourite book; and I have now just risen from my last (let me call it my fifth) perusal, having liked it better and admired it more seriously than ever. Perhaps I have a sense of ownership, being so well known in these six volumes. Perhaps I think that d'Artagnan delights to have me read of him, and Louis Quatorze is gratified, and Fouquet throws me a look, and Aramis, although he knows I do not love him, yet plays to me with his best graces, as to an old patron of the show.[11] Perhaps, if I am not careful, something may befall me like what befell George IV about the battle of Waterloo, and I may come to fancy the *Vicomte* one of the first, and Heaven knows the best, of my own works.[12] At least, I avow myself a partisan; and when I compare the popularity of the *Vicomte* with that of *Monte Cristo*, or its own elder brother, the *Trois Mousquetaires*, I confess I am both pained and puzzled.

To those who have already made acquaintance with the titular hero in the pages of *Vingt Ans Après*, perhaps the name may act as a deterrent. A man might well stand back if he supposed he were to follow, for six volumes, so well-conducted, so fine-spoken, and withal so dreary a cavalier as Bragelonne. But the fear is idle. I may be said to have passed the best years of my life in these six volumes, and my acquaintance with Raoul has never gone beyond a bow; and when he, who has so long pretended to be alive, is at last suffered to pretend to be dead, I am sometimes reminded of a saying in an earlier volume: '*Enfin, dit Miss Stewart,*' – and it was of Bragelonne she spoke – '*enfin il a fait quelquechose: ç'est, ma foi! bien heureux.*'[13] I am reminded of it, as I say; and the next moment, when Athos dies of his death, and my dear d'Artagnan bursts into his storm of sobbing, I can but deplore my flippancy.

Or perhaps it is La Vallière that the reader of *Vingt Ans Après* is inclined to flee.[14] Well, he is right there too, though not so right. Louise is no success. Her creator has spared no pains; she is well-meant, not ill-designed, sometimes has a word that rings out true; sometimes, if only for a breath, she may even engage our sympathies. But I have never envied the King his triumph. And so far from pitying Bragelonne for his defeat, I could wish him no worse (not, for lack of malice, but imagination) than to be wedded to that lady. Madame enchants me; I can forgive that royal minx her most serious offences; I can thrill and soften with the King on that memorable occasion when he goes to upbraid and remains to flirt; and when it comes to the '*Allons, aimez-moi donc*' it is my heart that melts in the bosom of de Guiche.[15] Not so with Louise. Readers cannot fail to have remarked that what an author tells us of the beauty or the charm of his creatures goes for nought; that we know instantly better; that the heroine cannot open her mouth but what, all in a moment, the fine phrases of preparation fall from round her like the robes from Cinderella, and she stands before us, self-betrayed, as a poor, ugly, sickly wench, or perhaps a strapping market-woman. Authors, at least, know it well; a heroine will too often start the trick of 'getting ugly' and no disease is more difficult to cure. I said authors; but indeed I had a side eye to one author in particular, with whose works I am very well acquainted, though I cannot read them, and who has spent many vigils in this cause, sitting beside his ailing puppets and (like a magician) wearying his art to restore them to youth and beauty.[16] There are others who ride too high for these misfortunes. Who doubts the loveliness of Rosalind?[17] Arden itself was not more lovely. Who ever questioned the perennial charm of Rose Jocelyn, Lucy Desborough, or Clara Middleton? fair women with fair names, the daughters of George Meredith.[18] Elizabeth Bennet has but to speak, and I am at her knees.[19] Ah! these are the creators of desirable women. They would never have fallen in the mud with Dumas and poor La Vallière. It is my only consolation that not one of all of them, except the first, could have plucked at the moustache of d'Artagnan.

Or perhaps, again, a proportion of readers stumble at the threshold. In so vast a mansion there were sure to be back stairs and kitchen offices where no one would delight to linger; but it was at least unhappy that the vestibule should be so badly lighted; and until, in the seventeenth chapter, d'Artagnan sets off to seek his friends, I must confess, the book goes heavily enough. But, from thenceforward, what a feast is spread! Monk kidnapped; d'Artagnan enriched; Mazarin's death; the ever delectable adventure of Belle Isle, wherein Aramis outwits d'Artagnan, with its epilogue (vol. v. chap. xxviii.), where d'Artagnan regains the moral superiority; the love adventures at Fontainebleau, with St. Aignan's story of the dryad and the business of de Guiche, de Wardes, and Manicamp; Aramis made general of the Jesuits; Aramis at the Bastille; the night talk in the forest of Sénart; Belle Isle again, with the death of Porthos; and last, but not least, the taming of d'Artagnan the untamable, under the lash of the young King. What other novel has such epic variety and nobility of incident? often, if you will, impossible; often of the order of an Arabian story; and yet all based in human nature. For if you come to that, what novel has more human nature? not studied with the microscope, but seen largely, in plain daylight, with the natural eye? What novel has more good sense, and gaiety, and wit, and unflagging, admirable literary skill? Good souls, I suppose, must sometimes read it in the blackguard travesty of a translation. But there is no style so untranslatable; light as a whipped trifle, strong as silk; wordy like a village tale; pat like a general's despatch; with every fault, yet never tedious; with no merit, yet inimitably right. And, once more, to make an end of commendations, what novel is inspired with a more unstrained or a more wholesome morality?

Yes; in spite of Miss Yonge, who introduced me to the name of d'Artagnan only to dissuade me from a nearer knowledge of the man, I have to add morality. There is no quite good book without a good morality; but the world is wide, and so are morals. Out of two people who have dipped into Sir Richard Burton's *Thousand and One Nights*, one shall have been offended by the animal details; another to whom these were harmless, perhaps even pleasing, shall yet have been shocked in his turn by the rascality and cruelty of all the characters.[20] Of two readers, again, one shall have been pained by the morality of a religious memoir, one by that of the *Vicomte de Bragelonne*. And the point is that neither need be wrong. We shall always shock each other both in life and art; we cannot get the sun into our pictures, nor the abstract right (if there be such a thing) into our books; enough if, in the one, there glimmer some hint of the great light that blinds us from heaven; enough, if, in the other, there shine, even upon foul details, a spirit of magnanimity. I would scarce send to the *Vicomte* a reader who was in quest of what we may call puritan morality. The ventripotent mulatto, the great eater, worker, earner and waster, the man of much and witty laughter, the man of the great heart and alas! of the doubtful honesty, is a figure not yet clearly set before the world; he still awaits a sober and yet genial portrait; but with whatever art that may be touched, and whatever indulgence, it will not be the portrait of a precisian.[21] Dumas was certainly not thinking of himself, but of Planchet, when he put into the mouth of d'Artagnan's old servant this excellent profession: '*Monsieur, j'étais une de ces bonnes pâtes d'hommes que Dieu a fait pour s'animer pendant un certain temps et pour trouver bonnes toutes choses qui accompagnent leur séjour sur la terre.*'[22] He was thinking, as I say, of Planchet, to whom the words are aptly fitted; but they were fitted also to Planchet's creator; and perhaps this struck him as he wrote, for observe what follows: '*D'Artagnan s'assit alors près de la fenêtre, et, cette philosophie de Planchet lui ayant paru solide, il y rêva.*'[23] In a man who finds all things good, you will scarce expect much zeal for negative virtues: the active alone will have a charm for him; abstinence, however wise, however kind, will always seem to such a judge entirely mean and partly impious. So with Dumas. Chastity is not near his heart; nor yet, to his own sore cost, that virtue of frugality which is the armour of the artist. Now, in the *Vicomte*, he had much to do with the contest of Fouquet and Colbert.[24] Historic justice should be all upon the side of Colbert, of official honesty, and fiscal competence. And Dumas knew it well: three times at least he shows his knowledge; once it is but flashed upon us and received with the laughter of Fouquet himself, in the jesting controversy in the gardens of Saint Mandé; once it is touched on by Aramis in the forest of Sénart; in the end, it is set before us clearly in one dignified speech of the triumphant Colbert. But in Fouquet, the waster, the lover of good cheer and wit and art, the swift transactor of much business, '*l'homme de bruit, l'homme de plaisir, l'homme qui n'est que parceque les autres sont*,' Dumas saw something of himself and drew the figure the more tenderly.[25] It is to me even touching to see how he insists on Fouquet's honour; not seeing, you might think, that unflawed honour is impossible to spendthrifts; but rather, perhaps, in the light of his own life, seeing it too well, and clinging the more to what was left. Honour can survive a wound; it can live and thrive without a member. The man rebounds from his disgrace; he begins fresh foundations on the ruins of the old; and when his sword is broken, he will do valiantly with his dagger. So it is with Fouquet in the book; so it was with Dumas on the battlefield of life.

To cling to what is left of any damaged quality is virtue in the man; but perhaps to sing its praises is scarcely to be called morality in the writer. And it is elsewhere, it is in the character of d'Artagnan, that we must look for that spirit of morality, which is one of the chief merits of the book, makes one of the main joys of its perusal, and sets it high above more popular rivals. Athos, with the coming of years, has declined too much into the preacher, and the preacher of a sapless creed; but d'Artagnan has mellowed into a man so witty, rough, kind and upright, that he takes the heart by storm. There is nothing of the copy-book about his virtues, nothing of the drawing-room in his fine, natural civility; he will sail near the wind; he is no district visitor – no Wesley or Robespierre; his conscience is void of all refinement whether for good or evil; but the whole man rings true like a good sovereign. Readers who have approached the *Vicomte*, not across country, but by the legitimate, five-volumed avenue of the *Mousquetaires* and *Vingt Ans Après*, will not have forgotten d'Artagnan's ungentlemanly and perfectly improbable trick upon Milady.[26] What a pleasure it is, then, what a reward, and how agreeable a lesson, to see the old captain humble himself to the son of the man whom he had personated! Here, and throughout, if I am to choose virtues for myself or my friends, let me choose the virtues of d'Artagnan. I do not say there is no character as well drawn in Shakespeare; I do say there is none that I love so wholly. There are many spiritual eyes that seem to spy upon our actions – eyes of the dead and the absent, whom we imagine to behold us in our most private hours, and whom we fear and scruple to offend: our witnesses and judges. And among these, even if you should think me childish, I must count my d'Artagnan – not d'Artagnan of the memoirs whom Thackeray pretended to prefer – a preference, I take the freedom of saying, in which he stands alone; not the d'Artagnan of flesh and blood, but him of the ink and paper; not Nature's, but Dumas's.[27] And this is the particular crown and triumph of the artist – not to be true merely, but to be lovable; not simply to convince, but to enchant.

There is yet another point in the *Vicomte* which I find incomparable. I can recall no other work of the imagination in which the end of life is represented with so nice a tact. I was asked the other day if Dumas made me laugh or cry. Well, in this my late fifth reading of the *Vicomte*, I did laugh once at the small Coquelin de Volière business, and was perhaps a thought surprised at having done so: to make up for it, I smiled continually.[28] But for tears, I do not know. If you put a pistol to my throat, I must own the tale trips upon a very airy foot – within a measurable distance of unreality; and for those who like the big guns to be discharged and the great passions to appear authentically, it may even seem inadequate from first to last. Not so to me; I cannot count that a poor dinner, or a poor book, where I meet with those I love; and, above all, in this last volume, I find a singular charm of spirit. It breathes a pleasant and a tonic sadness, always brave, never hysterical. Upon the crowded, noisy life of this long tale, evening gradually falls; and the lights are extinguished, and the heroes pass away one by one. One by one they go, and not a regret embitters their departure; the young succeed them in their places, Louis Quatorze is swelling larger and shining broader, another generation and another France dawn on the horizon; but for us and these old men whom we have loved so long, the inevitable end draws near and is welcome. To read this well is to anticipate experience. Ah, if only when these hours of the long shadows fall for us in reality and not in figure, we may hope to face them with a mind as quiet!

But my paper is running out; the siege guns are firing on the Dutch frontier; and I must say adieu for the fifth time to my old comrade fallen on the field of glory. *Adieu*, – rather *au revoir*! Yet a sixth time, dearest d'Artagnan, we shall kidnap Monk and take horse together for Belle Isle.[29]

A Chapter on Dreams

✳

Having been commissioned to write a series of twelve articles for *Scribner's Magazine* after his arrival in America, Stevenson began the project very quickly with this essay, written while at Saranac. The first paper, he states in a letter to Fanny (winter 1887–8, *Letters* III, p. 190) was written in five days; and of the first two essays he wrote that they 'are quite good . . . at least they are not dull, which is the great affair in such a task as I have undertaken.' It met with an enthusiastic response from the editor, Burlingame who replied: 'it has reproduced perfectly what nothing else has ever quite expressed for me . . . the whole paper hit quite the ideal that I had in mind for these essays'. Later Stevenson singled out this essay as one he would wish to select if compiling the best out of the *Scribner's* articles (*Letters* IV, p. 95). William Archer also complimented Stevenson on the essay in a subsequent review and queried his suggestion that the dream-romance described in it was 'unmarketable' (*Pall Mall Gazette*, 20 April 1892, Maixner, p. 385).

Swearingen convincingly suggests that much of this essay may have been inspired by the questions put to Stevenson by interviewers when he was greeted with such acclaim on his arrival in New York. Certainly an article in *The New York Herald*, 8 September 1887, entitled 'Evolved in Dreams: Robert Louis Stevenson Describes How He Finds His Plots', shows the author offering similar explanations of his creative processes: in response to the enquiry about the writing of *The Strange Case of Dr Jekyll and Mr Hyde* and *Deacon Brodie*, he replies: 'I am quite in the habit of dreaming stories.'

Even now the essay offers an intriguing and compelling account of the creative processes, spinning a tale about the making of fiction. As J. C. Furnas suggests in *Voyage to Windward*, Stevenson's thinking in the essay may be linked with developments in modern psychiatry, and in particular his relationship with F. W. H. Myers, of the Society for Psychical Research. Stevenson sent a letter to Myers from Valima in 1892, in which he details three more dream experiences, and he had already corresponded with Myers about *Jekyll and Hyde*. Stevenson's narrative about the 'Brownies' who create for him also allows for an artful evasion of creative responsibility, fuelling debates over conflicting accounts of the creation of his most famous story.

A Chapter on Dreams[1]

The past is all of one texture – whether feigned or suffered – whether acted out in three dimensions, or only witnessed in that small theatre of the brain which we keep brightly lighted all night, long after the jets are down, and darkness and sleep reign undisturbed in the remainder of the body. There is no distinction on the face of our experiences; one is vivid indeed, and one dull, and one pleasant, and another agonising to remember, but which of them is what we call true, and which a dream, there is not one hair to prove. The past stands on a precarious footing; another straw split in the field of metaphysic, and behold us robbed of it. There is scarce a family that can count four generations but lays a claim to some dormant title or some castle and estate: a claim not prosecutable in any court of law, but flattering to the fancy and a great alleviation of idle hours. A man's claim to his own past is yet less valid. A paper might turn up (in proper story-book fashion) in the secret drawer of an old ebony secretary, and restore your family to its ancient honours, and reinstate mine in a certain West Indian islet (not far from St. Kitt's, as beloved tradition hummed in my young ears) which was once ours, and is now unjustly someone else's, and for that matter (in the state of the sugar trade) is not worth anything to anybody.[2] I do not say that these revolutions are likely; only no man can deny that they are possible; and the past, on the other hand, is lost for ever: our old days and deeds, our old selves, too, and the very world in which these scenes were acted, all brought down to the same faint residuum as a last night's dream, to some incontinuous images, and an echo in the chambers of the brain. Not an hour, not a mood, not a glance of the eye, can we revoke; it is all gone, past conjuring. And yet conceive us robbed of it, conceive that little thread of memory that we trail behind us broken at the pocket's edge; and in what naked nullity should we be left! for we only guide ourselves, and only know ourselves, by these air-painted pictures of the past.

Upon these grounds, there are some among us who claimed to have lived longer and more richly than their neighbours; when they lay asleep they claim they were still active; and among the treasures of memory that all men review for their amusement, these count in no second place the harvests of their dreams. There is one of this kind whom I have in my eye, and whose case is perhaps unusual enough to be described. He was from a child an ardent and uncomfortable dreamer.[3] When he had a touch of fever at night, and the room swelled and shrank, and his clothes, hanging on a nail, now loomed up instant to the bigness of a church, and now drew away into a horror of infinite distance and infinite littleness, the poor soul was very well aware of what must follow, and struggled hard against the approaches of that slumber which was the beginning of sorrows. But his struggles were in vain; sooner or later the night-hag would have him by the throat, and pluck him, strangling and screaming, from his sleep. His dreams were at times commonplace enough, at times very strange: at times they were almost formless, he would be haunted, for instance, by nothing more definite than a certain hue of brown, which he did not mind in the least while he was awake, but feared and loathed while he was dreaming; at times, again, they took on every detail of circumstance, as when once he supposed he must swallow the populous world, and awoke screaming with the horror of the thought. The two chief troubles of his very narrow existence – the practical and everyday trouble of school tasks and the ultimate and airy one of hell and judgment – were often confounded together into one appalling nightmare. He seemed to himself to stand before the Great White Throne; he was called on, poor little devil, to recite some form of words, on which his destiny depended; his tongue stuck, his memory was blank, hell gasped for him and he would awake, clinging to the curtain-rod with his knees to his chin.[4]

These were extremely poor experiences, on the whole; and at that time of life my dreamer would have very willingly parted with his power of dreams. But presently, in the course of his growth, the cries and physical contortions passed away, seemingly for ever; his visions were still for the most part miserable, but they were more constantly supported; and he would awake with no more extreme symptom than a flying heart, a freezing scalp, cold sweats, and the speechless midnight fear. His dreams, too, as befitted a mind better stocked with particulars, became more circumstantial, and had more the air and continuity of life. The look of the world beginning to take hold on his attention, scenery came to play a part in his sleeping as well as in his waking thoughts, so that he would take long, uneventful journeys and see strange towns and beautiful places as he lay in bed. And, what is more significant, an odd taste that he had for the Georgian costume and for stories laid in that period of English history, began to rule the features of his dreams; so that he masqueraded there in a three-cornered hat, and was much engaged with Jacobite conspiracy between the hour for bed and that for breakfast. About the same time, he began to read in his dreams – tales, for the most part, and for the most part after the manner of G. P. R. James, but so incredibly more vivid and moving than any printed book, that he has ever since been malcontent with literature.[5]

And then, while he was yet a student, there came to him a dream-adventure which he has no anxiety to repeat; he began, that is to say, to dream in sequence and thus to lead a double life – one of the day, one of the night – one that he had every reason to believe was the true one, another that he had no means of proving to be false. I should have said he studied, or was by way of studying, at Edinburgh College, which (it may be supposed) was how I came to know him. Well, in his dream-life, he passed a long day in the surgical theatre, his heart in his mouth, his teeth on edge, seeing monstrous malformations and the abhorred dexterity of surgeons. In a heavy, rainy, foggy evening he came forth into the South Bridge, turned up the High Street, and entered the door of a tall *land*, at the top of which he supposed himself to lodge.[6] All night long, in his wet clothes, he climbed the stairs, stair after stair in endless series, and at every second flight a flaring lamp with a reflector. All night long, he brushed by single persons passing downward – beggarly women of the street, great, weary, muddy labourers, poor scarecrows of men, pale parodies of women – but all drowsy and weary like himself, and all single, and all brushing against him as they passed. In the end, out of a northern window he would see day beginning to whiten over the Firth, give up the ascent, turn to descend, and in a breath be back again upon the streets, in his wet clothes, in the wet, haggard dawn, trudging to another day of monstrosities and operations. Time went quicker in the life of dreams, some seven hours (as near as he can guess) to one; and it went, besides, more intensely, so that the gloom of these fancied experiences clouded the day, and he had not shaken off their shadow ere it was time to lie down and to renew them. I cannot tell how long it was that he endured this discipline; but it was long enough to leave a great black blot upon his memory, long enough to send him, trembling for his reason, to the doors of a certain doctor; whereupon with a simple draught he was restored to the common lot of man.

The poor gentleman has since been troubled by nothing of the sort; indeed, his nights were for some while like any other man's, now blank, now chequered with dreams, and these sometimes charming, sometimes appalling, but except for an occasional vividness, of no extraordinary kind. I will just note one of these occasions, ere I pass on to what makes my dreamer truly interesting. It seemed to him that he was in the first floor of a rough hill-farm. The room showed some poor efforts at gentility, a carpet on the floor, a piano, I think, against the wall; but, for all these refinements, there was no mistaking he was in a moorland place, among hill-side people, and set in miles of heather. He looked down from the window upon a bare farm-yard, that seemed to have been long disused. A great, uneasy stillness lay upon the world. There was no sign of the farm-folk or of any live-stock, save for an old, brown, curly dog of the retriever breed, who sat close in against the wall of the house and seemed to be dozing. Something about this dog disquieted the dreamer; it was quite a nameless feeling, for the beast looked right enough – indeed, he was so old and dull and dusty and broken down, that he should rather have awakened pity and yet the conviction came and grew upon the dreamer that this was no proper dog at all, but something hellish. A great many dozing summer flies hummed about the yard; and presently the dog thrust forth his paw, caught a fly in his open palm, carried it to his mouth like an ape, and looking suddenly up at the dreamer in the window, winked to him with one eye. The dream went on, it matters not how it went; it was a good dream as dreams go; but there was nothing in the sequel worthy of that devilish brown dog. And the point of interest for me lies partly in that very fact: that having found so singular an incident, my imperfect dreamer should prove unable to carry the tale to a fit end and fall back on indescribable noises and indiscriminate horrors. It would be different now; he knows his business better!

For, to approach at last the point: This honest fellow had long been in the custom of setting himself to sleep with tales, and so had his father before him; but these were irresponsible inventions, told for the teller's pleasure, with no eye to the crass public or the thwart reviewer: tales where a thread might be dropped, or one adventure quitted for another, on fancy's least suggestion. So that the little people who manage man's internal theatre had not as yet received a very rigorous training; and played upon their stage like children who should have slipped into the house and found it empty, rather than like drilled actors performing a set piece to a huge hall of faces. But presently my dreamer began to turn his former amusement of story-telling to (what is called) account; by which I mean that he began to write and sell his tales. Here was he, and here were the little people who did that part of his business, in quite new conditions. The stories must now be trimmed and pared and set upon all fours, they must run from a beginning to an end and fit (after a manner) with the laws of life; the pleasure, in one word, had become a business; and that not only for the dreamer, but for the little people of his theatre. These understood the change as well as he. When he lay down to prepare himself for sleep, he no longer sought amusement, but printable and profitable tales; and after he had dozed off in his box-seat, his little people continued their evolutions with the same mercantile designs. All other forms of dream deserted him but two: he still occasionally reads the most delightful books, he still visits at times the most delightful places; and it is perhaps worthy of note that to these same places, and to one in particular, he returns at intervals of months and years, finding new field-paths, visiting new neighbours, beholding that happy valley under new effects of noon and dawn and sunset. But all the rest of the family of visions is quite lost to him: the common, mangled version of yesterday's affairs, the raw-head-and-bloody-bones nightmare, rumoured to be the child of toasted cheese – these and their like are gone; and, for the most part, whether awake or asleep, he is simply occupied – he or his little people – in consciously making stories for the market. This dreamer (like many other persons) has encountered some trifling vicissitudes of fortune. When the bank begins to send letters and the butcher to linger at the back gate, he sets to belabouring his brains after a story, for that is his readiest money-winner; and, behold! at once the little people begin to bestir themselves in the same quest, and labour all night long, and all night long set before him truncheons of tales upon their lighted theatre. No fear of his being frightened now; the flying heart and the frozen scalp are things bygone; applause, growing applause, growing interest, growing exultation in his own cleverness (for he takes all the credit), and at last a jubilant leap to wakefulness, with the cry, 'I have it, that'll do!' upon his lips: with such and similar emotions he sits at these nocturnal dramas, with such outbreaks, like Claudius in the play, he scatters the performance in the midst.[7] Often enough the waking is a disappointment; he has been too deep asleep, as I explain the thing; drowsiness has gained his little people, they have gone stumbling and maundering through their parts; and the play, to the awakened mind, is seen to be a tissue of absurdities. And yet how often have these sleepless Brownies done him honest service, and given him, as he sat idly taking his pleasure in the boxes, better tales than he could fashion for himself.[8]

Here is one, exactly as it came to him. It seemed he was the son of a very rich and wicked man, the owner of broad acres and a most damnable temper. The dreamer (and that was the son) had lived much abroad, on purpose to avoid his parent; and when at length he returned to England, it was to find him married again to a young wife, who was supposed to suffer cruelly and to loathe her yoke. Because of this marriage (as the dreamer indistinctly understood) it was desirable for father and son to have a meeting; and yet both being proud and both angry, neither would condescend upon a visit. Meet they did accordingly, in a desolate, sandy country by the sea and there they quarrelled, and the son, stung by some intolerable insult, struck down the father dead. No suspicion was aroused; the dead man was found and buried, and the dreamer succeeded to the broad estates, and found himself installed under the same roof with his father's widow, for whom no provision had been made. These two lived very much alone, as people may after a bereavement, sat down to table together, shared the long evenings, and grew daily better friends; until it seemed to him of a sudden that she was prying about dangerous matters, that she had conceived a notion of his guilt, that she watched him and tried him with questions. He drew back from her company as men draw back from a precipice suddenly discovered; and yet so strong was the attraction that he would drift again and again into the old intimacy, and again and again be startled back by some suggestive question or some inexplicable meaning in her eye. So they lived at cross purposes, a life full of broken dialogue, challenging glances, and suppressed passion; until, one day, he saw the woman slipping from the house in a veil, followed her to the station, followed her in the train to the sea-side country and out over the sand-hills to the very place where the murder was done. There she began to grope among the bents, he watching her, flat upon his face; and presently she had something in her hand – I cannot remember what it was, but it was deadly evidence against the dreamer – and as she held it up to look at it, perhaps from the shock of the discovery, her foot slipped, and she hung at some peril on the brink of the tall sand-wreaths. He had no thought but to spring up and rescue her; and there they stood face to face, she with that deadly matter openly in her hand – his very presence on the spot another link of proof. It was plain she was about to speak, but this was more than he could bear – he could bear to be lost, but not to talk of it with his destroyer; and he cut her short with trivial conversation. Arm in arm, they returned together to the train, talking he knew not what, made the journey back in the same carriage, sat down to dinner, and passed the evening in the drawing-room as in the past. But suspense and fear drummed in the dreamer's bosom. 'She has not denounced me yet' – so his thoughts ran – 'when will she denounce me? Will it be to-morrow?' And it was not to-morrow, nor the next day, nor the next; and their life settled back on the old terms, only that she seemed kinder than before, and that, as for him, the burthen of his suspense and wonder grew daily more unbearable, so that he wasted away like a man with a disease. Once, indeed, he broke all bounds of decency, seized an occasion when she was abroad, ransacked her room, and at last, hidden away among her jewels, found the damning evidence. There he stood, holding this thing, which was his life, in the hollow of his hand, and marvelling at her inconsequent behaviour, that she should seek, and keep, and yet not use it; and then the door opened, and behold herself. So, once more, they stood, eye to eye, with the evidence between them; and once more she raised to him a face brimming with some communication; and once more he shied away from speech and cut her off. But before he left the room, which he had turned upside down, he laid back his death-warrant where he had found it; and at that, her face lighted up. The next thing he heard, she was explaining to her maid, with some ingenious falsehood, the disorder of her things. Flesh and blood could bear the strain no longer; and I think it was the next morning (though chronology is always hazy in the theatre of the mind) that he burst from his reserve. They had been breakfasting together in one corner of a great, parqueted, sparely furnished room of many windows; all the time of the meal she had tortured him with sly allusions; and no sooner were the servants gone and these two protagonists alone together, than he leaped to his feet. She too sprang up, with a pale face; with a pale face, she heard him as he raved out his complaint: Why did she torture him so? she knew all, she knew he was no enemy to her; why did she not denounce him at once? what signified her whole behaviour? why did she torture him? and yet again, why did she torture him? And when he had done, she fell upon her knees, and with outstretched hands: 'Do you not understand?' she cried. 'I love you!'

Hereupon, with a pang of wonder and mercantile delight, the dreamer awoke. His mercantile delight was not of long endurance; for it soon became plain that in this spirited tale there were unmarketable elements; which is just the reason why you have it here so briefly told. But his wonder has still kept growing; and I think the reader's will also, if he consider it ripely. For now he sees why I speak of the little people as of substantive inventors and performers. To the end they had kept their secret. I will go bail for the dreamer (having excellent grounds for valuing his candour) that he had no guess whatsoever at the motive of the woman – the hinge of the whole well-invented plot – until the instant of that highly dramatic declaration. It was not his tale; it was the little people's![9] And observe: not only was the secret kept, the story was told with really guileful craftsmanship. The conduct of both actors is (in the cant phrase) psychologically correct, and the emotion aptly graduated up to the surprising climax. I am awake now, and I know this trade; and yet I cannot better it. I am awake, and I live by this business; and yet I could not outdo – could not perhaps equal – that crafty artifice (as of some old, experienced carpenter of plays, some Dennery or Sardou) by which the same situation is twice presented and the two actors twice brought face to face over the evidence, only once it is in her hand, once in his – and these in their due order, the least dramatic first.[10] The more I think of it, the more I am moved to press upon the world my question: Who are the Little People? They are near connections of the dreamer's, beyond doubt; they share in his financial worries and have an eye to the bank-book; they share plainly in his training; they have plainly learned like him to build the scheme of a considerate story and to arrange emotion in progressive order; only I think they have more talent; and one thing is beyond doubt, they can tell him a story piece by piece, like a serial, and keep him all the while in ignorance of where they aim. Who are they, then? and who is the dreamer?

Well, as regards the dreamer, I can answer that, for he is no less a person than myself; as I might have told you from the beginning, only that the critics murmur over my consistent egotism; and as I am positively forced to tell you now, or I could advance but little farther with my story. And for the Little People, what shall I say they are but just my Brownies, God bless them! who do one-half my work for me while I am fast asleep, and in all human likelihood, do the rest for me as well, when I am wide awake and fondly suppose I do it for myself. That part which is done while I am sleeping is the Brownies' part beyond contention; but that which is done while I am up and about is by no means necessarily mine, since all goes to show the Brownies have a hand in it even then. Here is a doubt that much concerns my conscience. For myself – what I call I, my conscience ego, the denizen of the pineal gland unless he has changed his residence since Descartes, the man with the conscience and the variable bank-account, the man with the hat and the boots, and the privilege of voting and not carrying his candidate at the general elections – I am sometimes tempted to suppose he is no story-teller at all, but a creature as matter of fact as any cheesemonger or any cheese, and a realist bemired up to the ears in actuality; so that, by that account, the whole of my published fiction should be the single-handed product of some Brownie, some Familiar, some unseen collaborator, whom I keep locked in a back garret, while I get all the praise and he but a share (which I cannot prevent him getting) of the pudding. I am an excellent adviser, something like Molière's servant; I pull back and I cut down; and I dress the whole in the best words and sentences that I can find and make; I hold the pen, too; and I do the sitting at the table, which is about the worst of it; and when all is done, I make up the manuscript and pay for the registration; so that, on the whole, I have some claim to share, though not so largely as I do, in the profits of our common enterprise.

I can but give an instance or so of what part is done sleeping and what part awake, and leave the reader to share what laurels there are, at his own nod, between myself and my collaborators; and to do this I will first take a book that a number of persons have been polite enough to read, *The Strange Case of Dr. Jekyll and Mr. Hyde.*[11] I had long been trying to write a story on this subject, to find a body, a vehicle, for that strong sense of man's double being, which must at times come in upon and overwhelm the mind of every thinking creature. I had even written one, *The*

Travelling Companion, which was returned by an editor on
the plea that it was a work of genius and indecent, and which
I burned the other day on the ground that it was not a work
of genius, and that *Jekyll* had supplanted it.[12] Then came one
of those financial fluctuations to which (with an elegant
modesty) I have hitherto referred in the third person. For
two days I went about racking my brains for a plot of any
sort; and on the second night I dreamed the scene at the
window, and a scene afterwards split in two, in which Hyde,
pursued for some crime, took the powder and underwent the
change in the presence of his pursuers. All the rest was made
awake, and consciously, although I think I can trace in much
of it the manner of my Brownies. The meaning of the tale is
therefore mine, and had long pre-existed in my garden of
Adonis, and tried one body after another in vain; indeed I do
most of the morality, worse luck! and my Brownies have not
a rudiment of what we call a conscience. Mine too, is the
setting, mine the characters. All that was given me was the
matter of three scenes, and the central idea of a voluntary
change becoming involuntary. Will it be thought ungenerous, after I have been so liberally ladling out praise to my
unseen collaborators, if I here toss them over, bound hand
and foot, into the arena of the critics? For the business of the
powders, which so many have censured, is, I am relieved to
say, not mine at all but the Brownies'. Of another tale, in
case the reader should have glanced at it, I may say a word:
the not very defensible story of *Olalla*.[13] Here the court, the
mother, the mother's niche, Olalla, Olalla's chamber, the
meetings on the stair, the broken window, the ugly scene of
the bite, were all given me in bulk and detail as I have tried
to write them; to this I added only the external scenery (for
in my dream I never was beyond the court), the portrait, the
characters of Felipe and the priest, the moral, such as it is,
and the last pages, such as, alas! they are. And I may even say
that in this case the moral itself was given me; for it arose
immediately on a comparison of the mother and the
daughter, and from the hideous trick of atavism in the first.
Sometimes a parabolic sense is still more undeniably present
in a dream; sometimes I cannot but suppose my Brownies
have been aping Bunyan, and yet in no case with what
would possibly be called a moral in a tract; never with the

ethical narrowness; conveying hints instead of life's larger limitations and that sort of sense which we seem to perceive in the arabesque of time and space.

For the most part, it will be seen, my Brownies are somewhat fantastic, like their stories hot and hot, full of passion and the picturesque, alive with animating incident; and they have no prejudice against the supernatural. But the other day they gave me a surprise, entertaining me with a love-story, a little April comedy, which I ought certainly to hand over to the author of A *Chance Acquaintance*, for he could write it as it should be written, and I am sure (although I mean to try) that I cannot.[14] But who would have supposed that a Brownie of mine should invent a tale for Mr Howells?

The Lantern-Bearers

*

'The Lantern-Bearers', published in February 1888, was also written for *Scribner's Magazine* while Stevenson lived at Saranac, but shows the writer returning to memories of his childhood, recalling holidays in North Berwick, and games played with boyhood friends, as a springboard for a more theoretical assessment of the power of imagination. In later years his memories were confirmed and enhanced in two pieces written by 'A Lantern-Bearer': one, published in *Chambers's Journal*, 28 May 1910, pp. 410–11, titled 'Some Notes on the Boyhood of RLS', recalls an earlier adventure, before the lanterns had come into play. In the hagiographic tone found in many retrospective accounts of Stevenson's life, the piece paints him leader of the boys by virtue of his powers of imagination and persuasion rather than physical prowess: 'he invested everything with charm and glamour, or sometimes awe, such as appeals to childish minds. . . . Everything in his alchemist brain 'suffered a sea-change into something rich and strange' and left in the minds of the children with whom he talked and dreamed the power to see an ineffaceable glory on the common things of childhood.' The other recollection, which first appeared in *Chambers's Journal* September 1919, is called 'R.L.S. as Playmate', and is included in *I Can Remember Robert Louis Stevenson*, edited by Rosaline Masson. It too testifies to Stevenson's inventiveness in games of adventure.

Burlingame, *Scribner's* editor, who received the copy in October 1887, suggested 'New Lamps for Old' as a possible title, but the final version is perhaps more in keeping with the essay's focus on the specific as a means of exploring the abstract. As Richard le Gallienne claimed in the *Academy*: 'Mr Stevenson has never touched a home-spun theme to finer issues . . . His power . . . of transfiguring facts into symbols, is here seen in its triumph' (14 May 1892, Maixner, p. 389). Although William Archer, less positively, called it 'that ingenious, unconvincing plea for the realism of idealism' (*Pall Mall Gazette*, 20 April 1892), the essay nevertheless features several of Stevenson's striking literary characteristics: his power to re-create a dramatic incident; the use of personal recollection as a means of addressing more general issues; and the movement from the anecdotal to the theoretical. It also features several physical descriptions of scenery which echo memorable locations in *Kidnapped*, *Catriona* and *Treasure Island*.

The Lantern-Bearers[1]

I

These boys congregated every autumn about a certain easterly fisher-village, where they tasted in a high degree the glory of existence.[2] The place was created seemingly on purpose for the diversion of young gentlemen. A street or two of houses, mostly red and many of them tiled; a number of fine trees clustered about the manse and the kirkyard, and turning the chief street into a shady alley; many little gardens more than usually bright with flowers; nets a-drying, and fisher-wives scolding in the backward parts; a smell of fish, a genial smell of seaweed; whiffs of blowing sand at the street corners; shops with golf-balls and bottled lollipops; another shop with penny pickwicks (that remarkable cigar) and the *London Journal*, dear to me for its startling pictures, and a few novels, dear for their suggestive names: such, as well as memory serves me, were the ingredients of the town.[3] These, you are to conceive posted on a spit between two sandy bays, and sparsely flanked with villas – enough for the boys to lodge in with their subsidiary parents, not enough (not yet enough) to cocknify the scene: a haven in the rocks in front: in front of that, a file of grey islets: to the left, endless links and sand-wreaths, a wilderness of hiding-holes, alive with popping rabbits and soaring gulls; to the right, a range of seaward crags, one rugged brow beyond another; the ruins of a mighty and ancient fortress on the brink of one; coves between – now charmed into sunshine quiet, now whistling with wind and clamorous with bursting surges; the dens and sheltered hollows redolent of thyme and southernwood, the air at the cliff's edge brisk and clean and pungent of the sea –

in front of all, the Bass Rock, tilted seaward like a doubtful bather, the surf ringing it with white, the solan-geese hanging round its summit like a great and glittering smoke.[4] This choice piece of sea-board was sacred, besides, to the wrecker; and the Bass, in the eye of fancy, still flew the colours of King James; and in the ear of fancy the arches of Tantallon still rang with horse-shoe iron, and echoed to the commands of Bell-the-Cat.

There was nothing to mar your days, if you were a boy summering in that part, but the embarrassment of pleasure. You might golf if you wanted; but I seem to have been better employed. You might secrete yourself in the Lady's Walk, a certain sunless dingle of elders, all mossed over by the damp as green as grass, and dotted here and there by the stream-side with roofless walls, the cold homes of anchorites. To fit themselves for life, and with a special eye to acquire the art of smoking, it was even common for the boys to harbour there; and you might have seen a single penny pickwick, honestly shared in lengths with a blunt knife, bestrew the glen with these apprentices. Again, you might join our fishing-parties, where we sat perched as thick as solan-geese, a covey of little anglers, boy and girl, angling over each other's heads, to the much entanglement of lines and loss of podleys and consequent shrill recrimination – shrill as the geese themselves. Indeed, had that been all, you might have done this often; but though fishing be a fine pastime, the podley is scarce to be regarded as a dainty for the table; and it was a point of honour that a boy should eat all that he had taken. Or again you might climb the Law, where the whale's jawbone stood landmark in the buzzing wind, and behold the face of many counties, and the smoke and spires of many towns and the sails of distant ships.[5] You might bathe, now in the flaws of fine weather, that we pathetically call our summer, now in a gale of wind, with the sand scourging your bare hide, your clothes thrashing abroad from underneath their guardian stone, the froth of the great breakers casting you headlong ere it had drowned your knees. Or you might explore the tidal rocks, above all in the ebb of springs, when the very roots of the hills, were for the nonce discovered; following my leader from one group to another, groping in slippery tangle for the wreck of ships, wading in pools after

the abominable creatures of the sea, and ever with an eye
cast backward on the march of the tide and the menaced line
of your retreat. And then you might go Crusoeing, a word
that covers all extempore eating in the open air: digging
perhaps a house under the margin of the links, kindling a fire
of the sea-ware, and cooking apples there – if they were truly
apples, for I sometimes suppose the merchant must have
played us off with some inferior and quite local fruit, capable
of resolving, in the neighbourhood of fire, into mere sand
and smoke and iodine; or perhaps pushing to Tantallon, you
might lunch on sandwiches and visions in the grassy court,
while the wind hummed in the crumbling turrets; or
clambering along the coast, eat geans (the worst, I must
suppose, in Christendom) from an adventurous gean-tree
that had taken root under a cliff, where it was shaken with
an ague of east wind, and silvered after gales with salt, and
grew so foreign among its bleak surroundings that to eat of its
produce was an adventure in itself.[6]

There are mingled some dismal memories with so many
that were joyous. Of the fisher-wife, for instance, who had
cut her throat at Canty Bay; and of how I ran with the other
children to the top of the Quadrant, and beheld a posse of
silent people escorting a cart, and on the cart, bound in a
chair, her throat bandaged, and the bandage all bloody –
horror! – the fisher-wife herself, who continued thenceforth
to hag-ride my thoughts, and even today (as I recall the
scene) darkens daylight. She was lodged in the little old jail
in the chief street; but whether or no she died there, with a
wise terror of the worst, I never inquired. She had been
tippling; it was but a dingy tragedy; and it seems strange and
hard that, after all these years, the poor crazy sinner should
be still pilloried on her cart in the scrap-book of my memory.
Nor shall I readily forget a certain house in the Quadrant
where a visitor died, and a dark old woman continued to
dwell alone with the dead body; nor how this old woman
conceived a hatred to myself and one of my cousins, and in
the dread hour of the dusk, as we were clambering on the
garden-walls, opened a window in that house of mortality
and cursed us in a shrill voice and with a marrowy choice of
language. It was a pair of very colourless urchins that fled
down the lane from this remarkable experience! But I recall

with a more doubtful sentiment, compounded out of fear and exultation, the coil of equinoctial tempests; trumpeting squalls, scouring flaws of rain; the boats with their reefed lug-sails scudding for the harbour mouth, where danger lay, for it was hard to make when the wind had any east in it; the wives clustered with blowing shawls at the pierhead, where (if fate was against them) they might see boat and husband and sons – their whole wealth and their whole family – engulfed under their eyes; and (what I saw but once) a troop of neighbours forcing such an unfortunate homeward, and she squalling and battling in their midst, a figure scarcely human, a tragic Maenad.

These are things that I recall with interest; but what my memory dwells upon the most, I have been all this while withholding. It was a sport peculiar to the place, and indeed to a week or so of our two months' holiday there. Maybe it still flourishes in its native spot; for boys and their pastimes are swayed by periodic forces inscrutable to man; so that tops and marbles reappear in their due season, regular like the sun and moon; and the harmless art of knucklebones has seen the fall of the Roman Empire and the rise of the United States. It may still flourish in its native spot, but nowhere else, I am persuaded; for I tried myself to introduce it on Tweedside, and was defeated lamentably; its charm being quite local, like a country wine that cannot be exported.

The idle manner of it was this:

Toward the end of September, when school-time was drawing near and the nights were already black, we would begin to sally from our respective villas, each equipped with a tin bull's-eye lantern. The thing was so well known that it had worn a rut in the commerce of Great Britain; and the grocers, about the due time, began to garnish their windows with our particular brand of luminary. We wore them buckled to the waist upon a cricket belt, and over them, such was the rigour of the game, a buttoned top-coat. They smelled noisomely of blistered tin; they never burned aright, though they would always burn our fingers; their use was naught; the pleasure of them merely fanciful; and yet a boy with a bull's-eye under his topcoat asked for nothing more. The fishermen used lanterns about their boats, and it was from them, I suppose, that we had got the hint; but theirs were not bull's-eyes, nor did we ever play at being fishermen. The police carried them at their belts, and we had plainly copied them in that; yet we did not pretend to be policemen. Burglars, indeed, we may have had some haunting thoughts of; and we had certainly an eye to past ages when lanterns were more common, and to certain story-books in which we had found them to figure very largely. But take it for all in all, the pleasure of the thing was substantive; and to be a boy with a bull's-eye under his top-coat was good enough for us.

When two of these asses met, there would be an anxious 'Have you got your lantern?' and a gratified 'Yes!' That was the shibboleth, and very needful too; for, as it was the rule to keep our glory contained, none could recognise a lantern-bearer, unless (like the pole-cat) by the smell. Four or five would sometimes climb into the belly of a ten-man lugger, with nothing but the thwarts above them – for the cabin was usually locked; or choose out some hollow of the links where the wind might whistle overhead. There the coats would be unbuttoned and the bull's-eyes discovered; and in the chequering glimmer, under the huge windy hall of the night, and cheered by a rich steam of toasting tinware, these fortunate young gentlemen would crouch together in the cold sand of the links or on the scaly bilges of the fishing-boat, and delight themselves with inappropriate talk. Woe is me that I may not give some specimens – some of their foresights of life, or deep inquiries into the rudiments of man and nature, these were so fiery and so innocent, they were so richly silly, so romantically young.[7] But the talk, at any rate, was but a condiment; and these gatherings themselves only accidents in the career of the lantern-bearer. The essence of this bliss was to walk by yourself in the black night; the slide shut, the top-coat buttoned; not a ray escaping, whether to conduct your footsteps or to make your glory public; a mere pillar of darkness in the dark; and all the while, deep down in the privacy of your fool's heart, to know you had a bull's-eye at your belt, and to exult and sing over the knowledge.

II

It is said that a poet has died young in the breast of the most stolid. It may be contended, rather, that this (somewhat

minor) bard in almost every case survives, and is the spice of
life to his possessor. Justice is not done to the versatility and
the unplumbed childishness of man's imagination. His life
from without may seem but a rude mound of mud; there will
be some golden chamber at the heart of it, in which he
dwells delighted; and for as dark as his pathway seems to the
observer, he will have some kind of a bull's-eye at his belt. It
would be hard to pick out a career more cheerless than that
of Dancer, the miser, as he figures in the 'Old Bailey
Reports', a prey to the most sordid persecutions, the butt of
his neighbourhood, betrayed by his hired man, his house
beleaguered by the impish school-boy, and he himself
grinding and fuming and impotently fleeing to the law
against these pin-pricks.[8] You marvel at first that anyone
should willingly prolong a life so destitute of charm and
dignity; and then you call to memory that had he chosen,
had he ceased to be a miser, he could have been freed at
once from these trials, and might have built himself a castle
and gone escorted by a squadron. For the love of more
recondite joys, which we cannot estimate, which, it may be,
we should envy, the man had willingly forgone both comfort
and consideration. 'His mind to him a kingdom was'; and
sure enough, digging into that mind, which seems at first a
dust-heap, we unearth some priceless jewels.[9] For Dancer
must have had the love of power and the disdain of using it,
a noble character in itself; disdain of many pleasures, a chief
part of what is commonly called wisdom; disdain of the
inevitable end, that finest trait of mankind; scorn of men's
opinions, another element of virtue; and at the back of all, a
conscience just like yours and mine, whining like a cur,
swindling like a thimble-rigger, but still pointing (there or
thereabout) to some conventional standard. Here were a
cabinet portrait to which Hawthorne perhaps had done
justice; and yet not Hawthorne either, for he was mildly
minded, and it lay not in him to create for us that throb of
the miser's pulse, his fretful energy of gusto, his vast arms of
ambition clutching in he knows not what: insatiable, insane,
a god with a muck-rake.[10] Thus, at least, looking in the
bosom of the miser, consideration detects the poet in the full
tide of life, with more, indeed, of the poetic fire than usually
goes to epics; and tracing that mean man about his cold

hearth, and to and fro in his discomfortable house, spies within him a blazing bonfire of delight. And so with others, who do not live by bread alone, but by some cherished and perhaps fantastic pleasure; who are meat salesmen to the external eye, and possibly to themselves are Shakespeares, Napoleons, or Beethovens; who have not one virtue to rub against another in the field of active life, and yet perhaps, in the life of contemplation, sit with the saints. We see them on the street, and we can count their buttons; but Heaven knows in what they pride themselves! Heaven knows where they have set their treasure!

There is one fable that touches very near the quick of life; the fable of the monk who passed into the woods, heard a bird break into song, hearkened for a trill or two, and found himself on his return a stranger at his convent gates; for he had been absent fifty years, and of all his comrades there survived but one to recognise him. It is not only in the woods that this enchanter carols, though perhaps he is native there. He sings in the most doleful places. The miser hears him and chuckles, and the days are moments. With no more apparatus than an ill-smelling lantern I have evoked him on the naked links. All life that is not merely mechanical is spun out of two strands: seeking for that bird and hearing him. And it is just this that makes life so hard to value, and the delight of each so incommunicable. And just a knowledge of this, and a remembrance of those fortunate hours in which the bird has sung to us, that fills us with such wonder when we turn the pages of the realist. There, to be sure, we find a picture of life in so far as it consists of mud and of old iron, cheap desires and cheap fears, that which we are ashamed to remember and that which we are careless whether we forget; but of the note of that time-devouring nightingale we hear no news.

The case of these writers of romance is most obscure. They have been boys and youths; they have lingered outside the window of the beloved, who was then most probably writing to someone else; they have sat before a sheet of paper, and felt themselves mere continents of congested poetry, not one line of which would flow; they have walked alone in the woods, they have walked in cities under the countless lamps; they have been to sea, they have hated, they have feared, they have longed to knife a man, and maybe done it; the wild taste of life has stung their palate. Or, if you deny them all the rest, one pleasure at least they have tasted to the full – their books are there to prove it – the keen pleasure of successful literary composition. And yet they fill the globe with volumes, whose cleverness inspires me with despairing admiration, and whose consistent falsity to all I care to call existence, with despairing wrath. If I had no better hope than to continue to revolve among the dreary and petty businesses, and to be moved by the paltry hopes and fears with which they surround and animate their heroes, I declare I would die now. But there has never an hour of mine gone quite so dully yet; if it were spent waiting at a railway junction, I would have some scattering thoughts, I could count some grains of memory, compared to which the whole of one of these romances seems but dross.

These writers would retort (if I take them properly) that this was very true; that it was the same with themselves and other persons of (what they call) the artistic temperament; that in this we were exceptional, and should apparently be ashamed of ourselves; but that our works must deal exclusively with (what they call) the average man, who was a prodigious dull fellow, and quite dead to all but the paltriest considerations. I accept the issue. We can only know others by ourselves. The artistic temperament (a plague on the expression!) does not make us different from our fellow-men, or it would make us incapable of writing novels; and the average man (a murrain on the word!) is just like you and me, or he would not be average. It was Whitman who stamped a kind of Birmingham sacredness upon the latter phrase; but Whitman knew very well, and showed very nobly, that the average man was full of joys and full of poetry of his own.[11] And this harping on life's dulness and man's meanness is a loud profession of incompetence; it is one of two things: the cry of the blind eye, *I cannot see*, or the complaint of the dumb tongue, *I cannot utter*. To draw a life without delights is to prove I have not realised it. To picture a man without some sort of poetry – well, it goes near to prove my case, for it shows an author may have little enough. To see Dancer only as a dirty, old, small-minded, impotently fuming man, in a dirty house, besieged by Harrow

boys, and probably beset by small attorneys, is to show myself
as keen an observer as . . . the Harrow boys. But these
young gentlemen (with a more becoming modesty) were
content to pluck Dancer by the coat-tails; they did not
suppose they had surprised his secret or could put him living
in a book: and it is there my error would have lain. Or say
that in the same romance – I continue to call these books
romances, in the hope of giving pain – say that in the same
romance, which now begins really to take shape, I should
leave to speak of Dancer, and follow instead the Harrow
boys; and say that I came on some such business as that of my
lantern-bearers on the links, and described the boys as very
cold, spat upon by flurries of rain, and drearily surrounded,
all of which they were; and their talk as silly and indecent,
which it certainly was. I might upon these lines, and had I
Zola's genius, turn out, in a page or so, a gem of literary art,
render the lantern-light with the touches of a master, and lay
on the indecency with the ungrudging hand of love; and
when all was done, what triumph would my picture be of
shallowness and dulness! how it would have missed the
point! how it would have belied the boys![12] To the ear of the
stenographer, the talk is merely silly and indecent; but ask
the boys themselves, and they are discussing (as it is highly
proper they should) the possibilities of existence. To the eye
of the observer they are wet and cold and drearily
surrounded; but ask themselves, and they are in the heaven
of recondite pleasure, the ground of which is an ill-smelling
lantern.

III

For, to repeat, the ground of a man's joy is often hard to hit.
It may hinge at times upon a mere accessory, like the lantern,
it may reside, like Dancer's in the mysterious inwards of
psychology. It may consist with perpetual failure, and find
exercise in the continued chase. It has so little bond with
externals (such as the observer scribbles in his note-book)
that it may even touch them not; and the man's true life, for
which he consents to live, lie altogether in the field of fancy.
The clergyman, in his spare hours may be winning battles,
the farmer sailing ships, the banker reaping triumph in the

arts: all leading another life, plying another trade from that they chose; like the poet's housebuilder, who after all is cased in stone,

> By his fireside, as impotent fancy prompts,
> Rebuilds it to his liking.[13]

In such a case the poetry runs underground. The observer (poor soul, with his documents!) is all abroad. For to look at the man is but to court deception. We shall see the trunk from which he draws his nourishment; but he himself is above and abroad in the green dome of foliage, hummed through by winds and nested in by nightingales. And the true realism were that of the poets, to climb up after him like a squirrel, and catch some glimpse of the heaven for which he lives. And the true realism, always and everywhere, is that of the poets to find out where joy resides, and give it a voice far beyond singing.

For to miss the joy is to miss all. In the joy of the actors lies the sense of any action. That is the explanation, that the excuse. To one who has not the secret of the lanterns, the scene upon the links is meaningless. And hence the haunting and truly spectral unreality of realistic books. Hence, when we read the English realists, the incredulous wonder with which we observe the hero's constancy under the submerging tide of dulness, and how he bears up with his jibbing sweetheart, and endures the chatter of idiot girls, and stands by his whole unfeatured wilderness of an existence, instead of seeking relief in drink or foreign travel. Hence in the French, in that meat-market of middle-aged sensuality, the disgusted surprise with which we see the hero drift sidelong, and practically quite untempted, into every description of misconduct and dishonour. In each, we miss the personal poetry, the enchanted atmosphere, that rainbow work of fancy that clothes what is naked and seems to ennoble what is base; in each, life falls dead like dough, instead of soaring away like a balloon into the colours of the sunset; each is true, each inconceivable; for no man lives in the external truth, among salts and acids, but in the warm, phantasmagoric chamber of his brain, with the painted windows and the storied walls.

Of this falsity we have had a recent example from a man who knows far better – Tolstoi's *Powers of Darkness*.[14] Here is a piece full of force and truth, yet quite untrue. For before Mikita was led into so dire a situation he was tempted, and temptations are beautiful at least in part; and a work which dwells on the ugliness of crime and gives no hint of any loveliness in the temptation, sins against the modesty of life, and even when a Tolstoi writes it, sinks to melodrama. The peasants are not understood; they saw their life in fairer colours; even the deaf girl was clothed in poetry for Mikita, or he had never fallen. And so, once again, even an Old Bailey melodrama, without some brightness of poetry and lustre of existence, falls into the inconceivable and ranks with fairy tales.

IV

In nobler books we are moved with something like the emotions of life; and this emotion is very variously provoked. We are so moved when Levine labours in the field, when André sinks beyond emotion, when Richard Feverel and Lucy Desborough meet beside the river, when Antony, 'not cowardly, puts off his helmet', when Kent has infinite pity on the dying Lear, when, in Dostoieffsky's *Despised and Rejected*, the uncomplaining hero drains his cup of suffering and virtue.[15] These are notes that please the great heart of man. Not only love, and the fields, and the bright face of danger, but sacrifice and death and unmerited suffering humbly supported, touch in us the vein of the poetic. We love to think of them, we long to try them, we are humbly hopeful that we may prove heroes also.

We have heard, perhaps, too much of lesser matter. Here is the door, here is the open air. *Itur in antiquam silvam*.[16]

Some Gentlemen in Fiction

✳

This essay was one of several written for *Scribner's Magazine* in the late 1880s and was received enthusiastically by Burlingame in March 1888. It was republished in the collected works under *Lay Morals and Other Ethical papers* (Tusitala 26), rather than with the more obviously critical essays of other volumes; yet, while it purports to address questions of 'gentlemanliness', the essay centres around the relationship between writers and the characters they create, exploring the impact of a writer's background on their fictional characters, the effects of commercial pressures and the technical problems of constructing 'verbal puppets' through 'strings of words and parts of books'. As such, the essay offers fascinating insights into Stevenson's response to particular characters, and a map of literary influences, but it also reveals many of the ways in which 'one writer of fiction whom I have the advantage of knowing' operates.

Nevertheless, the essay did succeed in provoking a 'moral' response from at least one reader, the son of the novelist Charles Dickens, who objected to Stevenson's comments on his father's novels and published a piece to this effect in his magazine, *All the Year Round* on 15 February 1890, pp. 163–5. Although he implicitly endorses the judgements made by Stevenson on the fictional gentlemen in question, his tone is indignant: 'But surely of all the mob of gentlemen who write with ease, Mr R. L. Stevenson is the last one would expect to defame or soil the designation.' He proceeds to describe Stevenson's comments as 'the very mockery of criticism'. He later admitted, in what appears to be a response to a letter from Stevenson, that he may have responded too harshly, had read the piece 'overhastily', and that Stevenson was entitled to a 'frank apology'.

Some Gentlemen In Fiction[1]

I

To make a character at all – so to select, so to describe a few
acts, a few speeches, perhaps (though this is quite super-
fluous) a few details of physical appearance, as that these
shall all cohere and strike in the reader's mind a common
note of personality – there is no more delicate enterprise,
success is nowhere less comprehensible than here. We meet a
man, we find his talk to have been racy; and yet if every word
were taken down by shorthand, we should stand amazed at
its essential insignificance. Physical presence, the speaking
eye, the inimitable commentary of the voice, it was in these
the spell resided; and these are all excluded from the pages of
the novel. There is one writer of fiction whom I have the
advantage of knowing; and he confesses to me that his
success in this matter (small though it be) is quite surprising
to himself. 'In one of my books,' he writes, 'and in one only,
the characters took the bit in their mouth; all at once, they
became detached from the flat paper, they turned their backs
on me and walked off bodily; and from that time, my task
was stenographic – it was they who spoke, it was they who
wrote the remainder of the story. When this miracle of
genesis occurred, I was thrilled with joyous surprise; I felt a
certain awe – shall we call it superstitious? And yet how
small a miracle it was; with what a partial life were my
characters endowed; and when all was said, how little did I
know of them! It was a form of words they supplied me with;
it was in a form of words they consisted; beyond and behind
was nothing.' The limitation, which this writer felt and
which he seems to have deplored, can be remarked in the
work of even literary princes. I think it was Hazlitt who
declared that, if the names were dropped at press, he could
restore any speech in Shakespeare to the proper speaker; and
I daresay we could all pick out the words of Nym or Pistol,
Caius or Evans; but not even Hazlitt could do the like for the
great leading characters, who yet are cast in a more delicate
mould, and appear before us far more subtly and far more
fully differentiated, than these easy-going ventriloquial

puppets.[2] It is just when the obvious expedients of the barrel-organ vocabulary, the droll mispronunciation or the racy dialect, are laid aside, that the true masterpieces are wrought (it would seem) from nothing. Hamlet speaks in character, I potently believe it, and yet see not how. He speaks at least as no man ever spoke in life, and very much as many other heroes do in the same volume; now uttering the noblest verse, now prose of the most cunning workmanship; clothing his opinions throughout in that amazing dialect, Shakespearese. The opinions themselves, again, though they are true and forcible and reinforced with excellent images, are not peculiar either to Hamlet, or to any man or class or period; in their admirable generality of appeal resides their merit; they might figure, and they would be applauded, in almost any play and in the mouth of almost any noble and considerate character. The only hint that is given as to his physical man – I speak for myself – is merely shocking, seems merely erroneous, and is perhaps best explained away upon the theory that Shakespeare had Burbage more directly in his eye than Hamlet.[3] As for what the Prince does and what he refrains from doing, all acts and passions are strangely impersonal. A thousand characters, as different among themselves as night from day, should yet, under the like stress of circumstance, have trodden punctually in the footprints of Hamlet and each other. Have you read *André Cornélis?* in which M. Bourget handled over again but yesterday the theme of *Hamlet*, even as Godwin had already rehandled part of it in *Caleb Williams*.[4] You can see the character M. Bourget means with quite sufficient clearness; it is not a masterpiece, but it is adequately indicated; and the character is proper to the part, these acts and passions fit him like a glove, he carries the tale, not with so good a grace as Hamlet, but with equal nature. Well, the two personalities are fundamentally distinct: they breathe upon us out of different worlds; in face, in touch, in the subtile atmosphere by which we recognise an individual, in all that goes to build up a character – or at least that shadowy thing, a character in a book – they are even opposed: the same fate involves them, they behave on the same lines, and they have not one hair in common. What, then, remains of Hamlet? and by what magic does he stand forth in our brains, *teres atque rotundus*, solid to the touch, a man to praise, to blame, to pity, ay, and to love?[5]

At bottom, what we hate or love is doubtless some projection of the author; the personal atmosphere is doubtless his; and when we think we know Hamlet, we know but a side of his creator. It is a good old comfortable doctrine, which our fathers have taken for a pillow, which has served as a cradle for ourselves; and yet, in some of its applications, it brings us face to face with difficulties. I said last month that we could tell a gentleman in a novel.[6] Let us continue to take Hamlet. Manners vary, they invert themselves, from age to age; Shakespeare's gentlemen are not quite ours, there is no doubt their talk would raise a flutter in a modern tea-party; but in the old pious phrase, they have the root of the matter. All the most beautiful traits of the gentleman adorn this character of Hamlet: it was the side on which Salvini seized, which he so attractively displayed, with which he led theatres captive; it is the side, I think, by which the Prince endears himself to readers.[7] It is true there is one staggering scene, the great scene with his mother. But we must regard this as the author's lost battle; here it was that Shakespeare failed: what to do with the Queen, how to depict her, how to make Hamlet use her, these (as we know) were his miserable problem; it beat him; he faced it with an indecision worthy of his hero; he shifted, he shuffled with it; in the end, he may be said to have left his paper blank. One reason why we do not more generally recognise this failure of Shakespeare's is because we have most of us seen the play performed; and managers, by what seems a stroke of art, by what is really (I dare say) a fortunate necessity, smuggle the problem out of sight – the play, too, for the matter of that; but the glamour of the footlights and the charm of that little strip of fiddlers' heads and elbows, conceal the conjuring. This stroke of art (let me call it so) consists in casting the Queen as an old woman. Thanks to the footlights and the fiddlers' heads, we never pause to inquire why the King should have pawned his soul for this college-bedmaker in masquerade; and thanks to the absurdity of the whole position, and that unconscious unchivalry of audiences (ay, and of authors also) to old women, Hamlet's monstrous conduct passes unobserved or unresented. Were the Queen cast as she should be, a woman still young and beautiful, had she been coherently written by Shakespeare, and were she played with any spirit, even an audience would rise.

But the scene is simply false, effective on the stage, untrue of any son or any mother; in judging the character of Hamlet, it must be left upon one side; and in all other relations we recognise the Prince for a gentleman.

Now, if the personal charm of any verbal puppet be indeed only an emanation from its author, may we conclude, since we feel Hamlet to be a gentleman, that Shakespeare was one too?[8] An instructive parallel occurs. There were in England two writers of fiction, contemporaries, rivals in fame, opposites in character; one descended from a great house, easy, generous, witty, debauched, a favourite in the tap-room and the hunting field, yet withal a man of a high practical intelligence, a distinguished public servant, an ornament of the bench: the other, sprung from I know not whence – but not from kings – buzzed about by second-rate women, and their fit companion, a tea-bibber in parlours, a man of painful propriety, with all the narrowness and much of the animosity of the backshop and the dissenting chapel. Take the pair, they seem like types: Fielding, with all his faults, was undeniably a gentleman; Richardson, with all his genius and his virtues, as undeniably was not. And now turn to their works. In *Tom Jones*, a novel of which the respectable profess that they could stand the dulness if it were not so blackguardly, and the more honest admit they could forgive the blackguardism if it were not so dull – in *Tom Jones*, with its voluminous bulk and troops of characters, there is no shadow of a gentleman, for Allworthy is only ink and paper.[9] In *Joseph Andrews* I fear I have always confined my reading to the parson; and Mr Adams, delightful as he is, has no pretension 'to the genteel'.[10] In *Amelia*, things get better; all things get better; it is one of the curiosities of literature that Fielding, who wrote one book that was engaging, truthful, kind, and clean, and another book that was dirty, dull, and false, should be spoken of, the world over, as the author of the second and not the first, as the author of *Tom Jones*, not of *Amelia*.[11] And in *Amelia*, sure enough, we find some gentlefolk; Booth and Dr Harrison will pass in a crowd, I dare not say they will do more. It is very differently that one must speak of Richardson's creations. With *Sir Charles Grandison* I am unacquainted – there are many impediments in this brief life of man; I have more than once, indeed, reconnoitred the first volume with a flying party, but always decided not to break ground before the place till my siege guns came up; and it's an odd thing – I have been all these years in the field, and that powerful artillery is still miles in the rear.[12] The day it overtakes me, Baron Gibbon's fortress shall be beat about his ears, and my flag be planted on the formidable ramparts of the second part of *Faust*. Clarendon, too – But why should I continue this confession?[13] Let the reader take up the wondrous tale himself, and run over the books that he has tried, and failed withal, and vowed to try again, and now beholds, as he goes about a library, with secret compunction. As to Sir Charles at least, I have the report of spies; and by the papers in the office of my Intelligence Department, it would seem he was a most accomplished baronet. I am the more ready to credit these reports, because the spies are persons thoroughly accustomed to the business; and because my own investigation of a kindred quarter of the globe (*Clarissa Harlowe*) has led me to set a high value on the Richardsonians.[14] Lovelace – in spite of his abominable misbehaviour – Colonel Morden and my Lord M– are all gentlemen of undisputed quality. They more than pass muster, they excel; they have a gallant, a conspicuous carriage; they roll into the book, four in hand, in gracious attitudes. The best of Fielding's gentlemen had scarce been at their ease in M– Hall; Dr Harrison had seemed a plain, honest man, a trifle below his company; and poor Booth (supposing him to have served in Colonel Morden's corps and to have travelled in the post-chaise along with his commandant) had been glad to slink away with Mowbray and crack a bottle in the butler's room.

So that here, on the terms of our theory, we have an odd inversion, tempting to the cynic.

II

Just the other day, there were again two rival novelists in England: Thackeray and Dickens; and the case of the last is, in this connection, full of interest. Here was a man and an artist, the most strenuous, one of the most endowed; and for how many years he laboured in vain to create a gentleman! With all his watchfulness of men and manners, with all his fiery industry, with his exquisite native gift of characterisa- tion, with his clear knowledge of what he meant to do, there was yet something lacking. In part after part, novel after novel, a whole menagerie of characters, the good, the bad, the droll, and the tragic, came at his beck like slaves about an Oriental despot; there was only one who stayed away: the gentleman. If this ill fortune had persisted it might have shaken man's belief in art and industry. But years were given and courage was continued to the indefatigable artist; and at length, after so many and such lamentable failures, success began to attend upon his arms. David Copperfield scrambled through on hands and knees; it was at least a negative success; and Dickens, keenly alive to all he did, must have heaved a sigh of infinite relief.[15] Then came the evil days, the days of *Dombey* and *Dorrit*, from which the lover of Dickens willingly averts his eyes; and when that temporary blight had passed away, and the artist began with a more resolute arm to reap the aftermath of his genius, we find him able to create a Carton, a Wrayburn, a Twemlow.[16] No mistake about these three; they are all gentlemen: the sottish Carton, the effete Twemlow, the insolent Wrayburn, all have doubled the cape.

There were never in any book three perfect sentences on end; there was never a character in any volume but it somewhere tripped. We are like dancing dogs and preaching women: the wonder is not that we should do it well, but that we should do it at all. And Wrayburn, I am free to admit, comes on one occasion to the dust. I mean, of course, the scene with the old Jew.[17] I will make you a present of the Jew for a card-board figure; but that is neither here nor there: the ineffectuality of the one presentment does not mitigate the grossness, the baseness, the inhumanity of the other. In this scene, and in one other (if I remember aright) where it is echoed, Wrayburn combines the wit of the omnibus-cad with the good feeling of the Andaman Islander: in all the remainder of the book, throughout a thousand perils, playing (you would say) with difficulty, the author swimmingly steers

his hero on the true course.[18] The error stands by itself, and
it is striking to observe the moment of its introduction. It
follows immediately upon one of the most dramatic passages
in fiction, that in which Bradley Headstone barks his
knuckles on the churchyard wall. To handle Bradley (one of
Dickens's superlative achievements) were a thing impossible
to almost any man but his creator; and even to him, we may
be sure, the effort was exhausting.[19] Dickens was a weary
man when he had barked the schoolmaster's knuckles, a
weary man and an excited; but the tale of bricks had to be
finished, the monthly number waited; and under the false
inspiration of irritated nerves, the scene of Wrayburn and
the Jew was written and sent forth; and there it is, a blot
upon the book and a buffet to the reader.

I make no more account of this passage than of that other
in *Hamlet*: a scene that has broken down, the judicious
reader cancels for himself. And the general tenor of
Wrayburn, and the whole of Carton and Twemlow, are
beyond exception. Here, then, we have a man who found it
for years an enterprise beyond his art to draw a gentleman,
and who in the end succeeded. Is it because Dickens was not
a gentleman himself that he so often failed? and if so, then
how did he succeed at last? Is it because he was a gentleman
that he succeeded? and if so, what made him fail? I feel
inclined to stop this paper here, after the manner of
conundrums, and offer a moderate reward for a solution. But
the true answer lies probably deeper than did ever plummet
sound.[20] And mine (such as it is) will hardly appear to the
reader to disturb the surface.

These verbal puppets (so to call them once again) are
things of a divided parentage: the breath of life may be an
emanation from their maker, but they themselves are only
strings of words and parts of books; they dwell in, they
belong to, literature; convention, technical artifice, technical gusto, the mechanical necessities of the art, these are the
flesh and blood with which they are invested. If we look only
at Carton and Wrayburn, both leading parts, it must strike us
at once that both are most ambitiously attempted; that
Dickens was not content to draw a hero and a gentleman
plainly and quietly; that, after all his ill-success, he must still
handicap himself upon these fresh adventures, and make

Carton a sot, and sometimes a cantankerous sot, and Wrayburn insolent to the verge, and sometimes beyond the verge, of what is pardonable. A moment's thought will show us this was in the nature of his genius, and a part of his literary method. His fierce intensity of design was not to be slaked with any academic portraiture; not all the arts of individualisation could perfectly content him; he must still seek something more definite and more express than nature. All artists, it may be properly argued, do the like; it is their method to discard the middling and the insignificant, to disengage the charactered and the precise. But it is only a class of artists that pursue so singly the note of personality; and is it not possible that such a preoccupation may disable men from representing gentlefolk? The gentleman passes in the stream of the day's manners, inconspicuous. The lover of the individual may find him scarce worth drawing. And even if he draw him, on what will his attention centre but just upon those points in which his model exceeds or falls short of his subdued ideal – but just upon those points in which the gentleman is not genteel? Dickens, in an hour of irritated nerves, and under the pressure of the monthly number, defaced his Wrayburn. Observe what he sacrifices. The ruling passion strong in his hour of weakness, he sacrifices dignity, decency, the essential human beauties of his hero; he still preserves the dialect, the shrill note of personality, the mark of identification. Thackeray, under the strain of the same villainous system, would have fallen upon the other side; his gentleman would still have been a gentleman, he would have only ceased to be an individual figure.

There are incompatible ambitions. You cannot paint a Vandyke and keep it a Franz Hals.[21]

III

I have preferred to conclude my inconclusive argument before I touched on Thackeray. Personally, he scarce appeals to us as the ideal gentleman; if there were nothing else, perpetual nosing after snobbery at least suggests the snob; but about the men he made, there can be no such question of reserve. And whether because he was himself a gentleman in a very high degree, or because his methods were in a very high degree suited to this class of work, or from the common operation of both causes, a gentleman came from his pen by the gift of nature. He could draw him as a character part, full of pettiness, tainted with vulgarity, and yet still a gentleman, in the inimitable Major Pendennis.[22] He could draw him as the full-blown hero – in Colonel Esmond. He could draw him – the next thing to the work of God – human and true and noble and frail, in Colonel Newcome. If the art of being a gentleman were forgotten, like the art of staining glass, it might be learned anew from that one character. It is learned there, I dare to say, daily. Mr Andrew Lang, in a graceful attitude of melancholy, denies the influence of books.[23] I think he forgets his philosophy; for surely there go two elements to the determination of conduct: heredity, and experience – that which is given to us at birth, that which is added and cancelled in the course of life; and what experience is more formative, what step of life is more efficient, than to know and weep for Colonel Newcome? And surely he forgets himself; for I call to mind other pages, beautiful pages, from which it may be gathered that the language of *The Newcomes* sings still in his memory, and its gospel is sometimes not forgotten. I call it a gospel: it is the best I know. Error and suffering and failure and death, those calamities that our contemporaries paint upon so vast a scale – they are all depicted here, but in a more true proportion. We may return, before this picture, to the simple and ancient faith. We may be sure (although we know not why) that we give our lives, like coral insects, to build up insensibly, in the twilight of the seas of time, the reef of righteousness. And we may be sure (although we see not how) it is a thing worth doing.

Popular Authors

*

This essay was one of a series of twelve articles Stevenson wrote for *Scribner's Magazine* in the autumn, winter and spring of 1887–8: 'I am condemned to write twelve articles in *Scribner's Magazine* for the love of gain', he wrote (Christmas 1887, *Letters* III, p. 172). His letters to Charles Scribner show him requesting a number of the popular titles he discusses, in order to refresh his memory. At the time of writing Stevenson was involved in complex negotiations of his own literary affairs (see *Letters* III, p. 157) so the commercial aspects of publishing may have been of particular concern. Ironically, the series for *Scribner's* was itself part of that world of commercial enterprise: 'It was a project I went into with horrid diffidence; and lucre was my only motive. I get on better than I expected, but it is difficult to find an article of the sort required for each date, and to vary the matter and keep up (if possible) the merit' (to Edmund Gosse, 31 March, 1888, *Letters* III, p. 182). Yet, while writing with such a strong consciousness of his own role in the literary profession, Stevenson also succeeds in conveying the voice of a reader, and offers an extended exploration of the pleasures of reading, the power of imagination and the nature of readerly desires.

The essay itself is highly playful, demonstrating an evident enjoyment in recounting the absurd plots of the penny thrillers, but also makes the point, even through the presentational trick of highlighting author's names by capital letters, that cultural hierarchies should not be taken for granted and that a context of production exists beyond the text itself which may shape its identity and the readers' responses. Although the names may be unfamiliar to readers today, readers of Stevenson's time might also have found them different from the usual literary reference points scattered through *belle-lettriste* writing – a situation he clearly relished.

Popular Authors[1]

The scene is the deck of an Atlantic liner, close by the doors
of the ashpit, where it is warm: the time, night: the persons,
an emigrant of an inquiring turn of mind and a deck hand.
'Now,' says the emigrant, 'is there not any book that gives a
true picture of a sailor's life?' – 'Well,' returns the other, with
great deliberation and emphasis, 'there is *one*; that is *just* a
sailor's life. You know all about it, if you know that . . .
'What do you call it?' asks the emigrant. 'They call it *Tom
Holt's Log*,' says the sailor. The emigrant entered the fact in
his note-book: with a wondering query as to what sort of stuff
this *Tom Holt* would prove to be: and a double-headed
prophecy that it would prove one of two things: either a
solid, dull, admirable piece of truth, or mere ink and banditti.
Well, the emigrant was wrong: it was something more
curious than either, for it was a work by STEPHENS HAYWARD.[2]

I

In this paper I propose to put the authors' names in capital
letters; the most of them have not much hope of durable
renown; their day is past, the poor dogs – they begin swiftly
to be forgotten; and HAYWARD is of the number. Yet he was a
popular writer; and what is really odd, he had a vein of hare-
brained merit. There never was a man of less pretension; the
intoxicating presence of an ink-bottle, which was too much
for the strong head of Napoleon, left him sober and light-
hearted; he had no shade of literary vanity; he was never at
the trouble to be dull. His works fell out of date in the days of
printing. They were the unhatched eggs of Arab tales; made
for word-of-mouth recitation, certain (if thus told) to
captivate an audience of boys or any simple people –
certain, on the lips of a generation or two of public story-
tellers, to take on new merit and become cherished lore.
Such tales as a man, such rather as a boy, tells himself at
night, not without smiling, as he drops asleep; such, with the
same exhilarating range of incident and the same trifling
ingenuities, with no more truth to experience and scarcely
more cohesion, HAYWARD told. If we so consider *The*

Diamond Necklace, or The Twenty Captains, which is what I remember best of HAYWARD, you will find that staggering narrative grow quite conceivable.[3]

A gentleman (his name forgotten – HAYWARD had no taste in names) puts an advertisement in the papers, inviting nineteen other gentlemen to join him in a likely enterprise. The nineteen appear promptly, nineteen, no more, no less: see the ease of the recumbent story-teller, half-asleep, hanging on the verge of that country of dreams, where candles come alight and journeys are accomplished at the wishing! These twenty, all total strangers, are to put their money together and form an association of strict equality: hence its name – *The Twenty Captains*. And it is no doubt very pleasant to be equal to anybody, even in name; and mighty desirable (at least in the eyes of young gentlemen hearing this tale in the school dormitory) to be called captain, even in private. But the deuce of it is, the founder has no enterprise in view, and here, you would think, the least wary capitalist would leave his chair, and buy a broom and a crossing with his money, rather than place it in the hands of this total stranger, whose mind by his own confession was a blank, and whose real name was probably Macaire.[4] No such matter in the book. With the ease of dreaming, the association is founded; and again with the ease of dreaming (HAYWARD being now three parts asleep) the enterprise, in the shape of a persecuted heiress and a truly damnable and idiotic aristocrat, appears upon the scene. For some time, our drowsy story-teller dodges along upon the frontiers of incoherence, hardly at the trouble to invent, never at the trouble to write literature; but suddenly his interest brightens up, he sees something in front of him, turns on the pillow, shakes off the tentacles of slumber, and puts his back into his tale. Injured innocence takes a special train to Dover; damnable idiot takes another and pursues; the twenty captains reach the station five minutes after, and demand a third. It is against the rules, they are told; not more than two specials (here is good news for the railway traveller) are allowed at the same time upon the line. Is injured innocence, with her diamond necklace, to lie at the mercy of an aristocrat? Forbid it, Heaven and the Cheap Press! The twenty captains slip unobserved into the engine-house, steal an engine, and forth upon the Dover line! As well as I can gather, there were no stations and no pointsmen on this route to Dover, which must in consequence be quick and safe. One thing it had in common with other and less simple railways, it had a line of telegraph wires; and these the twenty captains decided to destroy. One of them, you will not be surprised to learn, had a coil of rope – in his pocket, I suppose; another – again I shall not surprise you – was an Irishman and given to blundering. One end of the line was made fast to a telegraph post; one (by the Irishman) to the engine: all aboard – full steam ahead – a double crash, and there was the telegraph post upon the ground, and here – mark my HAYWARD! – was something carried away upon the engine. All eyes turn to see what it is: an integral part of the machinery! There is now no means of reducing speed; on thunders the engine, full steam ahead, down this remarkable route to Dover; on speed the twenty captains, not very easy in their minds. Presently, the driver of the second special (the aristocrat's) looks behind him, sees an engine on his track, signals, signals in vain, finds himself being overhauled, pokes up his fire and – full steam ahead in flight. Presently after, the driver of the first special (injured innocence's) looks behind, sees a special on his track and an engine on the track of the special, signals, signals in vain, and he too – full steam ahead in flight. Such a day on the Dover line! But at last the second special smashes into the first, and the engine into both; and for my part, I think there was an end of that romance. But HAYWARD was by this time fast asleep: not a life was lost; not only that, but the various parties recovered consciousness and resumed their wild career (only now, of course, on foot and across country) in the precise original order: injured innocence leading by a length, damnable aristocrat with still more damnable valet (like one man) a good second, and the twenty captains (again like one man) a bad third; so that here was the story going on again just as before, and this appalling catastrophe on the Dover line reduced to the proportions of a morning call. The feelings of the company (it is true) are not dwelt upon.

Now, I do not mean that *Tom Holt* is quite such high-flying folly as *The Twenty Captains*; for it is no such thing, nor half so entertaining. Still it flowed from the same irresponsible brain; still it was the mere drowsy divagation of a man in bed, now tedious, now extravagant – always acutely untrue to life as it is, often pleasantly coincident with childish hopes of what life ought to be – as (for instance) in the matter of that little pleasure-boat, rigged, to every block and rope, as a full-rigged ship, in which Tom goes sailing – happy child! And this was the work that an actual tarry seaman recommended for a picture of his own existence!

II

It was once my fortune to have an interview with Mr HAYWARD's publisher: a very affable gentleman in a very small office in a shady court off Fleet Street. We had some talk together of the works he issued and the authors who supplied them; and it was strange to hear him talk for all the world as one of our publishers might have talked of one of us, only with a more obliging frankness, so that the private life of these great men was more or less unveiled to me. So and so (he told me, among other things) had demanded an advance upon a novel, had laid out the sum (apparently on spirituous drinks) and refused to finish the work. 'We had to put it in the hands of BRACEBRIDGE HEMMING,' said the publisher with a chuckle: 'he finished it.' And then with conviction: 'A most reliable author, BRACEBRIDGE HEMMING.'[5] I have no doubt the name is new to the reader; it was not so to me. Among these great men of the dust there is a touching ambition which punishes itself; not content with such glory as comes to them, they long for the glory of being bound – long to invade, between six boards, the homes of that aristocracy whose manners they so often find occasion to expose; and sometimes (once in a long lifetime) the gods give them this also, and they appear in the orthodox three volumes and are fleered at in the critical press, and lie quite unread in circulating libraries. One such work came in my mind: *The Bondage of Brandon*, by BRACEBRIDGE HEMMING. I had not found much pleasure in the volumes; but I was the more glad to think that Mr Hemming's name was quite a household word, and himself quoted for 'a reliable author,' in his own literary circles.

On my way westward from this interview, I was aware of a first floor in Fleet Street rigged up with wire window blinds, brass straps, and gilt lettering: Office for the sale of the works of PIERCE EGAN.[6] 'Ay, Mr EGAN,' thought I, 'and have you an office all to yourself!' And then remembered that he too had once revelled in three volumes: *The Flower of the Flock* the book was called, not without pathos for the considerate mind; but even the flower of Egan's flock was not good enough for the critics or the circulating libraries, so that I purchased my own copy, quite unread, for three shillings at a railway bookstall. Poor dogs, I thought, what ails you, that you should have the desire of this fictitious upper popularity, made by hack journalists and countersigned by yawning girls? Yours is the more true. Your butcher, the landlady at your seaside lodgings – if you can afford that indulgence, the barmaid whom you doubtless court, even the Rates and Taxes that besiege your door, have actually read your tales and actually know your names. There was a waiter once (or so the story goes) who knew not the name of Tennyson: that of HEMMING perhaps had brought the light into his eyes, or VILES perhaps, or ERRYM, or the great J. F. SMITH, or the unutterable Reynolds, to whom even here I must deny his capitals.[7] – Fancy if you can (thought I), that I languish under the reverse of your complaint; and being an upper class author, bound and criticised, long for the penny number and the weekly woodcut!

Well, I know that glory now. I have tried and on the whole I have failed: just as EGAN and HEMMING failed in circulating libraries. It is my consolation that Charles Reade nearly wrecked that valuable property, the *London Journal*, which must instantly fall back on Mr Egan; the king of us all, George Meredith, once staggered the circulation of a weekly newspaper.[8] A servant-maid used to come and boast when she had read another chapter of *Treasure Island*: that any pleasure should attend the exercise never crossed her thoughts. The same tale, in a penny paper of a high class, was mighty coldly looked upon by the delicate test of the correspondence column, I could see I was far to leeward; and there was one giant on the staff (a man with some talent, when he chose to use it) with whom I very early perceived it was in vain to rival. Yet I was thought well of on my penny paper for two reasons; one that the publisher was bent on raising the standard – a difficult enterprise in which he has to

a great extent succeeded; the other, because (like Bracebridge Hemming) I was 'a reliable author'. For our great men
of the dust are apt to be behind with copy.

III

How I came to be such a student of our penny press demands
perhaps some explanation. I was brought up on *Cassell's
Family Paper*; but the lady who was kind enough to read the
tales aloud to me was subject to sharp attacks of conscience.[9]
She took the *Family Paper* on confidence; the tales it
contained being Family Tales, not novels. But every now
and then, something would occur to alarm her finer senses;
she would express a well-grounded fear that the current
fiction was 'going to turn out a Regular Novel'; and the
family paper, with my pious approval, would be dropped. Yet
neither she nor I were wholly stoical; and when Saturday
came round, we would study the windows of the stationer
and try to fish out of subsequent woodcuts and their legends
the further adventures of our favourites. Many points are
here suggested for the casuist; definitions of the Regular
Novel and the Family Tale are to be desired; and quite a
paper might be written on the relative merit of reading a
fiction outright and lusting after it at the stationer's window.
The experience at least had a great effect upon my
childhood. This inexpensive pleasure mastered me. Each
new Saturday I would go from one newsvendor's window to
another till I was master of the weekly gallery and had
thoroughly digested 'The Baronet Unmasked,' 'So and so
approaching the Mysterious House,' 'The Discovery of the
Dead Body in the Blue Marl Pit,' 'Dr. Vargas Removing the
Senseless Body of Fair Lilias,' and whatever other snatch of
unknown story and glimpse of unknown characters that
gallery afforded.[10] I do not know that I ever enjoyed fiction
more; those books that we have (in such a way) avoided
reading, are all so excellently written! And in early years, we
take a book for its material, and act as own artists, keenly
realising that which pleases us, leaving the rest aside. I never
supposed that a book was to command me until, one
disastrous day of storm, the heaven full of turbulent vapours,
the streets full of the squalling of the gale, the windows

resounding under bucketfuls of rain, my mother read aloud to me *Macbeth*. I cannot say I thought the experience agreeable; I far preferred the ditch-water stories that a child could dip and skip and doze over, stealing at times materials for play; it was something new and shocking to be thus ravished by a giant, and I shrank under the brutal grasp. But the spot in memory is still sensitive; nor do I ever read that tragedy but I hear the gale howling up the valley of the Leith.

All this while I would never buy upon my own account; pence were scarce, conscience busy; and I would study the pictures and dip into the exposed columns, but not buy. My fall was brought about by a truly romantic incident. Perhaps the reader knows Neidpath Castle, where it stands, bosomed in hills, on a green promontory; Tweed at its base running through all the gamut of a busy river, from the pouring shallow to the brown pool.[11] In the days when I was thereabout, and that part of the earth was made a heaven to me by many things now lost, by boats, and bathing, and the fascination of streams, and the delights of comradeship, and those (surely the prettiest and simplest) of a boy and girl romance – in those days of Arcady there dwelt in the upper story of the castle one whom I believe to have been the gamekeeper on the estate. The rest of the place stood open to incursive urchins; and there, in a deserted chamber, we found some half-a-dozen numbers of *Black Bess, or the Knight of the Road*, a work by EDWARD VILES.[12] So far as we are aware, no one had visited that chamber (which was in a turret) since Lambert blew in the doors of the fortress with contumelious English cannon.[13] Yet it could hardly have been Lambert (in whatever hurry of military operations) who had left these samples of romance; and the idea that the gamekeeper had anything to do with them was one that we discouraged. Well, the offence is now covered by prescription; we took them away; and in the shade of a contiguous fir-wood, lying on blaeberries, I made my first acquaintance with the art of Mr Viles. From this author, I passed on to MALCOLM J. ERRYM (the name to my present scrutiny suggesting an anagram on Merry), author of *Edith the Captive*, *The Treasures of St. Mark*, *A Mystery in Scarlet*, *George Barington*, *Sea-drift*, *Townsend the Runner*, and a variety of other well-named romances.[14] Memory may play me false, but I believe there was a kind of merit about Errym. The *Mystery in Scarlet* runs in my mind to this day; and if any hunter after autographs (and I think the world is full of such) can lay his hands on a copy even imperfect, and will send it to me in the care of Messrs. Scribner, my gratitude (the muse consenting) will even drop into poetry. For I have a curiosity to know what the Mystery in Scarlet was, and to renew acquaintance with King George and his valet Norris, who were the chief figures in the work and may be said to have risen in every page superior to history and the ten commandments. Hence I passed on to Mr EGAN, whom I trust the reader does not confuse with the author of *Tom and Jerry*; the two are quite distinct, though I have sometimes suspected they were father and son.[15] I never enjoyed EGAN as I did ERRYM but this was possibly a want of taste, and EGAN would do. Thence again I was suddenly brought face to face with Mr Reynolds. A school-fellow, acquainted with my debasing tastes, supplied me with *The Mysteries of London*, and I fell back revolted.[16] The same school-fellow (who seems to have been a devil of a fellow) supplied me about the same time with one of those contributions to literature (and even to art) from which the name of the publisher is modestly withheld. It was a far more respectable work than *The Mysteries of London*. J. F. SMITH when I was a child, ERRYM when I was a boy, HAYWARD when I had attained to man's estate, these I read for pleasure; the others, down to SYLVANUS COBB, I have made it my business to know (as far as my endurance would support me) from a sincere interest in human nature and the art of letters.[17]

IV

What kind of talent is required to please this mighty public? that was my first question, and was soon amended with the words, 'if any.' J. F. SMITH was a man of undeniable talent, ERRYM and HAYWARD have a certain spirit, and even in EGAN the very tender might recognise the rudiments of a sort of literary gift; but the cases on the other side are quite conclusive. Take Hemming, or the dull ruffian Reynolds , or Sylvanus Cobb, of whom perhaps I have only seen unfortunate examples – they seem not to have the talents of a rabbit, and why any one should read them is a thing that passes wonder. A plain-spoken and possibly high-thinking critic might here perhaps return upon me with my own expressions. And he would have missed the point. For I and my fellows have no such popularity to be accounted for. The reputation of an upper-class author is made for him at dinner-tables and nursed in newspaper paragraphs, and, when all is done, amounts to no great matter. We call it popularity, surely in a pleasant error. A flippant writer in the *Saturday Review* expressed a doubt if I had ever cherished a 'genteel' illusion; in truth I never had many, but this was one – and I have lost it.[18] Once I took the literary author at his own esteem; I behold him now like one of those gentlemen who read their own MS. descriptive poetry aloud to wife and babes around the evening hearth; addressing a mere parlour coterie and quite unknown to the great world outside the villa windows. At such pigmy reputation, Reynolds or COBB, or Mrs SOUTHWORTH can afford to smile.[19] By spontaneous public vote, at a cry from the unorganic masses, these great ones of the dust were laurelled. And for what?

Ay, there is the question: For what? How is this great honour gained? Many things have been suggested. The people (it has been said) like rapid narrative. If so, the taste is recent, for both Smith and Egan were leisurely writers. It has been said they like incident, not character. I am not so sure. G. P. R. James was an upper-class author, J. F. Smith a penny pressman; the two are in some ways not unlike; but – here is the curiosity – James made far the better story, Smith was far the more successful with his characters. Each (to bring the parallel home) wrote a novel called *The Stepmother*; each introduced a pair of old maids; and let any one study the result! James's *Stepmother* is a capital tale, but Smith's old maids are like Trollope at his best.[20] It is said again that the people like crime. Certainly they do. But the great ones of the dust have no monopoly of that, and their less fortunate rivals hammer away at murder and abduction unapplauded.

I return to linger about my seaman on the Atlantic liner. I shall be told he is exceptional. I am tempted to think, on the other hand, that he may be normal. The critical attitude, whether to books or life – how if that were the true exception? How if *Tom Holt's Log*, surreptitiously perused by a harbour-side, had been the means of sending my mariner to sea? How if he were still unconsciously expecting the Tom Holt part of the business to begin – perhaps to-morrow? How, even, if he had never yet awakened to the discrepancy between that singular picture and the facts? Let us take another instance. *The Young Ladies' Journal* is an elegant miscellany which I have frequently observed in the possession of the barmaid.[21] In a lone house on a moorland, I was once supplied with quite a considerable file of this production and (the weather being violent) devoutly read it. The tales were not ill done; they were well abreast of the average tale in a circulating library; there was only one difference, only one thing to remind me I was in the land of penny numbers instead of the parish of three volumes: Disguise it as the authors pleased (and they showed ingenuity in doing so) it was always the same tale they must relate: the tale of a poor girl ultimately married to a peer of the realm or (at the worst) a baronet. The circumstance is not common in life; but how familiar to the musings of the barmaid! The tales were not true to what men see; they were true to what the readers dreamed.

Let us try to remember how fancy works in children; with what selective partiality it reads, leaving often the bulk of the book unrealised, but fixing on the rest and living it; and what a passionate impotence it shows – what power of adoption, what weakness to create. It seems to be not much otherwise with uneducated readers. They long, not to enter into the lives of others, but to behold themselves in changed situations, ardently but impotently preconceived. The imagination (save the mark!) of the popular author here comes to the rescue, supplies some body of circumstances to these phantom aspirations, and conducts the readers where they will. Where they will: that's the point; elsewhere they will not follow. When I was a child, if I came on a book in which the characters wore armour, it fell from my hand; I had no criterion of merit, simply that one decisive taste, that my fancy refused to linger in the middle ages. And the mind of the uneducated reader is mailed with similar restriction. So it is that we must account for a thing otherwise unaccountable: the popularity of some of these great ones of the dust. In defect of any other gift, they have instinctive sympathy with the popular mind. They can thus supply to the shop-girl and the shoe-black vesture cut to the pattern of their naked fancies, and furnish them with welcome scenery and properties for autobiographical romancing.

Even in readers of an upper class, we may perceive the traces of a similar hesitation; even for them a writer may be too exotic. The villain, even the heroine, may be a Feejee islander, but only on condition the hero is one of ourselves. It is pretty to see the thing reversed in the Arabian tale (Torrens or Burton – the tale is omitted in popular editions) where the Moslem hero carries off the Christian amazon; and in the exogamous romance, there lies interred a good deal of human history and human nature.[22] But the question of exogamy is foreign to the purpose. Enough that we are not readily pleased without a character of our own race and language; so that, when the scene of a romance is laid on any distant soil, we look with eagerness and confidence for the coming of the English traveller. With the readers of the penny-press the thing goes further. Burning as they are to penetrate into the homes of the peerage, they must still be conducted there by some character of their own class, into whose person they cheerfully migrate for the time of reading. Hence the poor governesses supplied in the *Young Ladies' Journal*. Hence these dreary virtuous *ouvriers and ouvrières* of Xavier de Montépin.[23] He can do nothing with them and he is far too clever not to be aware of that. When he writes for the *Figaro*, he discards these venerable puppets and doubtless glories in their absence; but so soon as he must address the great audience of the halfpenny journal, out come the puppets and are furbished up, and take to drink again, and are once more reclaimed, and once more falsely accused. See them for what they are – Montépin's decoys; without these he could not make his public feel at home in the houses of the fraudulent bankers and the wicked dukes.

The reader, it has been said, migrates into such characters for the time of reading: under their name escapes the narrow prison of the individual career, and sates his avidity for other lives. To what extent he ever emigrates again, and how far the fancied careers react upon the true one, it would fill another paper to debate. But the case of my sailor shows their grave importance. 'Tom Holt does not apply to me,' thinks our dully-imaginative boy by the harbour-side, 'for I am not a sailor. But if I go to sea it will apply completely.' And he does go to sea. He lives surrounded by the fact, and does not observe it. He cannot realise, he cannot make a tale of his own life; which crumbles in discrete impressions even as he lives it, and slips between the fingers of his memory like sand. It is not this that he considers in his rare hours of rumination, but that other life, which was all lit up for him by the humble talent of a Hayward – that other life which, God knows, perhaps he still believes that he is leading – the life of Tom Holt.

Letter To A Young Gentleman
Who Proposes To Embrace The Career Of Art

✳

This essay was again part of the series published in *Scribner's Magazine*, written while Stevenson was at Saranac. It appeared in September 1888, and was reprinted in *Across the Plains* and in Tusitala 28, under *Essays Literary and Critical*. There it is followed by an essay, 'On the Choice of a Profession', which includes a note from Lloyd Osbourne, explaining that while it had long been supposed to be a draft for 'Letter to a Young Gentleman', it is in fact a separate piece of work, hitherto unpublished, which he suggests had been suppressed by the author and others as being 'too cynical, too sombre in tone, too out of keeping with the helpful philosophy always associated with R.L.S.' (p. 12). The subject of a profession, and the value of that profession, was however a subject which had clearly preoccupied Stevenson for many years. Apart from the essays included here which touch on that issue, he had also submitted an essay of similar content to Sir Leslie Stephen at the *Cornhill* in 1879.

Stevenson's friend, W. H. Low, also wrote, at Stevenson's suggestion, 'A Letter to the Same Young Gentleman' to follow in the September issue of *Scribner's*. The subject as Low describes it in *A Chronicle of Friendships*, had been 'an old quarrel between us, a quarrel which, even today, I cannot recall without wonder, that one who, like him, loved as the breath of life every exercise of the artist's faculty . . . could in the same breath assimilate him with her who sells her honour, and call the artist a son of joy' (p. 413). Stevenson was excited by the idea, having felt that none of his essays in the magazine had prompted the level of debate raised around his dialogue with Henry James some years earlier, and which he had hoped for in these pieces. Both Low and Stevenson discuss the relationship between artistic standards, production, and commercial pressures – subjects of increasing concern in the period. Stevenson's image of the writer as prostitute, however, disturbed some of his critics.

Letter To A Young Gentleman Who Proposes To Embrace The Career Of Art[1]

With the agreeable frankness of youth, you address me on a point of some practical importance to yourself and (it is even conceivable) of some gravity to the world: Should you or should you not become an artist? It is one which you must decide entirely for yourself; all that I can do is to bring under your notice some of the materials of that decision; and I will begin, as I shall probably conclude also, by assuring you that all depends on the vocation.

To know what you like is the beginning of wisdom and of old age. Youth is wholly experimental. The essence and charm of that unquiet and delightful epoch is ignorance of self as well as ignorance of life. These two unknowns the young man brings together again and again, now in the airiest touch, now with a bitter hug; now with exquisite pleasure, now with cutting pain; but never with indifference, to which he is a total stranger, and never with that near kinsman of indifference, contentment. If he be a youth of dainty senses or a brain easily heated, the interest of this series of experiments grows upon him out of all proportion to the pleasure he receives. It is not beauty that he loves, nor pleasure that he seeks, though he may think so; his design and his sufficient reward is to verify his own existence and taste the variety of human fate. To him, before the razor-edge of curiosity is dulled, all that is not actual living and the hot chase of experience wears a face of a disgusting dryness difficult to recall in later days; or if there be any exception – and here destiny steps in – it is in those moments when, wearied or surfeited of the primary activity of the senses, he calls up before memory the image of transacted pains and pleasures. Thus it is that such an one shies from all cut-and-dry professions, and inclines insensibly toward that career of art which consists only in the tasting and recording of experience.

This, which is not so much a vocation for art as an impatience of all other honest trades, frequently exists alone; and so existing, it will pass gently away in the course of years. Emphatically, it is not to be regarded, it is not a vocation, but a temptation; and when your father the other day so fiercely and (in my view) so properly discouraged your ambition, he was recalling not improbably some similar passage in his own experience. For the temptation is perhaps nearly as common as the vocation is rare. But again we have vocations which are imperfect; we have men whose minds are bound up, not so much in any art, as in the general *ars artium* and common base of all creative work; who will now dip into painting, and now study counterpoint, and anon will be inditing a sonnet: all these with equal interest, all often with genuine knowledge.[2] And of this temper, when it stands alone, I find it difficult to speak; but I should counsel such an one to take to letters, for in literature (which drags with so wide a net) all his information may be found some day useful, and if he should go on as he has begun, and turn at last into the critic, he will have learned to use the necessary tools. Lastly we come to those vocations which are at once decisive and precise; to the men who are born with the love of pigments, the passion of drawing, the gift of music, or the impulse to create with words, just as other and perhaps the same men are born with the love of hunting, or the sea, or horses, or the turning-lathe. These are predestined; if a man love the labour of any trade apart from any question of success or fame, the gods have called him. He may have the general vocation too: he may have a taste for all the arts, and I think he often has, but the mark of his calling is this laborious partiality for one, this inextinguishable zest in its technical successes, and (perhaps above all) a certain candour of mind, to take his very trifling enterprise with a gravity that would befit the cares of empire, and to think the smallest improvement worth accomplishing at any expense of time and industry. The book, the statue, the sonata, must be gone upon with the unreasoning good faith and the unflagging spirit of children at their play. *Is it worth doing?* – when it shall have occurred to any artist to ask himself that question, it is implicitly answered in the negative. It does not occur to the child as he plays at being a pirate on the dining-room sofa, nor to the hunter as he pursues his quarry; and the candour of the one and the ardour of the other should be united in the bosom of the artist.

If you recognise in yourself some such decisive taste, there is no room for hesitation: follow your bent. And observe (lest I should too much discourage you) that the disposition does not usually burn so brightly at the first, or rather not so constantly. Habit and practice sharpen gifts; the necessity of toil grows less disgusting, grows even welcome in the course of years; a small taste (if it be only genuine) waxes with indulgence into an exclusive passion. Enough, just now, if you can look back over a fair interval, and see that your chosen art has a little more than held its own among the thronging interests of youth. Time will do the rest, if devotion help it; and soon your every thought will be engrossed in that beloved occupation.

But even with devotion, you may remind me, even with unfaltering and delighted industry, many thousand artists spend their lives, if the result be regarded, utterly in vain: a thousand artists, and never one work of art. But the vast mass of mankind are incapable of doing anything reasonably well, art among the rest. The worthless artist would not improbably have been a quite incompetent baker. And the artist, even if he does not amuse the public, amuses himself; so that there will always be one man the happier for his vigils. This is the practical side of art: its inexpugnable fortress for the true practitioner. The direct returns – the wages of the trade – are small, but the indirect – the wages of the life – are incalculably great. No other business offers a man his daily bread upon such joyful terms. The soldier and the explorer have moments of a worthier excitement, but they are purchased by cruel hardships and periods of tedium that beggar language. In the life of the artist there need be no hour without its pleasure. I take the author, with whose career I am best acquainted; and it is true he works in a rebellious material, and that the act of writing is cramped and trying both to the eyes and the temper; but remark him in his study, when matter crowds upon him and words are not wanting – in what a continual series of small successes time flows by; with what a sense of power as of one moving mountains, he marshals his petty characters; with what pleasures, both of the ear and eye, he sees his airy structure growing on the page; and how he labours in a craft to which the whole material of his life is tributary, and which opens a door to all his tastes, his loves, his hatreds, and his convictions, so that what he writes is only what he longed to utter. He may have enjoyed many things in this big, tragic playground of the world; but what shall he have enjoyed more fully than a morning of successful work? Suppose it ill paid: the wonder is it should be paid at all. Other men pay, and pay dearly, for pleasures less desirable.

Nor will the practice of art afford you pleasure only; it affords besides an admirable training. For the artist works entirely upon honour. The public knows little or nothing of those merits in the quest of which you are condemned to spend the bulk of your endeavours. Merits of design, the merit of first-hand energy, the merit of a certain cheap accomplishment which a man of the artistic temper easily acquires – these they can recognise, and these they value. But to those more exquisite refinements of proficiency and finish, which the artist so ardently desires and so keenly feels, for which (in the vigorous words of Balzac) he must toil 'like a miner buried in a landslip,' for which, day after day, he recasts and revises and rejects – the gross mass of the public must be ever blind.[3] To those lost pains, suppose you attain the highest pitch of merit, posterity may possibly do justice; suppose, as is so probable, you fail by even a hair's breadth of the highest, rest certain they shall never be observed. Under the shadow of this cold thought, alone in his studio, the artist must preserve from day to day his constancy to the ideal. It is this which makes his life noble; it is by this that the practice of his craft strengthens and matures his character; it is for this that even the serious countenance of the great emperor was turned approvingly (if only for a moment) on the followers of Apollo, and that sternly gentle voice bade the artist cherish his art.

And here there fall two warnings to be made. First, if you are to continue to be a law to yourself, you must beware of the first signs of laziness.[4] This idealism in honesty can only he supported by perpetual effort; the standard is easily lowered, the artist who says '*It will do*,' is on the downward path; three or four pot-boilers are enough at times (above all at wrong times) to falsify a talent, and by the practice of journalism a man runs the risk of becoming wedded to cheap finish. This is the danger on the one side; there is not less upon the other. The consciousness of how much the artist is (and must be) a law to himself, debauches the small heads. Perceiving recondite merits very hard to attain, making or swallowing artistic formulae, or perhaps falling in love with some particular proficiency of his own, many artists forget the end of all art: to please. It is doubtless tempting to exclaim against the ignorant bourgeois; yet it should not be forgotten, it is he who is to pay us, and that (surely on the face of it) for services that he shall desire to have performed. Here also, if properly considered, there is a question of transcendental honesty. To give the public what they do not want, and yet expect to be supported: we have there a strange pretension, and yet not uncommon, above all with painters. The first duty in this world is for a man to pay his way; when that is quite accomplished, he may plunge into what eccentricity he likes; but emphatically not till then. Till then, he must pay assiduous court to the bourgeois who carries the purse. And if in the course of these capitulations he shall falsify his talent, it can never have been a strong one, and he will have preserved a better thing than talent – character. Or if he be of a mind so independent that he cannot stoop to this necessity, one course is yet open: he can desist from art, and follow some more manly way of life.

I speak of a more manly way of life, it is a point on which I must be frank. To live by a pleasure is not a high calling; it involves patronage, however veiled; it numbers the artist, however ambitious, along with dancing-girls and billiard-markers. The French have a romantic evasion for one employment, and call its practitioners the Daughters of Joy.[5] The artist is of the same family, he is of the Sons of Joy, chose his trade to please himself, gains his livelihood by pleasing others, and has parted with something of the sterner dignity of man. Journals but a little while ago declaimed against the Tennyson peerage; and this Son of Joy was blamed for condescension when he followed the example of Lord Lawrence and Lord Cairns and Lord Clyde.[6] The poet was more happily inspired; with a better modesty he accepted the honour; and anonymous journalists have not yet (if I am to believe them) recovered the vicarious disgrace to their profession. When it comes to their turn, these gentlemen can do themselves more justice; and I shall be glad to think of it;

for to my barbarian eyesight, even Lord Tennyson looks somewhat out of place in that assembly. There should be no honours for the artist; he has already, in the practice of his art, more than his share of the rewards of life; the honours are pre-empted for other trades, less agreeable and perhaps more useful.[7]

But the devil in these trades of pleasing is to fail to please. In ordinary occupations, a man offers to do a certain thing or to produce a certain article with a merely conventional accomplishment, a design in which (we may almost say) it is difficult to fail. But the artist steps forth out of the crowd and proposes to delight: an impudent design, in which it is impossible to fail without odious circumstances. The poor Daughter of Joy, carrying her smiles and finery quite unregarded through the crowd, makes a figure which it is impossible to recall without a wounding pity. She is the type of the unsuccessful artist. The actor, the dancer, and the singer must appear like her person, and drain publicly the cup of failure. But though the rest of us escape this crowning bitterness of the pillory, we all court in essence the same humiliation. We all profess to be able to delight. And how few of us are! We all pledge ourselves to be able to continue to delight. And the day will come to each, and even to the most admired, when the ardour shall have declined and the cunning shall be lost, and he shall sit by his deserted booth ashamed. Then shall he see himself condemned to do work for which he blushes to take payment. Then (as if his lot were not already cruel) he must lie exposed to the gibes of the wreckers of the press, who earn a little bitter bread by the condemnation of trash which they have not read, and the praise of excellence which they cannot understand.

And observe that this seems almost the necessary end at least of writers. *Les Blancs et les Bleus* (for instance) is of an order of merit very different from *Le Vicomte de Bragelonne*; and if any gentleman can bear to spy upon the nakedness of *Castle Dangerous*, his name I think is Ham: let it be enough for the rest of us to read of it (not without tears) in the pages of Lockhart.[8] Thus in old age, when occupation and comfort are most needful, the writer must lay aside at once his pastime and his breadwinner. The painter indeed, if he succeed at all in engaging the attention of the public, gains great sums and can stand to his easel until a great age without dishonourable failure. The writer has the double misfortune to be ill-paid while he can work, and to be incapable of working when he is old. It is thus a way of life which conducts directly to a false position.

For the writer (in spite of notorious examples to the contrary) must look to be ill-paid. Tennyson and Montépin make handsome livelihoods; but we cannot all hope to be Tennyson, and we do not all perhaps desire to be Montépin.[9] If you adopt an art to be your trade, weed your mind at the outset of all desire of money. What you may decently expect, if you have some talent and much industry, is such an income as a clerk will earn with a tenth or perhaps a twentieth of your nervous output. Nor have you the right to look for more; in the wages of the life, not in the wages of the trade, lies your reward; the work is here the wages. It will be seen I have little sympathy with the common lamentations of the artist class. Perhaps they do not remember the hire of the field labourer; or do they think no parallel will lie? Perhaps they have never observed what is the retiring allowance of a field officer; or do they suppose their contributions to the arts of pleasing more important than the services of a colonel? Perhaps they forget on how little Millet was content to live; or do they think, because they have less genius, they stand excused from the display of equal virtues? But upon one point there should be no dubiety: if a man be not frugal, he has no business in the arts. If he be not frugal, he steers directly for that last tragic scene of *le vieux saltimbanque*; if he be not frugal, he will find it hard to continue to be honest.[10] Some day, when the butcher is knocking at the door, he may be tempted, he may be obliged, to turn out and sell a slovenly piece of work. If the obligation shall have arisen through no wantonness of his own, he is even to be commended; for words cannot describe how far more necessary it is that a man should support his family, than that he should attain to – or preserve – distinction in the arts. But if the pressure comes through his own fault, he has stolen, and stolen under trust, and stolen (which is the worst of all) in such a way that no law can reach him.

And now you may perhaps ask me, if the debutant artist is to have no thought of money, and if (as is implied) he is to

expect no honours from the State, he may not at least look
forward to the delights of popularity? Praise, you will tell me,
is a savoury dish. And in so far as you may mean the
countenance of other artists, you would put your finger on
one of the most essential and enduring pleasures of the career
of art. But in so far as you should have an eye to the
commendations of the public or the notice of the newspapers, be sure you would but be cherishing a dream. It is
true that in certain esoteric journals the author (for instance)
is duly criticised, and that he is often praised a great deal
more than he deserves, sometimes for qualities which he
prided himself on eschewing, and sometimes by ladies and
gentlemen who have denied themselves the privilege of
reading his work. But if a man be sensitive to this wild praise,
we must suppose him equally alive to that which often
accompanies and always follows it – wild ridicule. A man
may have done well for years, and then he may fail; he will
hear of his failure. Or he may have done well for years, and
still do well, but the critics may have tired of praising him, or
there may have sprung up some new idol of the instant, some
'dust a little gilt', to whom they now prefer to offer
sacrifice.[11] Here is the obverse and the reverse of that empty
and ugly thing called popularity. Will any man suppose it
worth the gaining?[12]

NOTES

*

Notes

✳

Child's Play

1 Written summer 1878 (according to Swearingen), published in the *Cornhill Magazine*, September 1878, vol. 38, pp. 352–9, and included in *Virginibus Puerisque* (1881), Tusitala 25.

2 'lie awake to listen to the wind': various biographers have commented on Stevenson's own night-terrors. Balfour quotes: 'Other night scenes connected with my ill-health were the little sallies of delirium that used to waken me out of a feverish sleep, in such agony of terror as, thank God, I have never suffered since.' (*Life* I, p. 34).

3 'it is surely no very cynical asperity': in a letter to Lord Chesterfield about his *Dictionary*, 7 February 1755, Samuel Johnson wrote: 'I hope it is no very cynical asperity not to confess obligations where no benefit has been received . . .'

4 'Not Théophile Gautier, not Flaubert . . .': Théophile Gautier (1811–72): French writer and romanticist, associated with 'art for art's sake' as a doctrine; Gustave Flaubert (1821–80): noted for narrative impersonality. 'The young man of Nain': biblical figure, about to be buried but raised from the dead by Christ (*Luke* 7:11–17).

5 'cousin': Robert Alan Mowbray Stevenson, known as Bob, Stevenson's friend in both childhood and adult life, and later an artist. The cousins first met in the winter of 1857.

6 Cormoran: Cornish giant who fell into pit dug by Jack the giant killer.

The Morality of the Profession of Letters

1 Written early in 1881 (Swearingen) and published in the *Fortnightly Review* 157, April 1881, pp. 513–20, and in *Essays Literary and Critical*, under 'Essays in the Art of Writing' (Tusitala 28). Very few changes were made, mainly punctuation; a few phrases were deleted.

2 'popular writer': the footnote to the Tusitala edition reveals the 'pleasant popular writer' to be James Payn. In 1881 Payn published an essay on 'Penny Fiction' in the *Nineteenth Century*. Payn (1830–98) was the editor of *Chambers's Journal* (1859–74) and the *Cornhill Magazine* (1882–96), as well as a highly successful novelist, essayist and poet.

3 'esurient': greedy.

4 'four great elders': the footnote in the *Fortnightly Review* reads: 'Since this

article was written, only three of these remain. But the other, being dead, yet speaketh.' Thomas Carlyle died in 1881.

5 'Corinthian': libertine/man about town.

6 'rare': 'rarer' in the *Fortnightly Review*.

7 'the fact which somebody': replaces 'what' in the *Fortnightly Review*. *Candide*: Voltaire's satire on optimism (1759).

8 'return of our representatives from Berlin': the Congress of Berlin (13 June–13 July 1878) was a significant gathering of European diplomats. Lord Beaconsfield (i.e. Disraeli) returned in triumph, claiming 'peace with honour'.

9 Stevenson's footnote reads: 'A footnote, at least, is due to the admirable example set before all young writers in the width of literary sympathy displayed by Mr Swinburne. He runs forth to welcome merit, whether in Dickens or Trollope, whether in Villon, Milton, or Pope. This is, in criticism, the attitude we should all seek to preserve, not only in that, but in every branch of literary work.'

10 Alfred de Musset: French playwright and poet (1810–57), known as a melancholic writer, the author of *Carmosine*; *Fantasia*.

11 'There is a time . . .': echoes of *Ecclesiastes* 3:1.

12 'Our fine old sea-captain': the popular author and naval officer, Captain Frederick Marryat (1792–1848), published *The King's Own* in 1830 and *Newton Forster, or the Merchant Service* in 1832.

13 '*entre-filet*': paragraph.

A Gossip on Romance

1 Written in February 1882 (Swearingen) and published in *Longman's Magazine* 1, November 1882, pp. 69–79. This was a new journal, the source of much excitement and secrecy as Stevenson described in his letters: 'It is destined for Longman who (dead secret) is bringing out a new Mag. (6d.) in the Autumn. Dead Secret: all his letters are three deep with masks and passwords, and I swear on a skull daily' (Letter to Sidney Colvin, February 1882, *Letters* II, p. 184). In March he was paid £9.00 for the article. When it was reprinted in *Memories and Portraits* (1887), few changes were made, except minor alterations to the punctuation. Part of one sentence, indicated below, was also rewritten. The essay is in Tusitala 29.

2 'an old wayside inn': inns, of course, are much featured in Stevenson's fiction, most notably in *Treasure Island* and *Kidnapped*.

3 'John Rann or Jerry Abershaw': Rann, known as 'Sixteen-string Jack Rann' was one of the last 'classic' highwaymen, and was hanged in 1774; Abershaw (1773–95) was an English highwayman who worked on Wimbledon Common and was hanged for shooting a constable. In 1885–6 Stevenson worked on a novel to be entitled *The Great North Road*, which was to have brought together a tale of highwaymen and the theme of Hamlet. It was, however, one of his many unfinished projects. In a letter of September 1881 he is also enthusiastic about *Jerry Abershaw: a Tale of Putney Heath* as a follow-up to *Treasure Island*: 'Jerry Abershaw – O what a title! Jerry Abershaw: d–n it sir, it's a poem.' (*Letters* II, p. 171).

4 *What Will He Do With It?*: a novel by Edward Bulwer-Lytton, published under the pseudonym of Pisistratus Caxton in 1858/9.

5 The (still unidentified) tale of a 'dark, tall, house at night, and people groping on the stairs' appears to prefigure the famous scene in *Kidnapped* when David

Balfour is sent (supposedly to his death) up an unlit and unfinished staircase in the House of Shaws.

6 Stevenson's own footnote to the *Memories and Portraits* edition reads: 'Since traced by many obliging correspondents to the gallery of Charles Kinglsey.' The reference is, however, to *Ravenshoe* by Henry Kingsley, ch. 48 (1862).

7 'Conduct is three parts of life, they say; but I think they put it high.' In *Longman's*: 'Conduct is three parts of life, but it is not all the four.'

8 'miching mallecho': sneaking mischief: *Hamlet* III,ii,134 (Arden edition).

9 'Burford Bridge', Stevenson had visited Burford in the Cotswolds with his parents in 1878, and made friends with George Meredith.

10 *The Antiquary*: Sir Walter Scott (1816).

11 'I think, a boat shall be put off . . .': Stevenson's own footnote to *Memories and Portraits* reads: 'Since the above was written I have tried to launch the boat with my own hands in *Kidnapped*. Some day perhaps, I may try a rattle at the shutters.'

12 'plastic part of literature': a phrase Stevenson used at the time in relation to visual arts. See October 1883, letter to Bob Stevenson: 'the problems of executive, plastic art'.

13 'of the present day': *Memories and Portraits* footnote: '1882'

14 'Sandy's Mull': this would appear to be a reference to the Scottish folk-song 'Sandy's Mill'.

15 'Mr Crawley': character in Trollope's *The Last Chronicle of Barset* (1867); 'Mr Melnotte': character in Trollope's *The Way We Live Now* (1875). A few years earlier Stevenson had written: 'Do you know who is my favourite author just now? How are the might fallen! Anthony Trollope. I batten on him; he is so nearly wearying you, and yet he never does . . .' (21 February 1878, *Letters* II, p. 45).

16 William Thackeray, *Vanity Fair* (1847–8); *The History of Henry Esmond, Esquire* (1852).

17 Daniel Defoe, *The Life And Strange And Surprising Adventures Of Robinson Crusoe*, (1719); Samuel Richardson, *Clarissa: or The History of a Young Lady* (1747–9). Defoe was part of the author's childhood reading, one of the writers to whom he played 'the sedulous ape' and, as he recognised, part of the inspiration for *Treasure Island*.

18 *Arabian Nights*: another strong influence from Stevenson's childhood reading. His own *New Arabian Nights*, published in serial form throughout 1878 and in book form in 1882, offers a much more ambiguous moral perspective than his source.

19 '*Monte Cristo*': Alexander Dumas, *The Count of Monte Cristo* (1844–5). Also part of his childhood reading, Dumas remained a powerful influence on Stevenson: see 'A Gossip on a Novel of Dumas's'.

20 'Lucy and Richard Feveril': George Meredith, *The Ordeal of Richard Feverel* (1859). Stevenson was greatly inspired by Meredith's fiction and encouraged in meetings with him. He rated *The Egoist* extremely highly. Spelling changes from 'Feverell' in *Longman's* to 'Feveril' in *Memories and Portraits*.

21 'Haydn and Consuelo': *characters in Consuelo* by George Sand (1842–3).

22 Clark Russell, *The Sailor's Sweetheart* (1881).

23 Johann David Wyss, *The Swiss Family Robinson*, published in German 1812–13 and translated into English a year later.

24 Jules Verne, *Mysterious Island* (1874).

25 'Eugène de Rastignac': one of the main characters in Balzac's *Comédie Humaine*.

26 *The Lady of the Lake*: Sir Walter Scott's romantic poem, published in 1810.

27 Sir Walter Scott, *The Pirate* (1821).

28 *Guy Mannering*, (1815): this Scott novel was one of the few novels kept by Stevenson's father at home in Heriot Row. The excerpt quoted is from Chapter 41.

29 Miss Braddon: this would appear to be one of several melodramatic version of *Guy Mannering* which were popular at the time.

'Mrs Todger's idea of a wooden leg': Mrs Todger is the owner of a London boarding-house in *Martin Chuzzlewit* by Charles Dickens. In Chapter 9, after Mr Pecksniff has imbibed too much and become rather sentimentally amorous, he states:

> 'The legs of the human subject, my friends, are a beautiful production. Compare them with wooden legs, and observe the difference between the anatomy of nature and the anatomy of art. Do you know . . . that I should very much like to see Mrs Todger's notion of a wooden leg, if perfectly agreeable to herself.'

30 'Elspeth of the Craigburnfoot': first appears as the Meiklebackit granny in *The Antiquary*, vol. 2, ch. 11 (ch. 26, *Edinburgh Edition of the Waverley Novels*) and as Elspeth o' the Craigburnfoot in ch. 27, *EEWN* (ch. 12. vol. 2).

A Note on Realism

1 'A Note on Realism' was written in the summer of 1883 and appeared in *The Magazine of Art*, 7 November 1883, pp. 24–8. Edited by W. E. Henley in the 1880s, the periodical promoted an aestheticism very much of its time, and drew upon graduates for its contributors, thus offering a new kind of journalistic writing. The essay, which Stevenson had just completed in October (see *Letters* II, pp. 270–2), was reprinted in *Essays Literary and Critical* without major changes, although the single footnote for the periodical piece was removed. The later version is followed here but the footnote is included under note 6 below.

2 'What to put in and what to leave out': the principle of selection and its importance is discussed in several essays: see 'A Humble Remonstrance' and 'A Chapter on Dreams'.

3 Sir Walter Scott (1771–1832), usually seen as the father of the historical novel, was a significant influence on Stevenson and he wrote much about his work: see 'A Gossip on Romance'. The fiction of Honoré de Balzac (1799–1850) was a frequent subject in Stevenson's letters at this time. In a letter to his cousin, he attacks Balzac's inclusion of detail as a misguided attempt to render the real:

> He was a man who never found his method. An inarticulate Shakespeare, smothered under forcible-feeble detail. It is astonishing to the riper mind how bad he is, how feeble, how untrue, how tedious; and of course, when he surrendered to his temperament, how good and powerful. And yet never plain nor clear. He could not consent to be dull, and thus became so. He would leave nothing undeveloped, and thus drowned out of sight of land amid the multitude of crying and incongruous details. (*Letters* II, pp. 270–2)

4 'At least in France': a reference to the French movement of Naturalism in prose fiction during the latter part of the nineteenth century, with Emile Zola as its

prime exponent, and Daudet and Maupassant as followers. It represented an attempt to move away from idealisation of experience, concentrating instead on everyday life and its documentation rather than the fabrication of plot. As Stevenson points out in the same paragraph, this led to an emphasis on what was seen as the 'sordid' (his phrase is 'rancid') elements of working-class life.

5 'Voltaire': pseudonym of Francois-Marie Arouet (1694–1778). Philosopher, satirist, poet, dramatist, his fiction is usually seen as an exposition of his philosophies, hence the quality of abstraction highlighted and admired by Stevenson.

6 Alphonse Daudet (1840–97). Of the Naturalist school, he depicted life in Paris and in his native Provence. A footnote in *The Magazine of Art* adds: 'There is an interesting chapter to be written on the history of this movement, with its deduction from Scott, through Balzac and Flaubert, to our own contemporaries, and in particular with the malign side-influence of Gautier.' (*The Magazine of Art* 26) Théophile Gautier was a Romantic poet, novelist and critic, associated with the 'art for art's sake' doctrine.

7 'Molière': Jean-Baptiste Poquelin (1622–73): Stevenson cites a range of characters used in Molière's classical French comedies.

8 Beulah: *Isaiah*, 62, 4. In *Pilgrim's Progress* the land of heavenly joy.

9 *Troilus and Cressida*: Shakespeare's tragi-comic reworking of Homer's tale.

10 'Ariel': spirit assistant to Prospero the magician in *The Tempest*.

11 'Mr Lang and Mr Dobson': Andrew Lang (1844–1912), essayist, poet, editor, reviewer, fellow-Scot and friend of Stevenson. After adverse criticism of an ambitious narrative poem, *Helen of Troy* (1882), he turned to increasingly light verse. Henry Austin Dobson (1840–1921), shared Lang's fondness for French verse forms, such as the triolet and rondeau.

12 *History of Henry Esmond, Esquire*: (1852) Thackeray's historical novel, retrospectively narrated by Esmond but mainly in the third person, and dealing with a series of historical episodes, including the Battle of the Boyne and the plot to restore the Old Pretender to the throne of Queen Anne. *Vanity Fair* (1847–8), offers a satirical picture of the Napoleonic wars, following the fortunes of a range of characters whom Thackeray himself describes as 'puppets'.

13 'tricks of workmanship': in galley proofs 'tricks of facture' was used but questioned in margins by Henley.

'A Penny Plain and Twopence Coloured'

1 Written, according to Swearingen, autumn 1883; first published in *The Magazine of Art*, April 1884, pp. 227–32; later included in *Memories and Portraits* (Tusitala, 29). *The Magazine of Art* was edited by W. E. Henley between 1881 and 1886. There is a letter from Henley in the Beinecke Collection describing an unfavourable reaction to the piece: 'The archangel thinks "Penny Plain" damn bad: hollow, put up, and ill written. So you may retire hurt.'(25 December 1883) The original essay included plentiful illustrations from Skelt, and a long paragraph referring to them, not included in the later version. (See note 13.)

2 'changed its name': Park's, Webb's, Redington's and Pollock's were among the fifty publishers who produced toy theatre sheets. As late as 1932 two shops in Hoxton, Webb's and Pollock's, still produced sheets from the original blocks.

3 'Mr Ionides': Alexander Ionides, described as a 'Victorian Onassis' was a wealthy Greek merchant. The Ionides family, expatriate in London, were sophisticated, wealthy and unconventional members of London artistic life. (See Ormond, pp. 98–102.)

4 These are all titles of popular melodramas. From Mullin *Victorian Plays: A Record of Significant Productions on the London Stage, 1837–90*, we can gain some idea of authorship and dates: *Aladdin*: n.a., performed Lyceum 1844; *The Red Rover*: E. Fitzball, perf. 1837; *The Blind Boy; or The Heir of Stanislaus*: J. Kenney, perf. 1839; *The Old Oak Chest*: J. M. Scott, perf. 1842; *The Wood Daemon*: n.a.; *Jack Sheppard*: J. B. Buckstone, perf. 1839; *The Miller and His Men*: I. Pocock, 1813; *Der Freischütz, or The Seven Charmed Bullets; The Smuggler, or The Innkeeper's Daughter*, n.a. perf. 1838; *The Forest of Bondy, or The Dog of Montergis*: W. Barrymore, perf. 1838; *Robin Hood, or The Hunters of Arlingford*, n.a., perf. 1838; *The Waterman*: C. Dibdin, 1774; *Richard I; My Poll and My Partner Joe*: J. T. Hawes, perf. 1837; *The Inchcape Bell, or The Dumb Sailor Boy of the Rocks*: E. Fitzball, perf. 1837; *Three-fingered Jack; The Maid of the Inn; The Battle of Waterloo*, and *The Conquest of Quatre Bras and Ligny*, n.a., perf. 1842.

5 The *crux* of Buridan's donkey: a philosophical question of whether a donkey placed exactly between two haystacks would starve to death, because it had no motive to go to one rather than the other, wrongly attributed to the French philosopher, Buridan.

6 'Much as I have travelled in these realms of gold': a slight paraphrase of the opening lines of Keats's 'On First Looking into Chapman's Homer'.

7 *The Floating Beacon, or The Wild Woman of the Wreck*: E. Fitzball, perf. 1838; *The Wreck Ashore, or The Bridegroom of the Sea*: J. B. Buckstone, perf. 1837; *Sixteen-String Jack*: various versions, perf. in 1840s: see also reference in 'A Gossip on Romance'. *Lodoiska*, n.a., perf. 1839; *Silver Palace . . .*; *The Echo of Westminster Bridge*, n.a., perf. 1838. (See Mullin.)

8 'O. Smith; Fitzball': O. Smith was an actor in melodrama, and the leading villain at the Adelphi Theatre, celebrated for his evil laugh. In his prefatory note to 'The Bottle Imp' in *Island Nights' Entertainments* (Tusitala 13), Stevenson refers to it as 'the root idea of a piece once rendered popular by the redoubtable O. Smith.' Edward Fitzball (1792–1873) was author of a vast number of popular English melodramas. Stevenson was shown a collection of melodramas, principally by Fitzball, when a guest of Sir Percy Shelley, which were then given to him after Shelley's death. Again in *Island Nights' Entertainments* mention is made of Fitzball by Fanny Stevenson in her introductory note, (Tusitala,13, pp. xi-xii), acknowledging his work as an influence on 'The Bottle Imp'.

9 'Transpontus': 'transpontine' – literally 'over the bridge' – came to refer to a style of drama made popular south of the Thames: melodramatic and sensationalist.

10 T. P. Cooke: Thomas Potter Cooke (1786–1864), an English actor known as 'Tippy Cooke', highly successful in melodramas such as *The Vampire* (1820) and *Black-Ey'd Susan* (1829).

11 Hyères: in the south of France, where the Stevensons lived between March 1883 and June 1884.

12 Cruikshank: George Cruikshank, caricaturist and illustrator; Jonathan Wild, English criminal, hanged at Tyburn in 1725, and inspiration for Fielding's satire, *Jonathan Wild*. *Jack Sheppard*, a melodrama by J. B. Buckstone, adapted from Harrison Ainsworth's novel of 1839, which depicted Jack's apprenticeship to Wild, was illustrated by Cruikshank.

13 *Der Freischütz*: a romantic opera by Weber.

14 The version in *The Magazine of Art* then contains the following paragraph, with numbered illustrations referred to in parentheses:

> From the treasures of Clarke of Garrick Street, that unrivalled merchant of Skeltery, we offer here for auld lang syne, a sheet or two of Skelt diminished. It was proper to recall the feeling of the sheets of characters; and to this end, as most familiar, that dear 'Miller and his Men' is put to contribution – even to Ravina the terrible (1), to Ribner's corpse (10), to a group of 'Robbers asleep' (14), to a trio of millers singing (12), to that terrific abduction piece (9), in which I call upon you to admire the extreme imbecility of the heroine's legs. Words could not palliate the cut-throat badness, nor words augment the charm, of these most innocent marionettes. I could not in honesty refuse you the explosion from the same romantic drama; it was always in the window, a decoy for children; here it is again (2), the old millstones flying as of yore. Follows from the 'Smuggler' (7) a sea and shore scape, delicately Skelty, ranking, I conceive, among his masterpieces. Please to remark the cottage architecture of Transpontus: the beacon, how nautical it is; the revenue cutter, how oak-hearted; and the clouds, on which I dare not dwell. Sea, rock and vegetation will equally reward the eye. I am capable myself of going on for ever: I have here an old street, a feast of gables; I have cots and castles, caves and forest glades, the rivers and the deep, roads winding and wooing the rapt eye, and vast and varied prospects rolled across by breeze and clouds; but I perceive the editor to frown on my exuberance, and I will conclude (6) with something in the grand style, prodigious wild, a true Salvator Skelt. It is a vile example, and had I the wood and cavern from 'The Old Oak Chest'(sc.1, pl.1) or the wolf's dingle from Der Freischütz, then indeed should you see Skelt assume the terrible and dip his brush in earthquake and eclipse. Then should you have the opportunity to appreciate my Skelt's idea of the mountain pine, a most romantic concept. But this tame and tasteless piece is the one example of his buskined Ossianic manner that my poor resources can command; and once more it should be welcome to your kind remembrance; for it is also one of the band of the immortal 'Miller'.

A Humble Remonstrance

1 Written in the autumn of 1884, 'A Humble Remonstrance' appeared in *Longman's Magazine* 5, December 1884, pp. 139–47. *Longman's Magazine*, a successor to *Fraser's Magazine*, ran from 1882–1905. As a monthly miscellany, it published fiction, including two serial novel instalments in each issue, poetry and critical articles. With its wide range of contributors, it was chiefly notable for its fiction. It was owned by the publishers, Longman's. The essay was reprinted in *Memories and Portraits* (1887), pp. 274–99, and it is this later version which is followed here. See Tusitala 29.

Stevenson's own note to the essay's title explains: 'This paper, which does not otherwise fit the present volume, is reprinted here as the proper continuation of the last.' The 'last' to which he refers is 'A Gossip on Romance'.

2 'recently': Stevenson's note indicates '1884' at this point. 'The Art of Fiction'

was published in *Longman's Magazine* 4, September 1884, pp. 502–21. 'Besant': Sir
Walter Besant (1836–1901) had already written several best-selling novels. His
most recent, *All Sorts and Conditions of Men* (1882), had drawn attention to the
terrible conditions of the poor. 'The Art of Fiction: A Lecture . . . With Notes and
additions' was published by Chatto & Windus in 1884. 'James': Henry James
(1843–1916) had by 1884 published several important novels, including *Roderick
Hudson* (1876), *The American* (1877), *Daisy Miller* (1879) and *Portrait of a Lady*
(1881). A full account of the correspondence between Stevenson and James can
be found in Janet Adam Smith (ed.) *Henry James and Robert Louis Stevenson: A
Record of Friendship and Criticism* (1948).

3 'Salvini': Tommaso Salvini (1829–1915) made an international reputation
playing Shakespeare's tragic heroes. In 1876 he played Macbeth in Edinburgh, in a
production not seen in London until 1884. Stevenson's review, 'Salvini's
Macbeth', was reprinted in *Essays Literary and Critical*. Mrs Florence A. MacCun
recalls sitting next to Stevenson at the production of Salvini's *Macbeth* in *I Can
Remember Robert Louis Stevenson*, ed. R. Masson, p. 19.

4 'Mr Mudie': Mudie's Lending Library was one of the great circulating libraries
of the second half of the nineteenth century. It played an important role, through
its influence on publication and distribution, in determining the range and nature
of fiction in popular circulation.

5 *The Lady of the Lake*: Sir Walter Scott's long narrative poem, published in
1810.

6 'Spenserian': Edmund Spenser (c. 1552–99), author of *The Faerie Queene*,
whose innovative stanza form was particularly appropriate to narrative verse.
'Gibbon': Edward Gibbon (1737–94), author of *The History of the Decline and Fall
of the Roman Empire* (1776–88), favoured a more wordy style of lengthy sentences.
'Reade': Charles Reade (1814–84), a popular novelist, adopted a style of cropped
prose for his fiction. At the time of writing, Reade, best-known for *The Cloister and
the Hearth* (1861), was a highly successful and respected novelist, seen as a major
figure by James and Swinburne, although his sensational fictions are now largely
unread.

7 *Don Juan*: the famous Spanish story of seduction, first dramatised by Gabriel
Tellez (1583–1648), and subsequently adapted by (among others) Mozart,
Pushkin, Bryon, Browning and Shaw. *Zanoni*: a novel of the occult by Edward
Bulwer-Lytton (1803–73), published in 1842. *The Scarlet Letter*: a romance of
conscience by the American Nathaniel Hawthorne (1804–64), published in 1850.
The Pilgrim's Progress: an allegory by John Bunyan, published between 1678 and
1684 – a major influence from Stevenson's early reading.

8 *Paradise Lost*: John Milton's famous epic, published in 1667, was translated into
French prose by Vicomte François-René de Chateaubriand (1768–1848). George
Gilfillan (1813–78) was an extremely prolific Scottish poet and critic with a wide
circle of literary acquaintances. The reference to *Paradise Lost*, however, remains
obscure. Gilfillan edited an edition of Milton's *Poetical Works* in 1853, and
reviewed Professor David Masson's *Life of John Milton*; he also corresponded with
the poet Sidney Dobell about Milton. None of these writers appears to have
produced a version in 'novel' form.

9 *Life of Johnson*: James Boswell (1740–95) produced *The Life of Samuel Johnson*, a
biographical account of his friend, in 1791. *Tom Jones*: Henry Fielding (1707–54)
published *Tom Jones* in 1749. This comic epic in prose, a departure from the
epistolary style of his contemporary, Richardson, presents a picaresque series of

adventures of its eponymous hero, from the perspective of a wry observer. Both texts, Stevenson appears to suggest, depend upon the organisation and selection of incidents, dialogue and character for the vivacity of their writing and the engagement they offer to the reader. Boswell's case is special because of his intimacy with his subject.

10 'Tacitus': Roman historian, b. AD 55, whose *Histories and Annals* offer insights into political events and human characters with the skills of a novelist or dramatist. 'Carlyle': Thomas Carlyle (1795–1881), historian and essayist, can also be seen as a figure who brought descriptive powers and literary skills to the writing of history. 'Michelet': Jules Michelet (1798–1874) was a French historian, whose *L'Histoire de France* is considered the most famous example of nineteenth-century romantic narrative history. 'Macaulay': Thomas Babington Macaulay (1800–59) was again a politician and historian who brought literary skills to the writing of history, acknowledging his debt to Scott. His *History of England* (1849–55) was a best-seller in the nineteenth century.

11 '*montibus aviis*': by flying too high – possibly a reference to Icarus.

12 'dazzle': in 'A Gossip on Romance' Stevenson uses a similar image to describe the process of reading: 'our mind filled with the busiest, kaleidoscopic dance of images, incapable of sleep or continuous thought'.

13 'told their stories round the savage camp-fire': E. M. Forster uses a similar example to illustrate the centrality of narrative in *Aspects of the Novel* (1927): 'The primitive audience was an audience of shock-heads, gaping round the camp-fire, fatigued with contending against the mammoth or the woolly rhinoceros, and only kept awake by suspense.' Stevenson's own point of reference might also have been that of the powerful Scottish oral tradition with which he (and literary predecessors such as Burns, Scott and Hogg) had been familiar.

14 'a little book about a quest for hidden treasure': *Treasure Island* was published in book form in 1883.

15 'Pisgah': mountain from which Moses saw the Promised Land. 'Get thee up into the top of Pisgah, and lift up thine eyes westward, and northward, and southward, and eastward, and behold it with thine eyes . . .' Deuteronomy 3. 27.

16 'a pirate is a beard, a pair of wide trousers and a liberal complement of pistols': in *Longman's* 5, 144: 'for him, a pirate is a beard in wide trousers and literally bristling with pistols'.

17 'the characters are portrayed only so far': again there are echoes of 'A Gossip on Romance' in which Stevenson claims: 'It is not character but incident that woos us out of our reserve.'

18 *Gil Blas*: picaresque narrative by the French novelists and playwright Alain-René Le Sage (1668–1747), translated into English by Tobias Smollett in 1749.

19 'The Author of Beltraffio': a story by Henry James first published in the June/ July issue of the *English Illustrated Magazine* in 1884. It was a particular favourite of Fanny Osbourne: the boy in the story reminded her of her own son who had died. It has been suggested that this story, about a marriage in which the wife despises her husband's writing and destroys her own son rather than let him be influenced by it, was inspired by the Stevensons' relationship, as an article in *Twentieth Century Magazine* by G. S. Hellman (January 1926), tried to argue. While certain descriptions of the writer's bohemian appearance may carry reminders of Stevenson, James's notebook for 1884 reveals that the idea came from an anecdote about J. A. Symonds. The story itself is, however, of particular interest in relation to the issues discussed in 'A Humble Remonstrance', in that 'Beltraffio' is

described as 'the most complete presentation that had yet been made of the gospel of art; it was a kind of aesthetic war-cry'. The story therefore explores issues of aesthetics in relation to literary form similar to those engaging Stevenson and James in debate.

20 *Rhoda Fleming*: George Meredith, a friend of, and influence upon, Stevenson, published *Rhoda Fleming* (to mixed responses) in 1865. In the later version of this essay Stevenson adds his own note to 'long out of print': 'Now no longer so, thank Heaven!'

Aldine: *The Aldine* was a journal of art and typography which ran from 1868 to 1879. It was consistently praised for its fine engravings and typography.

'Hardy's *Pair of Blue Eyes*': Thomas Hardy published *A Pair of Blue Eyes* in 1873. *Griffith Gaunt and The Double Marriage*: Charles Reade published the sensational fiction *Griffith Gaunt* in 1866. *The Double Marriage* (1867), a historical romance, first appeared in serial form as *White Lies* in the *London Journal* in 1857, but was based on a play, *The Double Marriage*, which was itself based on a play by Auguste Maquet entitled *Le Château Grantier*. Reade's play was first presented in London in 1867. 'Maquet': Auguste Maquet (1813–88) collaborated with Dumas in writing historical novels, mainly supplying the historical framework or bare bones of plot, and also published some novels of his own.

21 'Mrs Lovel': the 'fair witch' whose manipulative charms and duplicity are central to the plot of *Rhoda Fleming*.

22 *Duchesse de Langeais*: Honoré de Balzac wrote *The Duchesse de Langeais* as one of the 'scènes de la vie humaine' in his *Comédie Humaine*. The story is one of passion: a beautiful duchess in Paris society exploits the feelings of the Marquis de Montriveau but is broken-hearted when he appears to tire of her. She flees to a Carmelite convent where he eventually tracks her down. But when he attempts to kidnap her she is found dead in her cell, and is buried at sea. Stevenson had earlier criticised Balzac as a writer unable to select and organise his material: 'He would leave nothing undeveloped, and thus drowned out of sight of land amid the multitude of crying and incongruous details' (Letter to R. A. M. Stevenson, October 1883, *Letters* II, p. 271).

23 Of the essay Stevenson later wrote: 'I own I think the école bête, of which I am the champion, has the whip hand of the argument; but as James is to make a rejoinder, I must not boast. . . . I was terribly tied down to space, which has made the end congested and dull' (Letter to W. H. Low, 13 March 1885, *Letters* III, p. 40).

24 'since the above was written': Stevenson added the final section when the essay was reprinted in *Memories and Portraits* (1887).

'W. D. Howells': the American novelist William Dean Howells (1837–1920) began his writing career with comedies of manners but developed an interest in realistic characters grappling with ethical problems in such novels as *A Modern Instance* (1882) and *A Woman's Reason* (1883). He was a firm believer in literary realism and saw in it a democracy and equality lacking in other forms of writing. He also argued that art must serve morality. Howells had already had a slightly hostile encounter with Stevenson in 1882 when Stevenson – after reading *A Modern Instance* and deciding that the author's morality would prevent him from enjoying a planned visit in St-Marcel because Fanny was divorced – wrote to Howells that 'I desire to know no one who considers himself holier than my wife'. From 1886 to 1892 Howells wrote a literary column in *Harpers Monthly* under the title 'The Editor's Study'. In this he enjoyed attacking what he described as 'the babes of Romance'. In particular an essay of 1886 'Negative Realism: Stevenson, Balzac' indicated the limitations of romance. The clearest statement of Howell's position in the debate, however, comes in an essay from April 1887, entitled 'Realism: the moral issue' in which he writes:

> 'For our own part we confess that we do not care to judge any work of the imagination without first applying this test to it. We must ask ourselves before we ask anything else, Is it true – true to the motives, the impulses, the principles that shape the life of actual men and women? This truth, which necessarily includes the highest morality and the highest artistry – this truth given, the book *cannot* be wicked and cannot be weak; and without it all the graces of style and feats of invention and cunning of construction are so many superfluities of naughtiness.'

25 'Lemuel Barkers': Lemuel Barker was a character in W. D. Howell's novel, *The Minister's Charge*, serialized in the *Century Magazine* in 1886, and published in 1887. The character is that of young and untalented boy who believes himself to be a poet. (I am grateful to S. Ashton, T. Belanger and J. Dock for assistance with this reference.)

On Some Technical Elements of Style in Literature

1 Written in December 1884, and first published in the *Contemporary Review*, founded in 1866, which covered political and religious matters, and to a certain extent, literary subjects. In April 1885, when this essay appeared under the title 'On Style in Literature: its Technical Elements', it was edited by Sir Percy Bunting. Some minor changes in punctuation have been made between the *Contemporary Review* and the version included under '*Essays in the Art of Writing*' (Tusitala 28).

2 *Hudibras*: satire by Samuel Butler (1613–80), Stevenson slightly misquotes from c. 3.1.1: 'the hand' should read 'his hand'.

3 All these writers are recurring figures in Stevenson's writing: see 'Books Which Have Influenced Me'.

4 In the *Contemporary Review* there follows a representation in tabular form of these divisions:

	In time	In space	In time and space
Presentative	Music	Painting, Sculpture &c.	Dance
Representative	Literature	Architecture	Acting

5 'since Mr Anthony Trollope is dead, I will': Trollope, an enthusiast for and champion of Cicero, wrote a two-volume biography, *The Life of Cicero* (1880).

6 'from the same play': *As You Like It*.

7 'Fleeming Jenkin': Professor of Engineering at Edinburgh University, a family friend, polymath and strong influence on Stevenson, who later wrote his biography.

8 'All night the dreadless Angel unpursued': *Paradise Lost*, Bk VI, 1.

9 '*Aut Lacedaemonium Tarentum*': from Horace, *Odes*, III.5.56, in which Regulus,

going into exile, is seen to act as if he were a lawyer going on vacation in the watering-place of Tarentum.

10 'Athens, the eye of Greece, Mother of Arts': *Paradise Regained*, Bk IV, 240.

11 'Captain Reid': Mayne Reid (1818–83), popular author of adventure stories.

12 '*invita Minerva*': uninspiredly.

13 'unheard melodies': Keats, 'Ode on Grecian Urn' (1819): 'Heard melodies are sweet, but those unheard/Are sweeter'.

14 'I cannot praise . . .': Milton, *Areopagitica* (1644):

15 Stevenson's footnote in the *Contemporary Review* reads:

> As PVF will continue to haunt us through our English examples, take, by way of comparison, this Latin verse, of which it forms a chief adornment, and do not hold me answerable for the all-too-Roman freedom of the sense: '*Hanc volo, quae facilis, quae palliolata vagatur.*'

16 'In Xanadu . . .': Coleridge, 'Kubla Khan' (1816).

17 'The barge . . .': *Antony and Cleopatra*, II, ii, 199.

18 'A mole . . .': *Cymbeline*, II, ii, 36.

19 'But in the wind': *Troilus and Cressida*, I iii, 26

20 'Macaulay': Thomas Babington Macaulay, *History of England From the Ascension of James the Second* (1849), ch. XIII. In the five-volume edition of 1869 these lines can be found on p. 246.

21 'Macaulay': as above, ch. XIII, p. 372.

Books Which Have Influenced Me

1 Written April or May 1887 (Swearingen) and first published as part of a series in *The British Weekly* on 13 May 1887, no. 28, vol. II, 17–19. *The British Weekly*, subtitled 'A Journal of Social and Christian Progress' was mainly devoted to religious material, but had been running this series for some time; Stevenson's contribution was the eighth. Some details about the manuscript version, now untraced, appear in *The Bookman*, 8 January 1899. The essay is reprinted in *Essays Literary and Critical*, Tusitala 28. Only minor changes have been made from the journal article, mainly in punctuation.

2 'Mrs. Scott Siddons': this actress visited Edinburgh's Theatre Royal for a fortnight in 1874.

3 For further thoughts on D'Artagnan, see 'A Gossip on a Novel of Dumas's'.

4 *The Pilgrim's Progress*: Bunyan's text was an early influence on Stevenson: read aloud to him as a child by Cummy; acted out with dolls; and a model for his writing. It remained in his group of 'second favourite' books.

5 '*Essais* of Montaigne': published between 1580 and 1595. Stevenson read these as an undergraduate and learnt from their perspective on issues of morality. Montaigne was one of the writers to whom Stevenson described himself as playing 'the sedulous ape'.

6 'Whitman's *Leaves of Grass*': published in 1855. His poetry, brought to public attention in Britain by the likes of Rossetti and Swinburne, was also part of Stevenson's undergraduate reading and in 1878 he wrote an essay on his work, 'Walt Whitman', which was published in *Familiar Studies of Men and Books*. As a young man Stevenson had admired the centrality Whitman gave to the erotic.

7 'Herbert Spencer': evolutionary philosopher and ethical thinker (1820–1903).

The influence of his writing was seen by Stevenson's parents as one reason for his loss of faith.

8 '*caput-mortuum*': a thing from which all that makes it valuable has been distilled away.

9 '*Goethe's Life* by Lewes': George Henry Lewes (1817–78): his most distinguished work, his *Life of Goethe*, was published in 1855.

10 '*Werther*': Goethe's novel, *Die Leiden des Jungen Werthers* (1774). Werther became a hugely popular and fashionable figure, representative of artistic melancholy, loathing of the world and self, and suicide.

11 'Martial': Latin epigrammatist whom Stevenson worked at translating while in Davos 1881–2: 'I cannot conceive a person who does not love his Martial' (21 November 1887, *Letters* III, p. 161.)

12 *Meditations*: *Meditations* of Marcus Aurelius (121–80 ad): Roman Emperor, and Stoic philosopher. In mid-nineteenth century a writer highly popular with Matthew Arnold.

13 'the silence that is in the lonely hills': in 'Song at the Feast of Brougham Castle upon the Restoration of Lord Clifford, the Shepherd, to the Estates and Honours of his Ancestors' (1807), Wordsworth describes: 'The silence that is in the starry sky,/ The sleep that is among the lonely hills.' Stevenson may be conflating the quotation, although Sir Lewis Morris (1833–1907) also refers to 'the silence of the lonely hills' in 'A Vision of Saints' (1890).

14 'Mill': John Stuart Mill's *Autobiography* (1873) famously describes the effect reading Wordsworth had on him.

15 *The Egoist*: published in 1879, Meredith's novel is referred to frequently by Stevenson. (See also 'A Gossip on a Novel of Dumas's'.) Meredith was not only a friend but also one of the authors he most admired.

16 'Nathan': prophet and adviser to David.

17 'Willoughby is me!': Meredith did in fact base the character of Gower Woodseer in *The Amazing Marriage* (1895) on Stevenson.

18 Hazlitt, 'On the Spirit of Obligations': one of Hazlitt's more acerbic essays, published 1826. 'Penn': William Penn (1644–1718), Quaker and founder of Pennsylvania, published a collection of aphorisms, *Some Fruits of Solitude*, in 1693. Stevenson began an abortive essay on him in 1880. 'Mitford's, *Tales of Old Japan*': Algernon Bertram Freeman-Mitford published *Tales of Old Japan* in 1871.

A Gossip on a Novel of Dumas's

1 Written in the spring/summer of 1887 (Swearingen) and published in *Memories and Portraits*, November 1887, Tusitala 29.

2 This list might be compared with texts cited in 'Books Which Have Influenced Me'.

3 *The Bible in Spain*: narrative of travel by George Borrow, 1843.

4 'Their sometime selves the same through the year': this would appear to be a misquotation from Coventry Patmore's 'Mignonne' (1886): 'Thy sometime self the same throughout the year.'

5 'How often . . .': Stevenson's favourite Scott novels cited here include *Guy Mannering*, a copy of which had been in his father's library.

6 *The Egoist*: George Meredith, 1879: see also 'Books Which Have Influenced Me'.

The Vicomte de Bragelonne: the final musketeer adventure by Dumas, serialised betwen October and January 1850. (*The Three Musketeers* was serialised in *Le Siècle* 1843–4). The musketeers saga was continued in a number of volumes, and Stevenson appears here to refer, under the title of *The Vicomte de Bragelonne*, to those now published as *The Vicomte de Bragelonne*, *Louise de la Vallière* and *The Man in the Iron Mask*.

7 'in a hotel at Nice': in 1863 Stevenson travelled with his parents to the Riviera, Germany and Italy.

8 'a work of Miss Yonge's': an entry by Edward Latham, *Notes and Queries* 22 January, 1921, points to this as *The Young Stepmother* (first published in serial form, 1857–60), in which a character is found reading 'one of the worst and most fascinating of Dumas's romances', and is terrified lest his father discover this transgression. He is advised that 'there are some exciting pleasures that we must turn our backs on resolutely. I think this book is one of them.' (ch. IV)

9 'the rough-and-tumble in the Place de Grève': this is one of the most typically swashbuckling episodes in the book which Stevenson, as a boy, remembers better than the political machination of the rival financiers.

10 'alone upon the Pentlands': from 1867 the family rented Swanston cottage at Lothianburn in the Pentlands. One letter from there in 1871 describes himself as 'reading heaps of nice books'. (*Letters* I, p. 35)

11 'Fouquet'; charismatic but devious superintendent of finance to Louis XIV; 'Aramis': the most ambitious and scheming of the Musketeers.

12 George IV: liked to claim that his efforts were responsible for the overthrow of Napoleon. According to Fulford (1935; 1947), when George IV was taken by Wellington to see the battlefield of Waterloo he ordered an artillery-damaged tree to be cut down and made into a chair, upon which were carved the words 'Georgio Augusto Europae Liberatori'.

13 'Raoul': Vicomte de Bragelonne: first appears in *Vingt Ans Après* (serialised in 1845 in *Le Siècle*.) Miss Stewart's words are: 'At all events . . . he has done something; and a very good thing too, upon my word.' (*Louise de la Vallière*, LXXXV, World's Classics edition, tr. D. Coward.)

14 'La Vallière': Louise de la Vallière, one of the central female characters in *The Vicomte de Bragelonne*, extremely young at the start of the trilogy. Beloved by and betrothed to Raoul, she becomes the mistress of Louis XIV, and is seen as the cause of Raoul's death.

15 'Madame': Princess Henrietta, Phillippe's bride: lively, flirtatious and manipulative.

'de Guiche': courtier and favourite of Phillippe d'Orléans, who falls in love with Princess Henrietta.

16 As critics have noted, Stevenson had many problems with the creation of his (few) female characters, with the exception of 'Catriona'.

17.' Rosalind': *As You Like It*.

18 'Rose Jocelyn; Lucy Desborough, Clara Middleton': characters from Meredith's novels: *Evan Harrington* (1860); *The Ordeal of Richard Feverel* (1859); *The Egoist* (1879).

19 'Elizabeth Bennet': *Pride and Prejudice* (1813).

20 'Sir Richard Burton's *Thousand and One Nights*': unexpurgated version of the Arabian Nights, 1885–8.

21 'ventripotent Mulatto': a reference to Dumas, whose father was the child of a Frenchman and a woman from Haiti named Marie-Cessette Dumas.

22 'Planchet': 'Monsieur, I am one of those good-humoured sort of men Heaven created for the purpose of living a certain space of time, and of considering all things good which they meet with during their stay on earth.' (*Louise de la Vallière*, LIII, World's Classics edition, tr. D. Coward.)

23 'D'Artagnan sat down close to the window, and as there seemed to be something substantial in Planchet's philosophy, he mused over it.' (*Louise de la Vallière*, LIII, World's Classics edition, tr. D. Coward.)

24 'Fouquet and Colbert': the financial rivals who compete for the handling of the wealth of the kingdom.

25 'The noisy man, the man of pleasure, the man who exists only because others exist too.'

26 'trick upon Milady': impersonation by d'Artagnan of her lover in a darkened chamber.

27 'memoirs whom Thackeray pretended to prefer: *Memoirs of M. d'Artagnan* (1700) by Courtilz de Sandras, the source of Dumas's novel.

28 'Coquelin de Volière business': Porthos misnames the playwright Poquelin de Molière, who appears as a character in *The Man in the Iron Mask*, Coquelin de Volière.

29 'kidnap Monk': an episode in *The Vicomte de Bragelonne* in which the Musketeers kidnap General Monk and alter the course of history.

A Chapter on Dreams

1 Written in October 1887 (Swearingen) and published in *Scribner's Magazine* 3, January 1888, pp. 122–8, this essay formed part of Scribner's offer of $3,500 for twelve articles. The version published in *Across the Plains* (1892) and in Tusitala 30, under 'Random Memories', excludes a section from the original. This is given in note 9 below.

2 'restore your family to its ancient honours': McLynn comments: 'RLS's fantasies about having foreign blood were as far-fetched as his claim that the Stevensons descended from the Macgregors.' (*Robert Louis Stevenson: a biography*, p. 10)

3 'an ardent and uncomfortable dreamer': in 'Memoirs of Himself' Stevenson wrote: 'I suffered, at other times, from the most hideous nightmares . . . These were very strange; one that I remember seemed to indicate a considerable force of imagination.' (Tusitala 29, p. 150).

4 'hell 'gasped for him': 'gaped' in *Scribner's*.

5 'G. P. R. James': author of many romantic novels, biographies and histories (1799–1860).

6 '*land*': a house of different storeys, let out in tenements.

7 'like Claudius in the play': Stevenson's reference to *Hamlet* finds further echoes in the dream-story he later recounts.

8 'Brownies': benevolent household sprites, according to Chambers' *Scots Dictionary* – but J. C. Furnas notes that they should be seen as 'powerful' rather than 'quaint'.

9 In *Scribner's* the text continues:
    That he seemed himself to play a part in it, to be and suffer in the person of

the hero, is but an oddity of this particular dream; at which, indeed, I wonder a little, and which I seek to explain by analogy. In reading a plain tale, burthened with no psychology, and movingly and truthfully told, we are sometimes deceived for a moment, and take the emotions of the hero for our own. It is our testimony to the spirit and truth of the performance. So, perhaps, was this illusion of the dreamer's; and as he was asleep, he was doubtless the more easily and the more perfectly deceived. But observe . . .'

10 'could not perhaps equal': in *Scribner's*: 'could not even equal'.

'some Dennery or Sardou': Adolphe Philippe d'Ennery (1811–99), author of various melodramas, translated into English in the 1860s; Victorien Sardou (1831–1908), highly successful French dramatist, author of various comedies, historical plays and romantic melodramas.

11 *The Strange Case of Dr Jekyll and Mr Hyde*: Stevenson wrote that this story, published in 1886, was 'conceived, written, re-written, re-re-written, and printed inside ten weeks' (*Letters* III, p. 83). Accounts of its production have subsequently been much debated by critics and biographers.

12 *The Travelling Companion*: written at Hyères, 1882–4, and later burned.

13 *Olalla*: written November/December 1885, published Christmas 1885 in the *Court and Society Review*, then included among *Merry Men and Other Tales* (1887). As Balfour notes Stevenson was 'never well satisfied' with the story.' (*Life*, II, p. 15)

14 *A Chance Acquaintance*: a novel by W. D. Howells, an old enemy of Stevenson's, published in 1873. Stevenson makes further reference to Howells in 'A Humble Remonstrance'.

The Lantern-Bearers

1 Written early–mid October 1887 (Swearingen), and published in *Scribner's Magazine* 3, February 1888, pp. 251–6, as part of Stevenson's series of commissioned articles; reprinted in *Across the Plains* (1892), and in Tusitala 30. Some slight cuts and changes to punctuation took place from the original.

2 'certain easterly fishing-village': North Berwick, where Stevenson spent summers in the 1860s.

3 *London Journal*: an important periodical for the development of popular journalism (1845–1912).

4 'the Bass Rock': later to feature in *Catriona* (1893).

5 'the Law': Berwick Law, a local hill.

6 'geans': Stevenson's own footnote: 'wild cherries'.

7 The version in *Scribner's Magazine* continues: 'But there is a kind of fool abroad, whose folly is not even laughable; and it is this fool who gives the note of literary decency.'

8 'Dancer': Daniel Dancer (1716–94), a Pinner miser, who lived on a meagre subsistence but left a substantial amount of money. He was the subject of popular narratives such as 'The Strange and Unaccountable Life of Daniel Dancer' (1801).

9 'His mind to him a kingdom was': possibly a misquotation of 'My mind to me a kingdom is', Sir Edward Dyer, 1540–1607.

10 'Hawthorne': another writer to whom Stevenson had claimed to play 'the sedulous ape'.

11 Whitman: Stevenson comments in his essay 'Walt Whitman' (*Familiar Studies*

of Men and Books, Tusitala 27), that: 'he was a theoriser about society before he was a poet'. He also points out in that essay that 'the average man' was one of Whitman's favourite phrases.

12 'Zola's genius': for Stevenson's opinions on Zola and French Naturalism, see 'A Note on Realism'.

13 'By his fireside': a misquotation from Wordsworth's *Prelude*: 'Or as a man, who, when his house is built,/ A frame locked up in wood and stone, doth still,/ As impotent fancy prompts, by his fireside,/ Rebuilds it to his liking.' Bk VI, 291–4 (1850).

14 *Powers of Darkness*: Leo Tolstoy wrote this play in 1886.

15 References to: *Anna Karenina*; *War and Peace*; *The Ordeal of Richard Feverel*; *Antony and Cleopatra*; *King Lear*; and Dostoevsky, *The Despised and Rejected*.

16 *itur in antiquam silvam*: this appears to be a quotation from Virgil's *Aeneid*, Book VI, 179, in which Aeneas and his men set out to collect wood for a funeral pyre for Misenus: 'into the ancient forest'.

Some Gentlemen in Fiction

1 Written February 1888 (Swearingen), published in *Scribner's Magazine* 3, June 1888, pp. 764–8. Reprinted in *Lay Morals* (Tusitala 26).

2 Hazlitt: probably a reference to Hazlitt's *Characters of Shakespeare's Plays* (1817). The characters mentioned include: Nym, who appears in *The Merry Wives of Windsor* and *Henry V*, as a follower of Falstaff, as does Pistol, who was also in *Henry IV* pt. 2. Caius is a character in *The Merry Wives of Windsor*; so is Sir Hugh Evans.

3 'Burbage': Richard Burbage, leading tragic actor in Shakespeare's theatre.

4 'Have you read *André Cornélis?*': Paul Bourget (1852–1935) wrote this novel of psychological analysis in 1887, as a reworking of Shakepeare's tragedy. Stevenson admired his work and dedicated *Across the Plains* to him. *The Adventures of Caleb Williams*, (1794) by William Godwin (1756–1836) also parallels the scenarios of *Hamlet*, in the relationship of the eponymous hero to the murderer Falkland.

5 *teres atque rotundus*: Horace: 'a man polished and round'.

6 'last month': 'Gentlemen', published in *Scribner's*, May 1888, pp. 635–40, and in Tusitala 26. Although the two essays appear closely related by title, the earlier piece deals much more with explicitly moral questions of 'gentlemanliness'.

7 'Salvini': Tommaso Salvini (1829–1915) made an international reputation playing Shakespeare's tragic heroes. Stevenson wrote an essay about his performance.

8 'verbal puppet': a phrase similar to that used by Thackeray in *Vanity Fair* (1847/8) who describes his characters as puppets.

9 *Tom Jones*: Henry Fielding published *The History of Tom Jones* in 1749; Squire Allworthy is a leading character.

10 *Joseph Andrews*: *The History of the Adventures of Joseph Andrews and of his Friend, Mr Abraham Adams* (1742). Parson Adams is the moral hero but also faintly ridiculous.

11 *Amelia* (1751–2): characters include Captain Billy Booth and the parson, Dr Harrison.

12 *Sir Charles Grandison*: a novel by Samuel Richardson, published in 1754.

13 'Baron Gibbon's fortress': Edward Gibbon, *The History of the Decline and Fall of the Roman Empire* (1776–88); Clarendon, *The Life of Edward, Earl of Clarendon* (1759) and *The True Historical Narrative of the Rebellion and Civil Wars in England* (1702–4).

14 *Clarissa Harlowe*: Samuel Richardson, published 1748–9. Colonel Morden, Clarissa's cousin, kills her seducer Lovelace in a duel.

15 'David Copperfield': Dicken's novel, *David Copperfield*, published 1849–50; *Dombey and Son* (1847–8); *Little Dorrit* (1855–7): Stevenson is not chronologically accurate here in describing a pattern of development, if publication dates are taken into account.

16 Carton: *A Tale of Two Cities* (1859); Wrayburn: *Our Mututal Friend* (1864–5); Twemlow: in *Our Mutual Friend* is a put-upon and apparently insignificant character who makes an important statement about what it means to be a gentleman.

17 'the scene with the old Jew': *Our Mutual Friend*, ch. 15.

18 Andaman Islanders: primitive pygmy tribes from an island in Bay of Bengal.

19 Bradley Headstone: schoolmaster and would-be murderer in *Our Mutual Friend*.

20 'deeper than did ever plummet sound': *The Tempest*, V,i,50

21 Comparison of Franz Hals (1582/3–1666), portrait painter of highly individualised characters from a variety of walks of life, with Sir Anthony Vandyke (1599–1641) painter of stylised and aristocratic portraits.

22 'Major Pendennis': *The History of Pendennis* (1848–50): story of flawed hero, Arthur Pendennis; *The History of Henry Esmond* (1852); *The Newcomes* (1853–5): story told by Arthur Pendennis of descendants of self-made man, Thomas Newcome. Colonel Thomas Newcome: unworldly soldier.

23 'denies the influence of books': Andrew Lang favoured books that amused rather than those that attempted to deal with psychological or social issues.

Popular Authors

1 Written in February/March 1888 (Swearingen), this was published in *Scribner's Magazine* 4, July 1888, pp. 122–8, and reprinted in Tusitala 28. During this period, writing while living in the mountains at Saranac, Stevenson had requested Charles Scribner to send him a range of 'popular authors' for this piece, to refresh his memory. The 'three-volume novel' to which he refers in the essay represents the format imposed by 'serious' publishers and the circulating libraries. This is presented in contrast to the serial publication of cheap fiction in penny parts, and to popular journals which depended upon the serialisation of melodramatic fiction for their success. Some of the titles he refers to in the essay have indeed proved ephemeral, and difficult to trace.

2 'Stephens Hayward': William Stephens Hayward, author of a number of popular adventure stories, published *Tom Holt's Log: A Tale Of The Deep Sea* in 1868.

3 *The Diamond Necklace, or the Twenty Captains*: various novels entitled *The Diamond Necklace* were published around this time, although none meets Stevenson's description. Hayward also wrote *The Diamond Cross; And How I Won It* (1868) and *The Idol's Eye: Adventures in Search of a Big Diamond* (1883) but

I have been unable to trace *The Twenty Captains*. (See Allibone, Sadleir and Wolff.)

4 'Macaire': type from melodrama, immortalised in 1830 in the cartoons of Daumier: a cad and exploiter of fools. (Stevenson and Henley collaborated on a farce/melodrama entitled *Macaire* in January 1885.)

5 'Bracebridge 'Hemming': also spelt Hemying (1841–1901), author of *The Bondage of Brandon* (1881) and a number of romances. He also collaborated with Henry Mayhew on *The Prostitute Class Generally* (1861).

6 'Pierce Egan': Pierce Egan the elder (1772–1849) was author of *Life in London; or the day and night scenes of Jerry Hawthorn Esq. and Corinthian Tom* (1821). His son, Pierce Egan (1814–80) also wrote a vast number of novels including *The Flower of the Flock*.

7 See further details below.

8 *London Journal*: an important periodical for the development of popular journalism, aimed at working-class readers (1845–1912). The novelist Charles Reade serialised fiction for the *London Journal*; Meredith's novel *Evan Harrington* was serialised in *Once a Week*. It ran in competition with Wilkie Collins' *The Woman in White* in *All the Year Round*, and was not well received.

9 *Cassell's Family Paper*: a popular and improving miscellany read to Stevenson by his nurse, Cummy.

10 'Fair Lilias': one of the titles Stevenson told Charles Scribner he particularly wished for.

11 'Neidpath Castle': near Peebles in the Scottish borders.

12 'Edward Viles': author of *Black Bess; or, the Knight of the Road. A tale of the good old times* (1866–8), and a range of other titles about vagabonds and highwaymen.

13 'Lambert': John Lambert (1619–84) went with Cromwell to Scotland in 1650 as major-general.

14 'ERRYM': Stevenson is right in believing this to be an anagram, in fact of J. M. Rymer, author of *Edith the Captive; or the Robbers of Eppiney Forest* (1861) and a range of other titles.

15 Stevenson was correct in assuming the Egans were father and son. 'Tom and Jerry' refers to *Life in London; or the day and night scenes of Jerry Hawthorn Esq. and Corinthian Tom*.

16 *The Mysteries of London*: G. W. M. Reynolds (1814–79),was author of *The Mysteries of London* (1847–69). As editor of and journalist for the *London Journal*, Reynolds published a number of sensational sketches of London life in novel form. *The Mysteries of London* was a massive work of around four and a half million words, and a best-seller of its time. In particular it aimed to attract the new literate working classes with its vivid depictions of horrors and depravity amongst both high and low life circles in London.

17 'J. F. Smith': (1804–90), a contributor to the *London Journal* and author of *The Prelate: a Novel* (1860) and a range of other titles. 'Sylvanus Cobb': (1832–87), an American author, who wrote novelettes for newspapers such as *Gleason's Pictorial* and produced titles such as *The Heir and the Usurper* (c.1880) and *The Foundling of Estella* (c.1880). (See Allibone.)

18 *Saturday Review*: this would appear to be a reference to the review of *Prince Otto* published on 21 November 1885, in which the reviewer complained that the story 'deals with persons who have no high or romantic aspirations, no lofty ideals'. (Stevenson wrote several letters to friends about the injustice of the criticism.)

19 'Mrs Southworth': Emma Southworth (1819–90), prolific author of romances such as *The Lost Heiress* (1854); *The Missing Bride* (1855); and *The Fatal Marriage* (1863).

20 'G. P. R. James': George Payne Rainsford James (1801–60), highly prolific author of novels, popular histories and biographies. *The Step Mother; or, Evil Doings* was published in 1845. There is no reference to a novel by J. F. Smith entitled *The Stepmother* in the British Library Catalogue; the *National Union Catalog* however does cite a novel called *Die Stieftochter; oder Wer Gewinnt* of 1885, which may be the novel Stevenson is thinking of.

21 *The Young Ladies' Journal*: one of the increasing number of popular weekly periodicals directed toward specific groups in the 1880s.

22 'Torrens or Burton': Henry Whitelock Torrens published *The Book of the Thousand Nights and One Night* in 1838; Sir Richard Burton was the author of the unexpurgated version of the *Arabian Nights* published between 1885 and 1888.

23 Montépin: Xavier de Montépin (1823–1902), highly popular French journalist, playwright, and novelist.

'ouvriers and ouvrières': labourers.

A Letter To A Young Gentleman Who Proposes To Embrace The Career Of Art

1 Published in *Scribner's Magazine* 4, September 1888, pp. 377–81, under the title: 'A Letter to A Young Gentleman Who Proposes to Embrace the Career of Art', this was written in March/April 1888 (Swearingen). It was published with some cuts in *Across the Plains* (1892) and is included in Tusitala 28. The essay was followed in *Scribner's* by a response from Stevenson's friend W. H. Low. The *Scribner's* essay contains a final sentence excluded in the later version.

2 '*ars artium*': art of arts.

3 'toil like a miner buried in a landslip': Balzac, with reference to the young sculptor, Wenceslas Steinbock in *Cousine Bette*, writes: 'if the artist does not fling himself into his work . . . if once in this crater he does not work like a miner of whom the walls of the gallery have fallen . . . he is simply looking on the suicide of his own talents.'

4 'First': *Scribner's* version reads: 'And first. . . .'

5 'Daughters of Joy': this image of the artist as prostitute prompted much debate and was inspired, Stevenson claimed, by his reception in America. In an earlier letter to Edmund Gosse (2 January 1886) he used a similar image: 'We were full of the pride of life, and chose, like prostitutes, to live by a pleasure. We should be paid if we give the pleasure we pretend to give; but why should we be honoured?' (*Letters* III, p. 70).

6 'the Tennyson peerage': Tennyson was made a peer in 1884. Literary peerages were unusual and some sections of the press objected to the 'People's Poet' taking a title. (See Martin.)

7 'less agreeable: in *Scribner's*: 'more laborious'.

8 *Les Bleus et les Blancs*: a late novel by Dumas, dramatised in 1869; *The Vicomte de Bragelonne*: Stevenson's favourite Dumas novel. The *Scribner's* version continues: '*Denis Duval* is not written with the pen of *Esmond*.' *Denis Duval*: Thackeray's unfinished last novel, published in the *Cornhill* in 1864; *Castle*

Dangerous: a novel by Sir Walter Scott, 1831; J. G. Lockhart wrote *Memoirs of the Life of Scott* in 1837–8.

9   Montépin: Xavier de Montépin (1823–1902), hugely popular French journalist, playwright, and novelist.

10   *'le vieux saltimbanque'*: the old clown.

11   The essay in *Scribner's* continues:

I will be very bold and take a modern instance. A little while ago the name of Mr Howells was in every paper coupled with just laudations. And now it is the pleasure of the same journalists to pursue him daily with ineffective quips.

12   The essay in *Scribner's* then concludes:

Must not any man perceive that the reward of Mr Howells lies in the practice of his fine and solid art, not in the perusal of paragraphs which are conceived in a spirit to-day of ignorant worship and tomorrow of stupid injustice?

Stevenson speaks less postively of W. D. Howells in 'A Humble Remonstrance' and 'A Chapter on Dreams'.

Bibliography

✳

The Works of Robert Louis Stevenson (1923–4), Tusitala Edition, 35 vols, London: William Heinemann Ltd, is used throughout and referred to as 'Tusitala'.

References to *Letters* are also to the Tusitala edition, edited by Sir Sidney Colvin.

For a fuller and more recent edition of Stevenson's letters, see: Booth, Bradford A., and Ernest Mehew (1994–5), *The Letters of Robert Louis Stevenson*, 8 vols, New Haven and London: Yale University Press

A shorter version is also available in: Mehew, Ernest (1997), *Selected Letters of Robert Louis Stevenson*, New Haven and London: Yale University Press

Information on manuscript dating, publication dates etc., is taken from: Swearingen, Roger G. (1980) *The Prose Writings of Robert Louis Stevenson: A Guide*, London: Macmillan

Another important source of information on Stevenson is: Maixner, Paul (ed.) (1981) *Robert Louis Stevenson: The Critical Heritage*, London, Boston and Henley: Routledge and Kegan Paul

Essays and articles cited:

Anon. (1881), 'Magazines and Reviews', *The Academy*, 466, 9 April, p. 261

Besant, Walter (1884) 'The Art of Fiction: A Lecture', delivered 25 April 1884, London: Chatto and Windus

Collins, Wilkie (1858), 'The Unknown Public', *Household Words*, 439, pp. 217–22

Dickens, Charles (1890), *All the Year Round*, 15 February, pp. 163–5

Hammerton J. A. (ed.) (1907), 'Notes taken from *The Critic*, 10 September 1887', in *Stevensonia*, Edinburgh: John Grant, pp. 83–91

Howell, W. D. (1887), 'From the Editor's Study', *Harper's Monthly*, April

James, Henry (1884), 'The Art of Fiction', *Longman's Magazine*, 4, September, pp. 502–21

'Lantern-Bearer, A' (1910), 'Some Notes on the Boyhood of RLS', *Chambers's Journal*, 28 May, pp. 410–11

Latham, E. (1921), 'Stevenson and Miss Yonge', in *Notes and Queries*, 8 January, p. 30, and 22 January, p. 79

Lewes, G. H. (1858), 'Realism in Art: Recent German Fiction', *Westminster Review*, 70, October, pp. 488–518.

Low, W. H. (1888), 'A Letter to the Same Young Gentleman', *Scribner's Magazine*, vol. 4, September, pp. 381–4

Payn, James (1881), 'Penny Fiction', *Nineteenth Century*, January, vol. 9, pp. 145–54

Stevenson, R. L.:

(1874), 'Victor Hugo's Romances', *Cornhill Magazine* 30, pp. 179–94, Tusitala 27

(1876), 'Salvini's Macbeth', *The Academy*, 15 April, pp. 366–7, Tusitala 28

(1878), 'The Gospel According to Walt Whitman', *New Quarterly Magazine* 10 October, pp. 461–81, 'Walt Whitman', Tusitala 27

(1878), 'Child's Play', *Cornhill Magazine*, vol. 38, pp. 352–9

(1881), 'The Morality of the Profession of Letters', *Fortnightly Review*, vol. 157, April, pp. 513–20

(1881), 'Correspondence: "The Morality of the Profession of Letters"', *The Academy* 470, 7 May, p. 339

(1882), 'A Gossip on Romance', *Longman's Magazine* 1, pp. 69–79

(1883), 'A Note on Realism', *The Magazine of Art*, vol. 7, November, pp. 24–8

(1884), 'A Penny Plain and Twopence Coloured', *The Magazine of Art*, vol. 7, April, pp. 227–32

(1884), 'A Humble Remonstrance', *Longman's Magazine*, 5, December, pp. 139–47

(1885), 'Style in Literature: Its Technical Elements', *The Contemporary Review*, vol. 47, pp. 548–61

(1887), 'Books which Have Influenced me', *The British Weekly*, vol. II, 28, 13 May, pp. 17–19

(1887), 'A Gossip on a Novel of Dumas's', *Memories and Portraits* Tusitala 29

(1888), 'A Chapter on Dreams', *Scribner's Magazine*, vol. 3, January, pp. 122–8

(1888), 'The Lantern-Bearers', *Scribner's Magazine*, vol. 3, February, pp. 251–6

(1888), 'Gentlemen', *Scribner's Magazine*, vol. 3, May, pp. 635–40

(1888), 'Some Gentlemen in Fiction', *Scribner's Magazine*, vol. 3, June, pp. 764–8

(1888), 'Popular Authors', *Scribner's Magazine*', vol. 4, July, pp. 122–8

(1888), 'A Letter to a Young Gentleman Who Proposes To Embrace the Career of Art', *Scribner's Magazine*, vol. 4, September, pp. 377–81

(1893) 'Rosa Quo Locorum', *Random Memories*, Tusitala 30

Stevenson: biographical

Balfour, Graham (1901), *The Life of Robert Louis Stevenson*, 2 vols, London: Methuen

Bell, Ian (1992; 1993) *Robert Louis Stevenson: Dreams of Exile*, London: Headline; Edinburgh: Mainstream

Calder, Jenni (1980), *RLS: A Life Study*, London: Hamish Hamilton

Furnas, J. C. (1952), *Voyage to Windward: the Life of Robert Louis Stevenson*, London: Faber and Faber

Hennessy, James Pope (1974), *Robert Louis Stevenson*, London: Cape

Lang, Andrew (1905), *Adventures Among Books*, London: Longmans

Low, Will H. (1908), *A Chronicle of Friendships, 1873–1900*, London: Hodder and Stoughton

McLynn, Frank (1993; 1994), *Robert Louis Stevenson: A Biography*, London: Hutchinson; London: Pimlico

Masson, Rosaline (ed.) (1922), *I Can Remember Robert Louis Stevenson*, Edinburgh: W. and R. Chambers Ltd

Smith, Janet Adam (ed.) (1948), *Henry James and Robert Louis Stevenson: A Record Of Friendship And Criticism*, London: Rupert Hart-Davis

Thwaite, Ann (ed.) (1991), *Portraits from Life by Edmund Gosse*, Aldershot: Scolar Press

Stevenson: critical

Anderson, Carol (1991) 'No Single Key: The Fiction of Robert Louis Stevenson and Italo Calvino', in J. J. Simon and A. Sinner (eds), *English Studies 3: Proceedings of the Third Conference on the Literature of Region and Nation*, Luxembourg: Publications du Centre Universitaire de Luxembourg, pp. 15–34

Balderston, Daniel (1981) 'Borges' Frame of Reference: The Strange Case of Robert Louis Stevenson', Ph.D. thesis, Princeton University: Ann Arbor Mi. University Microfilms

Borges, J. L. (1974), *Borges on Writing* London: Allen Lane

Calder, Jenni (ed.) (1981), *Stevenson and Victorian Scotland*, Edinburgh: Edinburgh University Press

Chesterton, G. K. (1927), *Robert Louis Stevenson*, London: Hodder and Stoughton

Clunas, Alex (1981), 'R. L. Stevenson: Precursor of the Post-Moderns?', *Cencrastus* 6, pp. 9–11

Craig, Cairns (1996), *Out of History: Narrative Paradigms in Scottish and British Culture*, Edinburgh: Polygon

Daiches, David (1951), *Stevenson and the Art of Fiction* (a Frances Bergen memorial lecture delivered in the Yale University Library, 18 May), New York: privately printed

Eigner, Edwin (1966), *Robert Louis Stevenson and Romantic Tradition*, Princeton: Princeton University Press

Fiedler, Leslie (1971), 'RLS Revisited', in *Collected Essays*, vol. 1, New York: Stein and Day, pp. 297–311

Gelder, Kenneth (ed.) (1989), *Robert Louis Stevenson: The Scottish Short Stories and Essays*, Edinburgh: Edinburgh University Press

Gifford, Douglas (1981) 'Stevenson and Scottish Fiction: The Importance of *The Master of Ballantrae*', in J. Calder (ed.), *Stevenson and Victorian Scotland*, Edinburgh: Edinburgh University Press

Graham, Kenneth (1983), 'Stevenson and Henry James: A Crossing', in Andrew Noble (ed.) (1983), *Robert Louis Stevenson* London: Vision Press Ltd; USA: Barnes and Noble, pp. 23–46

Hamilton, Ian (1992), *Keepers of the Flame: Literary Estates and the Rise of Biography* London: Hutchinson

Hammond, J. R. (1984), *A Robert Louis Stevenson Companion: A Guide to the Novels, Essays and Short Stories*, London: Macmillan

Hart, James D. (ed.) (1966), *From Scotland to Silverado: Robert Louis Stevenson*, Cambridge, Mass: The Belknap Press of Harvard University Press

Hubbard, Tom (1995), *Seeking Mr Hyde: Studies in Robert Louis Stevenson, Symbolism, Myth and the Pre-Modern*, Frankfurt-am-Main: Peter Lang Gmbh

Kiely, Robert (1964), *Robert Louis Stevenson and the Fiction of Adventure*, Cambridge, Mass.: Harvard University Press

Mackenzie, Sister Mary Louise (1974), 'Experiments in Romance: Theory and Practice in the Fiction of Robert Louis Stevenson', Unpublished Ph.D. thesis: University of Toronto

Nabokov, Vladimir (1980), 'Dr Jekyll and Mr Hyde', in F. Bowers (ed.), *Lectures on Literature*, London: Weidenfeld and Nicolson, pp. 179–205

Noble, Andrew (ed.) (1983), *Robert Louis Stevenson* London: Vision Press Ltd; USA: Barnes and Noble

Sandison, Alan (1996), *Robert Louis Stevenson and the Appearance of Modernism* London: Macmillan

Bibliography: general

Allibone, S. Austin (1859), A Critical Dictionary of English Literature and British and American Authors, 2 vols, Philadelphia: Childs and Peterson; (1891) Supplement, Philadelphia: J. B. Lippincott and Co.

Altick, Richard (1957), The English Common Reader: A Social History of the Mass Reading Public 1800–1900, Chicago: University of Chicago Press

Baker, Herschel (1962), William Hazlitt, Cambridge, Mass.: Harvard University Press

Blake, Andrew (1989), Reading Victorian Fiction: the Cultural Context and Ideological Content of the Nineteenth-Century Novel, London: Macmillan

Bodleian Library (1994), Nineteenth-Century Short Title Catalogue, London: Avero

Booth, Michael (1991), Theatre in the Victorian Age, Cambridge: Cambridge University Press

Brewers' Dictionary of Phrase and Fable (14th edn) (1989), revised by Ivor H. Evans, London: Guild Publishing

Cady, Edwin H. (ed.), (1973) W. D. Howells as Critic, London: Routledge and Kegan Paul

Calvino, Italo (1980), Our Ancestors, trs. I. Quigley, London: Picador

Cox, R. G. (1982), 'Reviews and Magazines', in Boris Ford (ed.), The New Pelican Guide to English Literature, vol. 6, Harmondsworth: Penguin

Daugherty, Sarah B. (1981), The Literary Criticism of Henry James, Athens, Ohio: Ohio University Press

Drabble, M. (1985), The Oxford Companion to English Literature, London: Guild Publishing/Oxford University Press

Edel, Leon (1963), Henry James: the Middle Years, London: Rupert Hart-Davis

Edel, Leon (1963), The Complete Tales of Henry James: Volume 5 1883–4, London: Rupert-Hart Davis

Eigner, M. and G. Worth (eds) (1985), Victorian Criticism of the Novel, Cambridge: Cambridge University Press

Faller, Lincoln B. (1987), Turned to Account: The Forms and Functions of Criminal Biography in late Seventeenth- and early Eighteenth-century England, Cambridge: Cambridge University Press

Flint, Kate (1993), The Woman Reader 1837–1914, Oxford: Clarendon Press

Furst, Lilian (1992), Realism, Longman: London

Furst, Lilian, and Peter Skrine (1971), Naturalism, London: Methuen

Gibbons, Tom (1973), Rooms in the Darwin Hotel: Studies in English Literary Criticism and Ideas 1880–1920, Nedlands, Western Australia: University of Western Australia Press

Glendinning, Victoria (1992), *Trollope*, London: Hutchinson

Graham, Kenneth (1965), *English Criticism of the Novel 1865–1900*, Oxford: Clarendon Press

Graham, Walter (1930), *English Literary Periodicals*, New York: Thomas Nelson and Sons

Green, Roger Lancelyn (1946), *Andrew Lang: A Critical Biography*, Leicester: Edmund Ward

Gross, John (1969), *The Rise and Fall of the Man of Letters: Aspects of English Literary Life since 1800*, London: Weidenfeld and Nicholson

Guérard, Albert Léon (1916), *Five Masters of French Romance*, London: T. Fisher Unwin

Hartnoll, Phyllis (1983), *The Oxford Companion to the Theatre*, Oxford: Oxford University Press

Harvey, Sir Paul, and J. C. Heseltine (1959), *The Oxford Companion to French Literature*, Oxford: Clarendon Press

James, Louis (1976), *Print and the People 1819–1851*, London: Lane

Jameson, Frederic (1981), *The Political Unconscious: Narrative as a Socially Symbolic Act*, London: Methuen

Jordan, John O., and Robert L. Patten (eds) (1995), *Literature in the Marketplace: Nineteenth-Century British Publishing and Reading Practices*, Cambridge: Cambridge University Press

Keating, Peter (1989) *The Haunted Study: A Social History of the English Novel 1875–1914*, London: Secker and Warburg

Martin, Robert Bernard (1980), *Tennyson: the Unquiet Heart*, Oxford: Faber and Faber, Clarendon Press

Mullin, Donald C. (1987), *Victorian Plays: A Record of Significant Productions on the London Stage 1837–1901*, Connecticut: Greenwood Press

Olmsted, J. C. (ed.) (1979) *A Victorian Art of Fiction: Essays on the Novel in British Periodicals 1870–1900*, New York and London: Garland Publications Inc.

Radway, Janice (1987), *Reading the Romance: Women, Patriarchy and Popular Culture*, London: Verso

Reynolds, G. W. M. (1996), *The Mysteries of London*, edited and with an introduction by Trefor Thomas, Keele: Keele University Press

Riley, H. T. (ed.) (1871), *A Dictionary of Latin and Greek Quotations, Proverbs, Maxims and Mottoes*, London: Bell and Daldy

Rose, Jonathon, (1992) 'Rereading the English Common Reader: A Preface to a History of Audiences', *Journal of the History of Ideas*, 53.1, pp. 47–70

Rowell, George (1956), *The Victorian Theatre: A Survey*, Oxford: Oxford University Press

Sadleir, M. (1951) *XIX Century Fiction: A Bibliographic Record Based on his Own Collection*, 2 vols, Cambridge: Cambridge University Press

Sandars, Mary (1904), *Honoré de Balzac: His Life and Writing*, London: Stanley Paul

Showalter, Elaine (1990), *Sexual Anarchy: Gender and Culture at the Fin de Siècle*, London: Virago

Smith, Elton Edward (1976), *Charles Reade*, London: George Prior Publishers

Steedman, Carolyn (1989), *Landscape for a Good Woman: A Story of Two Lives*, London: Virago

Stevens, D. H. (1928), *A Reference Guide to Milton from 1800 to the Present Day*, Chicago: University of Chicago Press

Sutherland, John (1976), *Victorian Novelists and Publishers*, London: Athlone Press

Sutherland, John (1995), *Victorian Fiction: Writers, Publishers, Readers*, London: Macmillan

Taylor, George (1989), *Plays and Performances in the Victorian Theatre*, Manchester: Manchester University Press

Williams, Ioan (1971), *Meredith: The Critical Heritage*, London: Routledge and Kegan Paul

Wolff, Robert Lee (1982), *Nineteenth-century Fiction: A Bibliographical catalogue Based on the Collection Formed By Robert Lee Wolff*, New York: Garland Publishing Inc.

Wright, Austin (ed.) (1961), *Victorian Literature: Modern Essays in Criticism*, New York: Oxford University Press

Wright, R. G. (1973), *Author Bibliography of English Language Fiction in the Library of Congress Through 1950*, Boston: G. K. Hall and Co.

Index

✳